Dawson Turner, after a drawing by J.P. Davis, 1816.

DAWSON TURNER

A Norfolk Antiquary and his Remarkable Family

Edited by
Nigel Goodman

Phillimore

2007

Published by
PHILLIMORE & CO. LTD
Shopwyke Manor Barn, Chichester, West Sussex, England
www.phillimore.co.uk

ISBN 978-1-86077-445-4

Printed and bound in Great Britain

Contents

List of Illustrations

Preface

Having had the good fortune to inherit the residue of Dawson Turner's library and family papers, I had for some while been considering the idea of producing a book about this remarkable man, who was my great great great grandfather. Besides being a banker, he was a husband, father of 11 children, and notable as a patron of the arts, botanist, antiquary and collector of manuscripts. So in many respects he was an interesting figure in his time: born in 1775, his adult life spanned the first half of the 19th century.

Druery's *History of Yarmouth* includes the following account of him. 'Few individuals have been more distinguished by literary honors, either foreign or domestic, than this gentleman.' He was elected Fellow of the Linnean Society in 1797 at the age of 22, and of the Royal Society in 1803. Subsequently he was chosen as member of many learned societies, not only in London, but also in Göttingen, Edinburgh, Dublin, Stockholm, Rouen, Caen and Leipzig.

He was elected to The Athenaeum at the first meeting, held in the rooms of the Royal Society on 16 February 1824, thus being in the very first wave of 'founder members' and quite actively involved in its earliest days. In the same year there were also admitted: Francis (later Sir Francis) Palgrave, who had married Turner's daughter Elizabeth; and Hudson Gurney, his close friend and business partner.

His tastes, his talents and his hospitality were long remembered.

Thus I was more than pleased when Nigel Goodman, whose late wife was my cousin and also a direct descendant of Turner, offered to help over compiling and editing this volume.

Virtually every letter that Dawson Turner received was dutifully bound and protected. In 1890 my great grandfather, Sir Inglis Palgrave, was concerned about the future of this material, comprising some 82 volumes of correspondence, which he thought might have some historic interest. Thus he wrote to a don he knew at Trinity College, Cambridge, asking if they could give it a home. Since then it has reposed for over a century in their fine Wren Library, where it has been splendidly cared for and indexed, at the same time being readily accessible to the many people who have wished to see it.

Thus, on behalf of the family, I wish here to record our gratitude to the successive Librarians who have ensured its preservation. Now our special thanks go to the present Librarian, Professor David McKitterick, who has probably shown greater interest in this correspondence than any of his predecessors, and contributes a valuable article to this book.

In similar vein I wish to express our sincere appreciation to the Castle Museum at Norwich, and especially the current custodian, Dr Andrew Moore, and his faithful assistant, Norma Watt, for having taken such care and interest in all the Dawson Turner and Cotman material that they hold. We remember too, with admiration, Miklos Rajnai, who was Curator there for some years and partly responsible for arousing my own concern for my ancestor.

Likewise, we are grateful to the four other people who have done much research to contribute further chapters.

CHRISTOPHER PALGRAVE BARKER
March 2007

Contributors

Nigel Goodman, M.A., B.Sc.Econ., Dip.Ed.
formerly of Eton College, lecturer in Fine Arts

Dr Andrew Moore, M.A., Ph.D.
Keeper of Art and Senior Curator,
Norwich Museums and Archaeology Service

Dr Anne Secord, M.Sc., Ph.D.
Affiliated Research Scholar in the Department of History and
Philosophy of Science, University of Cambridge

Professor David McKitterick, F.B.A., Litt.D.
Librarian, Trinity College, Cambridge

Jessie Cambell, M.A., Dip.Arch.Admin.
former Archivist, Barclays Bank Group

Jane Knowles, M.A.
Exhibitions Organiser, National Gallery, London

Wendy Kett, B.A.Hons, Cert.inEd.
researcher on Mary Turner

CHAPTER ONE

Introduction

'This house is the most agreeable I ever visited. No visit could be unpleasantly long here,' wrote the barrister Henry Crabb Robinson in his diary on 26 October 1826. 'The moment breakfast was over Mr Turner went to the bank, Mrs Turner to her writing desk, and every one of the young ladies to drawing or some other tasteful occupation.'[1]

1 *Sir Joseph Banks, friend of Dawson Turner, etched by Mary Turner from a drawing by Thomas Phillips RA, 1816.*

The Bank House was on the South Quay at the very heart of the busy, attractive and prosperous town of Great Yarmouth. It was the happy home of Dawson Turner (1775-1858) and his exceptionally talented family. The house is described in some detail by a grandson, R.H. Inglis Palgrave.[2] It faced west looking out over the river Yare, which at that point was crossed by a drawbridge that carried a constant stream of traffic and was raised periodically to allow the passage of ships and fishing boats down to the sea. From the windows could be seen a forest of masts of ships at moorings and in the yards. All day long could be heard the tapping of the caulkers at work on the decks.

The Bank occupied the ground floor of this Georgian house. On the first floor was a long corridor from which doors opened into the elegant, panelled 30-foot drawing room, which had most of the finest paintings in Dawson Turner's collection of Old Masters, and the library, which had the family portrait by Thomas Phillips RA above the fireplace. This was

2 *Thomas Phillips RA, etching by Mary Turner after a self-portrait drawing, 1815. He was a portrait painter and a close friemd of the Turner family.*

3 *William Jackson Hooker, etched by Mary Turner from a drawing by J.S. Cotman, 1813.*

where the members of the family were almost constantly and happily at work, studying languages, drawing, etching, cataloguing and indexing, at the scene of Cotman's teaching. Every inch of wall space was covered with paintings and bookcases. Long before he had ceased to collect books he had run out of shelf space. As Dawson Turner wrote in March 1831, 'Not only have I with my books invaded every closet in every room in my house but in this library where I am writing all the chairs but three are covered with books: the same is the case with the sofa, the same with the four tables and window seats, and then on the floor I have 60 volumes which have been there for months and for which I have no place whatever.'

The main staircase had paintings by Van Dyk, Canaletto, Hondekoeter, Crome, and *Lady at her Toilet* attributed to Titian. A child's gate cut off the happy playground of the nursery and its annexe from the main staircase. This was very much a house filled with children and grandchildren. There was also a south wing whose walls were crowded not with Old Masters of European schools but with family portraits of past generations. Here there was also a curiosities room with spears from Pacific islands and strange artefacts brought back from far-off places by friends, botanists and travellers.

Dawson Turner was the eldest surviving child of James Turner, a merchant and banker. He was educated at North Walsham Grammar School and subsequently as a private pupil of the Rev Robert Forby of Barton who fostered his interest in botany. From 1792-4 he was at Pembroke College, Cambridge, where his uncle was Master. He had been destined for the Church but in 1794 was obliged to give up his calling, leave Cambridge prematurely, and, his father having died, take up his father's partnership at the bank. At this time he was only 18 but had inherited an ample fortune. What he was to make of his life was truly remarkable and is the subject of this book.

4 *Antonio Canova, Italian sculptor, etched by Mary Turner from a drawing by Thomas Phillips RA, 1816.*

By the time Henry Crabb Robinson visited the Bank House Dawson Turner had been living there for more than 30 years. In 1796 he had married the highly cultivated, charming and vivacious Mary Palgrave of Coltishall. It was a brilliantly successful marriage and they produced 11 children between 1797 and 1815, of whom three died early. Those who came to visit were enchanted by the house and its inhabitants, and by the scene of the family at work in this domestic academy. In 1826 there were four unmarried daughters living at home as Robinson noted, 'all very interesting and accomplished young women, full of talent which has left their personal attractions unimpaired. He has sons – the youngest at home – a nice boy.' The daughters had a

5 *W.H.C. Edwards, engraver who gave a great deal of help to Mary Turner, etched by Mary Turner and Edwards himself, from a drawing by J.P. Davis, 1815.*

truly exceptional education at home in Latin and Greek, French, German and Italian, all under the tutelage of their father who was an excellent linguist. Music and dancing were also taught, and the girls became thoroughly acquainted with history of art, history and literature. Above all they were trained to be talented artists, in part by their drawing master during the years 1812-23, John Sell Cotman, who was paid generously at £200 p.a. and who attended at the Bank House almost daily. The principal method of instruction, the one prevalent at the time, was to copy the work of the teacher. Dawson's wife Mary gained such proficiency and skill in this that her watercolours and drawings are hard to distinguish from those of Cotman,[3] such was her sympathetic understanding of his individual vision. She was outstanding too at etching, which she had

6 *Drawing of the Bank House, Great Yarmouth, the Turner family home. Photographed by Stephen Bates.*

7 *Elizabeth Turner, etched by Mary Turner after a drawing by J.P. Davis, 1816.*

8 *Maria Hooker, etched by Mary Turner from a drawing by Thomas Phillips RA, 1814.*

learnt from James Sowerby in 1804 when he was executing plates for Dawson Turner's *Muscologiae Hibernicea Spicilgium* while he was staying at the house. She also received unstinting long-term help in etching from William Camden Edwards of Bungay. One of her most brilliant etchings is a portrait of Cotman that surpasses the original drawing by J.P. Davis (fig. 19). Of the six known portraits of Cotman, this is perhaps the most convincing likeness and conveys his sensitive, reflective and somewhat brooding nature.

The educational regime at the Bank House was systematic and rigorous. There was incessant activity: never was a moment to be lost. Charles Lyell, the geologist, stayed with the Turners in 1817 and recorded in his diary[4], 'Mrs Turner has been etching with her daughters in the parlour every morning this week since half past six. Harriet [who was then 11] has as much talent as all the others united, and her knowledge of Latin is astonishing. She has a more perfect conception of Virgil than I had at 14, and earns a shilling at least three times a week by doing her Latin composition without a fault, and does it all with energy and goodwill.' Similarly, in the same year Benjamin Robert Haydon records how the house was run like a school: 'One seized a drawing, another a French grammar, a third a spelling book, a fourth her etching needle.'[5] The children were studying and drawing all day; they were highly motivated and

9 *Hannah Sarah Turner, etched by Mary Turner after a drawing by Elizabeth Palgrave, 1818.*

caught the infectious enthusiasm of their father. He was of course the driving force. Mother and daughters were fully involved and absorbed in Turner's publishing projects and his shifting preoccupations and interests. The output of this domestic academy was truly extraordinary. The number of drawings and watercolours produced was prodigious: for the extra-illustrated copy of Blomefield's *History of Norfolk* the family is thought to have provided 4,000 of the 7,000 total. Similarly, the number of etchings painstakingly executed was very great. In 1830 Mary had a limited edition of *One Hundred Etchings* published. At the sale of 1859 one lot consisted of 'Five Volumes of Etchings executed in the House of Dawson Turner'. There were 667 etchings from 1812-24, which are described thus: 'As a series this collection is probably un-exampled as a monument of the Artistic Skill in one family.' There is another folio scrapbook with 200 etchings entitled 'A Mother's Exemplar'. Many of the books in the library had extra illustrations by Mary and the daughters. The 51 lithograph illustrations of Dawson Turner's picture collection for *Outlines of Lithography* (1840) were executed by Mary Anne and Hannah Sarah.

Dawson Turner was perhaps a schoolteacher at heart who was left with a great thirst for knowledge after his early departure from Cambridge. He was stimulating company and his children were extremely intelligent, lively and charming. They were capable of responding to the inspiration provided by their father. There were frequent trips to draw and paint local churches and antiquities and, after 1814, when the first Treaty of Paris was signed, there were frequent visits to the Continent to see the great European picture galleries, Roman antiquities and splendid Gothic cathedrals. The children were enthusiastic and dedicated to their studies. They enjoyed a very close relationship with their devoted father for whom they had a touchingly deep affection. Of course the studies and work on the Dawson Turner collections went on long after school age and even marriage. By the time of Sir Frederick Madden's visit in 1832 the three unmarried daughters were teaching in schools or studying all day. Some of the illustrations in this book show the studious atmosphere at the Bank

10 *The four sons of Sir Francis Palgrave saying multiplication tables to their governess. Sketched by their mother Lady Palgrave (née Elizabeth Turner). Photographed by Stephen Bates.*

House, the girls in Empire-line long flowing dresses bent over their books and drawing boards, ringlets of hair falling beside their pretty faces.

Dawson and Mary Turner's children had full and interesting lives. The eldest daughter, Maria, at the age of 18, married Dawson Turner's botanist protégé William Jackson Hooker in 1815. He was to become the celebrated director of the Royal Botanic Gardens at Kew where his son Joseph, who was also knighted, succeeded him. The second daughter, Elizabeth, married Francis Palgrave in 1823. He was Jewish and before consenting to the marriage Dawson insisted that Francis change his name from Cohen to Palgrave and embrace the Christian religion. Francis was a barrister with exceptional talents who shared with his father-in-law a common interest in the antiquities of Norfolk and Normandy. He was to become Deputy Keeper of Public Records, the creator of the Public Records Office. He was knighted in 1831. He was something of an infant prodigy, having at the age of eight translated Homer's *Battle of the Frogs and Mice* from a Latin version into perfect French: this work was privately printed by his father in 1879. Francis and Elizabeth's children were all very distinguished: Francis Turner Palgrave as author of the *Golden Treasury* and Professor of Poetry at Oxford, Sir Robert Henry Inglis Palgrave as banker and editor of *The Economist*, Sir Reginald Francis Douce Palgrave as Clerk to the House of Commons, and William Gifford Palgrave as a traveller and diplomat of note, later known as 'Palgrave of Arabia'.

If Elizabeth was the most talented of Cotman's pupils (she benefited from his tuition throughout his 12 years at Yarmouth), Mary Anne, the third daughter, was the most industrious. She never married, stayed at home and became her father's general literary factotum. He records his deep gratitude to her in his *Guide to the Historian* (1848) with a touching dedication 'to his very dear daughter, Miss Mary Anne Turner, his constant companion and unwearied assistant; to whom his Norfolk collections owe their existence, his autographs their arrangement and their beauty; the author as a lasting testimony of his obligations, most gladly and gratefully dedicates this volume; which without her help, had never been prepared or completed.' She was largely responsible for his *History of Caister Castle* (1842), including all the illustrations. The delightful portrait *The Two Sisters* (1824), by the close family friend Thomas Phillips is of Elizabeth and Mary Anne. This painting hung among the Old Masters in the drawing room.

Harriet was to marry the locally well-known geologist and antiquarian The Reverend John Gunn. Hannah Sarah married a partner in the Bank, Thomas Brightwen, who was also a great benefactor in the town of Yarmouth. Eleanor Jane, known as Ellen, married the Reverend William Jacobson, Professor of Divinity at Oxford and later Bishop of Chester. Gurney became a surgeon with the East India Company and was to die in Calcutta at the early age of thirty-five. And lastly there was William Dawson who was a scholar and the Headmaster of the Royal Institution School, Liverpool. He was author of a number of works on the histories of England, Rome, Greece and Germany. It is noteworthy how Dawson Turner's passionate interests were shared and followed by his children and celebrated sons-in-law.

Dawson Turner was to remain a partner of the Bank (known as the Yarmouth and Suffolk Bank or the Turner Gurney Bank) until his death in 1858. It was one of the Gurney group of Banks in East Anglia, originally set up in 1781. Cautious and careful management enabled it to survive the periodic financial crises that caused many other country banks to fail, notably in 1825. After peace was finally signed in 1815 the Bank especially prospered with the expanding Yarmouth population and herring fishery industry. The number of clients trebled in the 30 years after Dawson Turner took over. His duties at the Bank did not stop him from making prolonged visits to parts of the British Isles, and from 1814 to the Continent. The only exception was in 1818 when he was delayed for nearly two months from joining his family in Normandy by affairs of the Halesworth branch. His younger brother was in charge and had become deranged, so that there was much to be sorted out. One of his partners at the Bank became a lifelong friend. This was the poet, MP and banker, Hudson Gurney (1775-1864). In 1844 Dawson Turner described him as 'the friend of my youth; we came into the bank on the same day as partners; and our friendship, I am most thankful to say, has continued to this hour unbroken.'[6] They shared many interests, including book collecting. Hudson Gurney's library contained 15,000 books and he claimed to have read them all.

Hudson Gurney was only one of Dawson Turner's very many friends who included many leading figures in his chosen fields of interest: botany, science, picture collecting, the fine arts, autograph and book collecting, literature, history and the antiquities of Norfolk and Normandy. He carried on a massive correspondence with his friends and acquaintances. His last surviving daughter, Eleanor Jacobson, gave 82 volumes of this correspondence with about 16,000 letters of general correspondence to Trinity College Cambridge in 1890. In addition there were many other bound volumes of correspondence including one with 728 letters from his son-in-law, Sir William Hooker. His *Account of a Tour in Normandy* in two volumes in 1820 was based on letters received from his family and from Cotman.

If he was the friendliest of men and a great correspondent, he was also extremely hospitable. The Puttick and Simpson sale catalogue of 1859 in relation to the Blomefield *History of Norfolk* says, 'This Book, perhaps the finest illustrated County History ever formed, is well known,

11 *Mary Turner, engraved by W.H.C. Edwards from a portrait by Thomas Phillips RA, 1814.*

for few there are of men of any standing in literature, science, or the arts, during the last thirty years or more, who have not at one time or another enjoyed the hospitality of its late possessor, and profited by his ever ready disposition to display the treasures in his library.' And the same generosity was shown to artists and connoisseurs who were equally willingly shown the picture collection.

Among his many friends were James Heath ARA, the leading line engraver in London, and his son Charles. The close relationship was mutually beneficial. Dawson Turner lent them money facilitating their illustrated publishing projects. He frequently sent presents to the Heaths by stagecoach: pheasants and barrels of oysters and herrings. In return James Heath would send bundles of autograph letters by distinguished people and, when they visited Yarmouth, would help Mary Turner with her etching. In her *One Hundred Etchings* there is a portrait of James Heath based on a drawing by the sculptor William Behnes. In 1820 James was unable to accept Dawson Turner's invitation to join his party visiting Paris. When Charles took over the business he showered Dawson Turner with first proofs of engravings including those for J.M.W. Turner's 1838 *Picturesque views in England and Wales*.[7]

In the early years at Bank House Dawson Turner devoted his great energies to botany, especially mosses, lichens, seaweeds and algae. Between 1800 and 1808 he produced four major publications quite apart from nine papers for the Linnean Society and the Annals of Botany. He was elected a Fellow of the Linnean Society in 1797 and a Fellow of the Royal Society in 1802. Elsewhere he was elected to Academies in Edinburgh, Dublin, Stockholm, Rouen, Caen, Leipzig and Berlin.

In the second decade of the century Dawson Turner assembled most of his collection of Old Master paintings at a cost of around £2,000. His favourite painting here was his *Landscape* by Hobbema. Before he went to sleep each night he would bring to mind the image of this lovely painting. It was about this time that he also developed a passionate interest in the antiquities of Norfolk and Normandy. His books on Normandy were published in 1820 and 1822. The latter in two volumes, *Architectural Antiquities of Normandy*, comprised a text by him and etchings by Cotman. He was particularly interested in medieval buildings that could be securely dated, with a view to discovering how architecture evolved stylistically in the Middle Ages. This he never managed to do but he did establish himself as a respected authority on the subject that was taken much further later in the century.

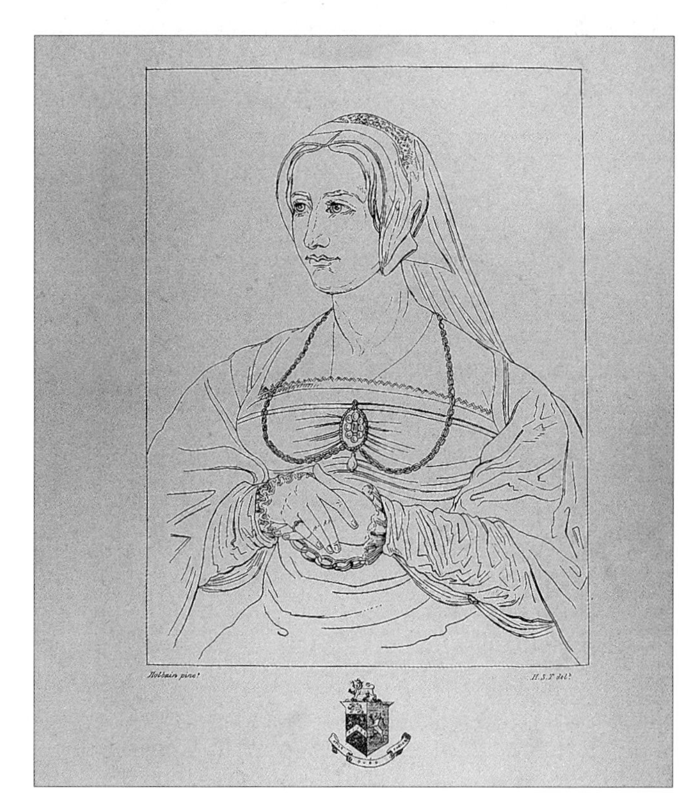

12 *Queen Catherine Parr, lithograph by Hannah Sarah Turner from an original in the collection of Dawson Turner by Hans Holbein.*

Autograph collecting was begun about 1816 when he first had contact with someone who was to become his mentor and friend, William Upcott. It became an important collection in 1820 when, in partnership with Hudson Gurney, he bought for £700 a substantial part of the manuscript collection that had belonged to the celebrated 18th-century collector, Cox Macro. Dawson Turner's share included over 900 letters and papers that constituted Macro's autograph collection. The letters of Kings and Queens from the 15th century onwards were particularly important. After this there was a dramatic increase in the purchase of autograph letters, that were eventually to number in excess of 40,000 items. They became a passion. He thought they threw a light on the character of the writer that was particularly interesting where celebrities and great historical figures were concerned. As he said in his 1848 *Guide to the Historian*, 'an autograph appears at the present time a no less indispensable accompaniment to biography than a portrait; and both for the same cause, as clues to the deciphering of character.'

13 *Archduke Albert, lithograph by Mary Anne Turner after an original in the collection of Dawson Turner by Jan van Bockhorst.*

14 *Dr Waagen, art critic, inspecting Dawson Turner's picture collection, 2 October 1850.*

Dawson Turner also had a passion for portraiture. He collected countless prints of celebrities, which were used to illustrate books in his library. His family album in two volumes now in the Victoria & Albert Museum contained over a hundred pencil portraits, many by Cotman, Phillips and Elizabeth Palgrave, and a few by John Varley who stayed at the Bank House in 1822. His collection of portraits of botanists is now at Kew. And, of course, Dawson Turner encouraged his wife and the children to produce drawn and etched portraits.

Mary Turner died on 17 March 1850 after 54 years of an exceptionally happy marriage. Life at the Bank House might have continued very much as before with the unmarried daughter, Mary Anne, taking complete charge of the household but for two dramatic events that brought the old rhythm of family life and business to an abrupt end.

Completely unexpectedly at the age of 76 Dawson Turner eloped to Gretna Green with Rosamund Matilda Duff, a widow of relatively humble birth, modest education and 35 years his junior. Their marriage at Gretna Green in September 1851 was followed by a more conventional ceremony at St James, Piccadilly, in December. This was to lead to a temporary estrangement from his family, the loss of many friends, disagreements with his partners at the Bank and a move away from Yarmouth to avoid social ostracism, first to Barnes and then to Old Brompton in London. Rather surprisingly, this proved a successful marriage: she nursed him admirably in his old age, and he taught her Latin and Hebrew to improve her education. Francis Palgrave (whose wife Elizabeth died in 1852) remained in contact and gradually there was reconciliation with the family. Towards the end of his life Sir William Hooker was in regular attendance.

The second drama was in 1852 when Dawson Turner became financially overstretched, necessitating the sale of assets. There had been signs of financial stress in the 1840s but he had not avoided his great horror of 'full house and empty purse' reaching such an unfortunate extremity. In May 1852 the picture collection was sold by Christie and Manson in 79 lots for £2,058. Giovanni Bellini's *Virgin and Child with Saints* went for £378 against a purchase price in 1814 of £54. In the following year Sothebys sold about half the library of printed books for £4,560: that, he said, was about half what he paid for them. Some of the manuscripts were later sold to the British Museum. After his death the remainder of the library was sold in an eight-day sale by Puttick and Simpson, and the

15 *Isaac Mouchereon,* Rocky Landscape, *watercolour copy by Hannah Sarah Turner of an original in the collection of Dawson Turner.*

16 *Peter Paul Rubens,* Peace and Plenty embracing each other, *watercolour copy by Elizabeth Palgrave of an original in the collection of Dawson Turner.*

same auctioneers sold the manuscripts and autographs for over £6,000. This included £460 for the extra-illustrated Blomefield (which is now in the British Library).

It is almost impossible to imagine how Dawson Turner managed to accomplish so much as banker, businessman, JP for the counties of Norfolk and Suffolk, educator, collector, author and traveller. Munby's admirable monograph ends with the description of Dawson Turner as 'this friendly, amiable and industrious man'.[8] Perhaps as good a summary as any by a contemporary was recorded by John William Burgon in his journal on 16 April 1838: 'Dawson Turner is an extra-ordinary man; he combines the banker with the man of letters. He is a classic and a botanist, a picture-fancier, an autograph collector … a pleasant companion, a kind host, a zealous abettor in literary enquiries, the tenderest of husbands, and the very kindest of fathers.'[9]

To analyse the various strands of his life and career this book brings together the scholarship of distinguished contributors who have studied

17 *Attributed to David Teniers junior,* Gardener and his wife, *watercolour copy by Hannah Sarah Turner of an original in the collection of Dawson Turner.*

Dawson Turner and his family in great depth. It is now nearly 150 years since his death and it is only surprising that this remarkable man and his extremely talented, captivating family have not been the subject of a book before now.

I wish to express my deeply felt thanks to all the contributors for their research and for writing so interestingly about their subjects. Special thanks are also due to Christopher Barker for having the idea to produce this book and for doing so much to propel the project forward. His Dawson Turner archive has provided a rich source of material. My thanks are also due to my son Rupert Goodman for allowing us to reproduce here the celebrated family portrait by Thomas Phillips RA and to my daughter Alexandra Abberton for permission to reproduce some of the girls' copies of paintings at the Bank House.

Nigel Goodman

CHAPTER TWO

Dawson Turner: Art Patron, Connoisseur and Collector

Introduction

Dawson Turner, an accomplished scholar and antiquary, was the leading patron among a group of collectors centred in Great Yarmouth, Norfolk in the first half of the 19th century. His inherited family banking business provided him with the means to activate his passions. He was able to devote time to scholarly pursuits, all of which fed his central passion as a collector and patron. His interests in botany led to his election as a Fellow of the Linnean Society in 1797 and also provided him with an entrée into London circles. He was passionately interested in the study of Norfolk history as well as antiquities, on which he published a number of books and pamphlets, gaining him admittance to further circles of influential people. He gathered an extensive library of botanical and historical books and collections of manuscripts, letters and autographs and in 1828 succeeded Sir Edward Smith as President of the Norfolk and Norwich Museum. Today significant survivals from his collections of manuscripts and books reside in public collections, notably the British Museum, Trinity College Cambridge and Norwich Castle Museum & Art Gallery. These holdings are of more than simply antiquarian interest, being testimony to the passions of a collector who may be seen to have reinvented the role of patron and connoisseur for the mercantile classes of the early 19th century.

Turner developed his understanding of art by consorting with some of the leading artists and professional minds of the day, also going out of his way to visit exhibitions in London and Paris, acquiring a massive collection of exhibition and gallery catalogues. He educated his taste by visiting the art collections of his neighbours in Norfolk, notably that of the Earl of Leicester at Holkham Hall. He carefully garnered the opinions not only of those connoisseurs and collectors whom he admired, but also those of artists whom he befriended, notably John Crome, John Sell Cotman and Thomas Phillips RA, with whom he travelled to Paris to visit the Palais de Louvre. His professional awareness of money values and market prices gave him acumen in his collecting, but not in his personal finances. In 1853 he suffered the dispersal of his library and collections through Christie's. His collection at this time included a choice group of paintings by Norwich School artists and also Dutch, Flemish and Italian School pictures. He had published his collection of paintings in *Outlines in Lithography* (1840), the text of which is a detailed catalogue that combines aesthetic appreciation tempered with provenance history and a smattering of anecdote and considered opinion as to attributions.

This essay outlines Dawson Turner's very real place in the pantheon of British polymaths whose mania for collecting was driven by a passion for the arts. That passion was fuelled by a practical and pragmatic approach to art appreciation that embraced an antiquarian attitude to the arts, tempered by a ready willingness to learn from contemporary artists, from looking at paintings by the established European masters as well as from the contents of his library. His desire to employ a Drawing Master (over two decades) to instruct and inspire his wife and daughters was fuelled as much by the need to develop his antiquarian and bibliophile interests as to sign up to the prevailing fashion for ladies to learn the art of drawing. His bookish projects were crucial to his desire to stamp his personality upon the arts but also to explore his understanding of the world. No sooner had John Crome left his employ than he inveigled Cotman to move his family to Great Yarmouth and continue the work of his household. This was traditional, self-serving patronage to which Cotman himself was nevertheless drawn, even as Crome bowed out. Cotman's personality required a careful and sustaining hand of friendship and this was what Turner proffered.

Patronage

The relationship of Turner with three key figures in the British art scene of the early 19th century is crucial in establishing the pedigree of Turner's claim to being a patron of the arts. These three artists, John Crome (1768-1821), John Sell Cotman (1782-1842) and Thomas Phillips RA (1770-1845) all held a special place in the comings and goings at Bank House. The first two were both engaged as Drawing Masters to help Mary Turner and her daughters learn to draw and paint in watercolour. The women sought a proficient standard in order not only to conform with the fashion for drawing but also to engage upon the task of helping Dawson Turner in the classification and recording of his many cultural pursuits, notably creating what became something of a 'paper museum' of artefacts and visual images as well as the written word. Thomas Phillips, meanwhile, was the artist who most closely enabled Turner to act as friend rather than employer – even when commissioning him to paint portraits of the family.

18 *Hannah Gurney, 1786-1850, portrait of John Crome, pencil with grey wash, heightened with white. Norwich Castle Museum and Art Gallery.*

Turner's patronage of John Crome (fig.19) included the purchase of works by him for his growing collection, but his support for Crome also extended well beyond the artist's death in 1821. It was Turner's memoir of the artist, together with his posthumous publication of the complete oeuvre of Crome's etchings, which was to provide the single most influential record of the artist in the 19th century. It was this memoir that established so many of the facts and also beneficent myths around the sketchily understood life of John Crome, an artist who was at the centre of an industry that established a 'School' of painting in early 19th-century Norwich. When John Crome died in 1821 the Rev William Gunn (1750-1841) wrote to John Flaxman RA that 'people are now crazy for his pictures which are bought with avidity and sell high.'[1] This has all the flavour of a worldly remark borrowed from his close acquaintance Dawson Turner, whose daughter Harriet was to marry Gunn's son, John. Turner not only provided Crome with employment as a Drawing Master but also acquired seven paintings for Bank House directly from the artist. At the same time the relationship between patron and artist was not, it seems, altogether a happy one.

Although the evidence is slim, it does seem that Cotman provides the key to believing that there may have been a stormy end to Turner's patronage of John Crome. Early in December 1811 Cotman wrote to

19 *Mary Turner, after J.P. Davis, portrait of John Sell Cotman; etching 1818. Norwich Castle Museum and Art Gallery.*

Dawson Turner: 'Crome, I think, is acting very wrong every way, and at some future time he may be sorry for it – should he propose bringing up his son to the same profession – for then by degrees he might have left it off to him.'[2] It is likely that Crome had effectively given up his teaching post at Bank House, for it was immediately after this – and effectively in the same letter – that Cotman was in negotiation with Dawson Turner over the prospect of moving himself and his family wholesale to Yarmouth so that he might assume the role of Drawing Master for the ladies of Bank House.

Turner's relationship with Crome is less substantiated during Crome's lifetime, but it is the memoir that leaves us in no doubt as to his patronage of the artist. In addition Turner records some well-chosen facts about his protégé in the entries for Crome's seven paintings in his catalogue of the Bank House collection, *Outlines in Lithography* (1840):

> Those figured in this volume were purchased by me from the artist himself. Some of them were painted expressly for me. I had the greatest regard for him when living. I enjoyed his society; I admired his talents; I valued the man; and I highly appreciated the good sense which led him to confine himself exclusively to the representation of nature, and to be satisfied with her as she offered herself to his eyes. Feelings of this description have probably induced me to give place to more of his works than I should otherwise have admitted. They are selected from eleven in my possession.[3]

If only half of this retrospective expression of feelings towards the artist shone through in Turner's dealings with Crome during his lifetime he would have felt well supported by his patron.

The second artist who is most consistently identified with Turner's patronage is John Sell Cotman (fig.19), who was in his salaried employ while living in Great Yarmouth. While Cotman was based in Norwich Turner offered a salary of £200 per annum to encourage him to move to Yarmouth and Cotman was gradually persuaded to make the move, finally settling there in January 1812. Cotman certainly acted as far more than Drawing Master to the household. The artist was to focus almost his entire output for over a decade in etching and drawing for Turner's publication projects. His teaching style also suited the needs of the ladies of the house, helping them to fulfill Turner's insatiable demand for illustrations to his many manuscripts and published book projects. Turner's relationship with Cotman is coloured by the fact that the artist was not only Turner's salaried employee but Turner was also his banker

20 *John Sell Cotman 1782-1842, Walsingham Abbey Gate, from* The Antiquities of Norfolk; *etching 1818.*

21 *Mary Anne Turner, after John Sell Cotman. View in the Town of Alençon, watercolour, 1825.*

effectively in charge of his financial affairs, including the mortgage that Cotman struggled to maintain. In consequence Turner was to receive numerous bleak reports on the artist's manic moods, which conflicted with the charm with which Cotman set about teaching Mary Turner and her daughters. Cotman brought out the best in creative terms from the ladies of Bank House. Some of their finest work as copyists relates to drawings in watercolour, which were not exclusively related to Dawson Turner's publications, notably a set of Normandy landscapes in monochrome and watercolour dating from 1822 that, although based upon Cotman's compositions, show great sensitivity towards his creative style (fig.21).[4]

Cotman did regard Turner as a friend and paid tribute to him often enough. One comment may here stand for almost 40 years of correspondence between them both: 'Without such a friendship I must have sunk under the intolerable load of bodily and mental affliction.'[5] Cotman dedicated the first plate – *The South Gate at Yarmouth* – in his first book, *Miscellaneous Etchings* (published 1811), to Turner (fig.22) and an equally accomplished plate in the same volume, *St Benet's Abbey*, to 'Mrs Dawson Turner' (fig.23). For his part Turner paid a similar compliment, typically, in an inscription to a copy of his book *One Hundred Etchings* (1830) in which he wrote a dedication:

> Of the very few copies of this the present is, with the greatest pleasure, given to J.S. Cotman Esq., not only as a memento of the regard entertained for him by all my family and of our high respect for his talents, but also as a proof of my thankfulness for the very great advantages which my daughters have derived from his very valuable instructions. D.T.[6]

Turner found numerous ways to encourage Cotman and provided him with an entrée to other patrons, notably his banking partner Hudson Gurney. Cotman paid tribute to that relationship, commenting that 'he supplied me with money like a prince.'[7] The extended Turner family all sought to patronise him in the best sense, including the daughters and their husbands. Towards the end of his life Cotman received another gift of a book from Turner, to which he responded: 'Your kind note accompanying the present pierced me to the quick. You said you would visit me and shake me by the hand once again before we died. It spoke volumes. It shall be sincerely clasped. I know of no man, save Hudson Gurney, whose esteem I more truly value and always did, than yourself.'[8]

It was with the Royal Academician Thomas Phillips that Turner forged his third most important of artist friendships. While he commissioned Phillips to paint a small group of family portraits that survive as testimony to his direct patronage, he also developed a friendship with him during their travels in France in the autumn of 1815. Their mutual friendship

22 *John Sell Cotman, 1782-1842, South Gate at Yarmouth, dedicated to Dawson Turner; etching, 1811.*

23 *John Sell Cotman, 1782-1842, St Benet's Abbey, dedicated to Mrs Dawson Turner; etching 1811.*

led to both the Turner and Phillips families becoming close friends, with Elizabeth Turner meeting her future husband, Francis Palgrave, at the Phillips's home. Perhaps the most tangible product of their friendship is the family portrait of Dawson Turner with his wife Mary and two of their daughters, Maria and Elizabeth, painted in 1814.[9] It is a successful portrait that subtly pays tribute to the head of the family standing at the apex of the composition, to Mary as next in the family hierarchy, while the two daughters are equally suitably placed within the composition. Seated to the fore is the elder of the two, Maria, who was shortly to marry William Jackson Hooker and holds a paper in reference to her artistic attributes. Seated on the ground is Elizabeth, the youngest, whose own marriage was a few years off but who symbolically proffers a celebratory circlet of flowers to her sister. The portrait, when exhibited at the Royal Academy, was pronounced 'a gem'.[10] In his catalogue entry for this portrait Turner professed 'it impossible to speak of this excellent friend of mine, or of his works, in any terms which would not be liable to be suspected of partiality'.[11] He chose instead to consider portraiture as a genre: 'If portraits be not of themselves actually history, they are assuredly the legitimate materials for it; and even where the objects they represent are destitute of any high pretensions, they are calculated to call forth affection, and so cultivate some of the best feelings of the human heart.'[12] Turner was subtly paying tribute to Phillips's talents in that his portrait had engendered his discussion of the art of portraiture at its finest.

This commission was followed in 1824 by that for the *Two Sisters*,[13] Lady Palgrave (née Elizabeth Turner) and Mary Anne Turner, a portrait Gustav Waagen was to admire during his visit to Bank House in 1850.[14] Phillips also painted portraits of Sir William and Lady Hooker (née Maria Turner), which hung in the dining room at Bank House.[15] Phillips in addition supplied drawings for Mrs Mary Turner to etch: 15 such drawings were the basis for etchings by Mary in Turner's *One Hundred Etchings* issued in 1830. Phillips's intimacy also extended to commenting to Turner on Cotman's mood swings: 'I lament with you the turns in Cotman's mind.'[16] One more area in which Phillips had some influence was as a London contact within the metropolitan art scene, particularly as a mediator with dealers. When Alexis Delahante wrote to Turner to inform him that he had bought Dou's *Old Woman and Goose* he specifically mentioned that it was 'because Mr Phillips recollected to have heard said that you did like the picture'.[17] It was Phillips who brought the Rubens studio sketch *Peace and Plenty* (fig.16) from the dealer Philip Panné: 'I have got your picture from Panné and think it a very fine specimen of the master.'[18] Phillips, meanwhile, would himself turn to Turner to seek his help. After their return from a trip to Italy in 1826 Phillips wrote to Turner asking: 'If you have any memo of the Pictures you saw which you think might be serviceable to me and could find time to transcribe them I should be obliged to you.'[19] We see an intimate friendship at work between the two men that fully justifies the assertion that Dawson Turner knew well how to extend both patronage and friendship to artists within his circle. We also see the degree to which it is not necessarily helpful to divide Turner's activities into those of patron and collector. Just as Crome was both painter and dealer, so was Phillips an artist who provided an entrée to both metropolitan artist friendships and art networks by which Turner could extend his patronage and understanding, including his connoisseurship and collecting networks.

Connoisseurship

Dawson Turner achieved some distinction as a connoisseur, being rather more than simply the 'immense living index' described by Benjamin Robert Haydon RA.[20] He effectively created a manufactory of the arts at Bank House, driving his entire family towards a shared goal of record-making and illustration: making archives and books and creating inventories and collections of ephemera and works of art. His architectural interests led to his projects to record the antiquities of Norfolk and then Normandy, while his employment of Cotman as his illustrator raised the level of his publications beyond their being of merely antiquarian and archival interest. At the same time he undertook a deliberate study and appreciation of artworks that belies his 'bookishness'. Indeed, his study of botany may be seen as a parallel interest to that of his connoisseurship, with its similar appreciation of typology and systematic reasoning.

Dawson Turner twice travelled to Paris, principally to view the works of art brought back by Napoleon from his campaigns and displayed in the Palais de Louvre. Of his visit to the Louvre in 1814 he wrote: 'I shall never forget the effect produced upon me by them, when I first visited the Louvre in June 1814.'[21] His visit at that time was in the company of his family,[22] while his principal travelling companion the following year was his friend Thomas Phillips RA. The trip is fastidiously recorded in Turner's journal of the three-week tour, which remains in the family collection and includes sketches from Phillips's notebook. We therefore learn of the genesis of the trip from Turner himself:

> It fortunately happened that at this time Mr Phillips was in Yarmouth, kindly awaiting the return of Mr & Mrs Hooker from Ireland; and few persuasions were necessary to induce a man so truly attached to an art in which he is justly eminent, to cross the channel once more, to take a look, however hasty, at the treasures of a collection avowedly unrivalled and now about to be dispersed, most probably for ever. For my part, I felt but too happy to place myself under the guidance of such a friend ... looking to no other object than that of improving my judgement in works of art by listening to his observations ... tho the name of Mr Phillips will not be formally appended to each remark, it must be understood that for almost every one I am indebted to him.[23]

The travellers set out from Norfolk on 24 September and, although they were in London for only a few hours, still found time to see 'a collection of pictures now on sale at Pall Mall'. While waiting for an improvement in the weather for their crossing at Brighton they met William Beechey who was just back from his own trip to see the pictures at the Palais de Louvre (26 September) and soon after landing at Dieppe they met up with Francis Chantrey.[24] Both Beechey and Chantrey reported that the paintings and sculptures at the Louvre were in the process of being removed by troops aiming to return them to their countries of origin. Their journey was from that moment indeed a 'hasty' one, under pressure to reach Paris in time before the walls of the Palais de Louvre were stripped bare. Soon after arrival at the Louvre they met Canova, who was overseeing the packing of works and informed them of his current commission by the Duke of Bedford for a sculpture of the Three Graces. Canova was evidently not enjoying his official role overseeing the packing: 'He entered readily into conversation with us, said he never was before employed in so painful & unthankful a task.' Turner and Phillips found the walls of some of the galleries stripped of works of art, many paintings on the floor or leaning against walls. The immediacy of special access made a deep impression on Turner as he experienced in a visceral sense the immediacy of works of art out of their frames and casually left for close scrutiny:

> All was confusion; more than half the French paintings, above seven eighths of the German and full two thirds of the Italian were already gone. In the German department those that remained looked at a distance like mere spots upon the wall ... In the Schools of Italy workmen were employed taking down the paintings from their places. *The Transfiguration* & the *Communion of St. Jerome* were lying side by side upon the floor, out of their frames, at the moment we got there. The *Madonna di Foligno*, the *St. Cecilia* & many other of Raphael's paintings were standing against the walls ... nor could the scene before us be so aptly assimilated to any thing as to the appearance of Christie's auction room the day succeeding a sale.[25]

Choosing to compare the Louvre with the auction house in this way suggests that Turner was used to seeing the auction house after a sale – presumably to collect a new purchase. The fate of individual works of art is much rumoured and debated in the pages of the journal, as the travellers meet up with other visitors such as the poet and art connoisseur Samuel Rogers (1763-1855), author of *Pleasures of Memory* (1792) and also the dealer Delahante,[26] and the artist Philip Reinagle (1749-1833) who was in Paris with his son.[27] Turner and Phillips also visited the Bibliothèque, where they met the curator M. Millin and then moved on to meet M. Bonnemaison (and also Delahante once again), where they saw the Giustiniani Collection:

> Mr Phillips, who had never seen it before, was disappointed at it to a degree which I certainly did not expect, tho I own that the impression which it had made upon Mrs Turner & me last year prepared me as little for any high approbation on his part. He pronounced the collection in general very bad, and was of opinion that the best pictures must have been taken out & replaced by copies. Perhaps however, without going so far, the difference between the real & supposed worth of this gallery may be sufficiently accounted for by admitting that the latter rested more upon a long accredited character, which no one would be disposed to controvert than upon its true merit; that seen as paintings usually are in palaces, little opportunity is afforded of carefully examining them & that with these, as with Lucien Bonaparte's collection in London, a public exhibition only was wanted to enable the public to form a just estimate of them, nor would anything else have destroyed the illusion caused by the high character of the possessors.[28]

Here we see Dawson Turner trying to account for a difference of opinion concerning the quality of paintings between the general consensus and that of Phillips, whose opinion he respected. His solution – that a difference of opinion can only be resolved through public exhibition in unproblematic circumstances where paintings are readily viewed – is entirely pragmatic. We sense that Turner is writing his journal for public consumption rather than for private record.

Turner does seem to have developed an eye for the quality of a painting and was well able to make judgements in the marketplace as much as in the gallery:

> On our way from the Institute to the Luxembourg we passed a number of old picture-shops, the contents of which and all others we have seen in Paris, are full as bad, or even worse than of similar shops in London; nor do their proprietors belie the character they have established themselves with us. They are equally exorbitant in their demands & equally ready to vouch for any thing. One of them this morning gave us a pretty good proof of the latter, by offering his guarantee for the originality of a vile copy of the *Temptation of St Anthony* by Teniers, & of one still worse of a female after Titian.[29]

Turner was ever ready to record an opinion about any work of art he came across and the journal is peppered with his comments and judgements, which make for fascinating reading as they occur at a time of such upheaval for the collections at the Palais de Louvre and elsewhere in Paris. His points of comparison were expanding all the time. With characteristic Norfolk fervour Turner considered the *Danae* by Titian at the Luxembourg 'not a favourable proof of his talents: it wants that lightness of pencilling, for which Mr Coke's *recumbent female* by him at Holkham is conspicuous.'[30] Turner was here adopting a well-known critique by Michelangelo as recorded by Vasari when referring to Titian's celebrated *Danae* painted for Cardinal Farnese. Turner was comparing the *Danae* then in Paris to a version of its presumed pendant, *Venus and a Lute Player* at Holkham Hall, a painting now recognised as by Titian and his workshop. This strikes as an opinion formed through critical reading but tested by personal scrutiny of individual works.

Dawson Turner was also aware that this historic moment in the fortunes of the aristocratic collections was likely to have ramifications for the supply and demand of European Masters:

> It is above a twelvemonth since there was a private sale of pictures here, & those of even a secondary class are caught up with avidity. This confirms me in the opinion I have long maintain'd that, would the present troubles but subside, the good will be dearer than ever or rather will be no longer to be procured. They will gradually withdraw, as before the Revolution, into Palaces, where they will be kept as heir-looms; & they will disappear the more rapidly from the following causes: because the taste for works of art is more diffused; because money is more plentiful; and because the number of prime paintings is reduced by the destruction caused in the troubles of the last 30 years.[31]

Turner was both tutoring himself as a man of taste in the model of the established connoisseur and collector, while also exercising a banker's eye for the fluctuations of the market. Turner made it his business to study the local art collections of Norfolk, notably those of Thomas Harvey of

Catton, Norwich and the mercantile collections of Great Yarmouth as well as the Earl of Leicester at Holkham Hall, further up the coast in north Norfolk.[32] With the help of Mary Turner over a sustained period he recorded the reactions of visitors to the Earl of Leicester's picture collection at Holkham. This strikes as being a somewhat proprietorial attention to the Holkham Collection, but is a reflection of a serious intention to record and assimilate in a consistent manner the opinions of visiting artists, scholars and connoisseurs to one of the greatest private collections in Britain.

An indication of the degree to which Turner's connoisseurship may be considered successful can be adjudged in part from an inventoried list of valuations that remains in the family collection.[33] Although undated, this was almost certainly compiled prior to the sale of Turner's picture collection in 1852.[34] The inventory was probably compiled around 1819,[35] at which time the collection was valued at £1,929 11s. 0d. The pictures included two miniatures after Titian valued at eight guineas and a Crome drawing (five guineas), acquired from John Crome himself; a drawing of *Fountain's Abbey* by Cotman (six guineas) and six gouache drawings attributed to Clippart, valued at 12 guineas. The most highly valued paintings were that after Leonardo da Vinci, the Gaspard Poussin *Tivoli*, a landscape by Richard Wilson from Thomas Harvey's collection and Hobbema's *Landscape*, which were all valued at £150 each. The important Bellini was valued at just £54. The latter was less an indication of the quality of the Bellini (colour plate VIII), but rather of the level of perceived value of early Renaissance masters at that time. As such it is a genuine marker for the quality of Turner's aesthetic judgement for the period and its perceived low value is in no way a reflection of Turner's connoisseurship. The values for Phillips's family portraits were highly priced at £105 for the *Group Portrait* and £80 for his portrait of William Hooker and his wife. Interestingly, the values of paintings acquired just eight years earlier from the Rev John Homfray all showed only modest increases over their original acquisition values.[36] When Dawson Turner's collection was finally sold in 1852, a total of 79 lots sold for £2,051 18s. While this seems to show little to no profit, it was a protected investment of significant value. Just as a point of comparison, the day following Turner's sale saw the collection of the Earl of Shaftesbury (63 lots) go for £2,058.[37]

Another indication of Turner's connoisseurship was his engagement with architecture. Although this stemmed from antiquarian leanings, his understanding developed far beyond the simply bookish. He toured Normandy in 1814, 1815 and 1818 in order to assess at first hand the architecture about which he wished to write, while he employed John Sell Cotman to record the churches of Normandy for him as beautiful

24 *John Sell Cotman, 1782-1842, Cathedral Church of Notre-Dame, at Rouen, West Front, published in* The Antiquities of Normandy; *etching 1822.*

antiquarian illustrations to his text. Admirers of the work of Cotman tend to see Turner's letterpress about each plate as simply illustrative of those plates made by Cotman as a result of his own three tours (in the summers of 1817, 1818 and 1820), but the genesis of the entire project was of course the reverse. Turner engaged the help of acquaintances in France, notably Jean-Vincent-Félix Lamouroux (1779-1825), Professor of Natural History at Caen, who was to meet Cotman on each of his tours. Turner's main contact in France when preparing Cotman's tours was an archaeologist, Auguste Le Prevost (died 1859), a member of a number of learned societies at Bernay. Turner effectively used an enormous network of contacts across a broad spectrum of learning to enable his projects to blossom and Cotman benefited from this expansive approach even in Normandy. The relationship between artist and family was a symbiotic one: Mary Turner wrote to her husband in June 1818 while she awaited Cotman's arrival to join the family in Normandy: 'I long for Mr Cotman's arrival ... He will be very useful both as a man and an artist.'[38] Dawson Turner was himself to join them all shortly afterwards at Caen and we may see Turner's eagerness to train his eye as a connoisseur as symptomatic of his appreciation of the arts in general. His interests extended to the field of architecture as well as to works of art he could afford to collect and also those he could not afford but which nevertheless were a focus of his study.

Collecting Art

Dawson Turner's study of his collection as published through his own catalogue, *Outlines in Lithography*, provides a fascinating glimpse into his approach to collecting. This reveals that most of his principal paintings were purchased in Norfolk, from visiting dealers targeting local collectors and from those collectors themselves. The quality of art within his reach was relatively high, and his acquisitions included fine examples of contemporary art as well as works by Giovanni Bellini (and studio), Jan Steen and Rubens' studio. Although his purchasing power was not as high as was that of more aristocratic purses, Turner used his inherited fortune from his father and a network of contacts to increase his collection to full effect.

He in fact could acquire paintings through more usurious means. Correspondence between Turner and the Minister of Yarmouth, the Rev John Homfray (1768-1842), shows that in 1811 Turner took on three paintings from Homfray's collection for six months, by which time Homfray hoped to redeem them: 'I have sent the following Pictures, which you will allow to remain with you until the 1st Janury 1812 by which time I hope to redeem them at the prices offered.'[39] Homfray's pictures

25 *Portrait of Thomas Harvey, 1748-1819, after John Opie. Oil on canvas. Norwich Castle Museum & Art Gallery.*

were a *King of Spain* (valued at £20); a *Landscape* by Crome (tentatively valued at £5) and a *Crucifixion* (£20). A month later he added two more paintings to the group, *The Queen*, valued at £50, and a 'Breughel' valued at £5. Homfray's expectations of income seem to relate to an expected inheritance: the paintings 'are to remain with you until I can redeem them or they are to become your property if they are not taken from your custody by three months after the death of Mrs (Spurgeon) … P.S. As you have mentioned the subject I must add for your satisfaction that whilst they hang in your home, they hang at my risqué should I ever be able to redeem them.'[40] Turner's catalogue *Outlines in Lithography* reveals that of these pictures at least four duly entered his collection: *The Queen* was Catharine Parr, attributed to Holbein; *The Crucifixion*, attributed to Van Dyck; and the King of Spain, presumably the *Portrait of the Archduke Albert*, attributed to Jan van Boeckhorst. The 'Breughel' may well have been the small landscape on copper for which Turner gives no provenance details in his catalogue,[41] while the Crome *Landscape* could also have remained with Turner.

Outlines in Lithography, privately published in 1840, identifies – according to its title page – 'a small collection of pictures'. At that time the collection numbered 51 oil paintings, consisting of 13 British School paintings, 16 Dutch School paintings, six from the Flemish School, three French School pictures, nine Italian School paintings and one each from the German and Spanish Schools. Turner confessed to being completely stumped as to the origins of just two of his oil paintings, a *View in the Campagna di Roma* and a *Vase of Flowers*, both for well-judged reasons.

Turner's British School paintings, comprised principally of his collection of seven works by John Crome[42] and his patronage of Crome, came at a relatively early stage in his career as a collector. Turner also regarded the Royal Academician Thomas Phillips as a true friend and owned two commissioned family portraits by him.[43] This friendship with Phillips was cemented by their trip to Paris in 1815 and his tour journal[44] records the degree to which he came into contact with Phillips's opinions on artistic matters during this formative time. Two more British School works were those by Sir David Wilkie,[45] which came into his possession through the amateur painter Perry Nursey, a family friend to Wilkie, who lived in Little Bealings near Woodbridge, Suffolk. Turner broke his own rule of not commenting upon the talents of the living by comparing Wilkie favourably with both the Dutch School and Hogarth, recognising in the process the relative rarity of his own landscape oil by Wilkie. The only other British School painting that Turner chose to record in the *Outlines* was Henry Bone's reduced copy in enamels on copper of Leonardo da Vinci's *Christ the Redeemer*.[46]

The largest number of works in the Bank House collection from any one school of painting was of the Dutch masters. In this respect Dawson Turner is a litmus test for the thesis that the European master collections of East Anglia were formed by the region's close proximity to the Low Countries, with its resulting direct mercantile links aiding the growth of both local collections and a taste for landscape painting in particular. Although almost all of Turner's collection was acquired from local sources, notably the painters John Crome and Robert Ladbrooke, the collectors Thomas Harvey of Catton (fig.25), Norwich, the Rev Thomas Ellison, Rector of Haddiscoe and the Rev John Homfray MA FAS (1768-1842). Only Harvey directly imported works of art. Homfray, Minister at St George's Chapel, Great Yarmouth 1821-39, had purchased his paintings principally from the London dealer Thomas Moore Slade, as had Ellison. At the same time, Turner's Dutch works of art were not exclusively landscape paintings. Although he owned landscapes attributed to Isaac Moucheron (fig.15),[47] Adam Pynacker,[48] David Teniers II[49] and notably Meindert Hobbema,[50] some of his most significant works of art in terms of quality were those attributed to Adriaen van der Werff,[51] Jan Steen,[52] Adriaen Brouwer,[53] Gerrit Dou[54] and Aelbert Cuyp.[55]

Reading the pages of Turner's *Outlines* it becomes clear that he used a close network of connections, local and national, to acquire his collection. Two of his five Flemish works were attributed to Van Dyck and one to Rubens. Although Turner argued cogently for Rubens' full authorship, his oil sketch for one of the panels commissioned by Charles I for the ceiling of the Banqueting House in Whitehall, *Peace Embracing Plenty* (fig.16), is now considered as by Rubens' studio.[56] Turner had purchased this oil sketch from the London dealer Philip Panné, while his *Crucifixion* attributed to Van Dyck was one of a group of pictures that had come to him from John Homfray who in turn had acquired a good number of his pictures from Thomas Moore Slade. Another Flemish work, Gaspar de Crayer's *Musical Party*,[57] formerly in the collection of the London banker William G. Coesvelt, was one of a number of paintings purchased directly by Turner from Alexis Delahante, one of the key importers of European master paintings from leading continental collections at the turn of the century. It was also through Delahante that Turner acquired his one Spanish School painting, attributed to del Mazo (also from the collection of William Coesvelt); two French School pictures, *Madame de Maintenon and her Niece*, attributed to Mignard, and a *Young Girl*, attributed to Greuze; and two Dutch paintings, his *Landscape* attributed to Teniers and his Dou panel painting, *Old Woman and Goose*.

Panné and Slade were two dealers who were known for their connections, able to bring to England some of the old family collections of Europe. The dealer William Buchanan, himself of considerable reputation in the field, wrote of Slade: 'Mr Slade, who has ever been a most enthusiastic admirer of works of art, was among the first of those gentlemen who set an example of giving liberal prices, which alone could draw those treasures from foreign countries.' While Homfray was a key Norfolk buyer of paintings from Slade, Turner did himself buy one small panel painting direct from Slade, which purported to be a self-portrait by David Teniers II. Turner went to some lengths in his *Outlines* to clarify whether Teniers could indeed have been the painter of his portrait and whether it was actually a self portrait: 'My authority for venturing to designate this picture as I have done, is, that it was so called by Mr Slade, by whom it was brought to Yarmouth shortly after he had completed the purchase of the Flemish, Dutch and German portions of the Orleans Gallery.'[58]

Dawson Turner also purchased a work direct from Buchanan, *The Rape of Europa* attributed to Titian, a reduced version of the composition well known from the fine original in the Orleans Collection that had passed to the ownership of the Earl of Darnley.[59] According to Buchanan this had formerly been in the collection of Citizen Robit, then passed through the hands of the connoisseurs Sir Simon Clarke and George Hibbert, then Sir M.M. Sykes and William Young Ottley before being purchased back by Buchanan in 1814. Turner carefully documents all these marks of status and authenticity in an entry typical of his thorough approach, which reflects well his methodology. He reveals all the twists and turns of the debate over authorship and attribution, is well aware that he is dealing with a copy after a celebrated original, while at the same time weighing the evidence of as many opinions as he can muster. This method is typical of the man that Benjamin Robert Haydon described as 'a living index' yet it is by no means a mere catalogue of opinion without research and assessment of his own. Typically he called upon numerous volumes to support his researches, most of which were in his own library. He also wrote up the opinions he learned, seeking them from correspondents as well as visitors to Bank House.

Turner's Italian School paintings were all attributed to distinguished painters and, while he carefully detailed their attributions, the number of differing opinions he records suggests the likelihood that some may be wrongly attributed. Nevertheless, Turner takes care to record all opinions and in the process gives alternatives that suggest that the quality of the Italian works is deserving, if not of the top quality. His prize possession was Giovanni Bellini's *The Virgin & Child with Saints*, now recognised by the fuller title of *The Madonna and Child enthroned with Saint Peter and Saint Paul and a Donor* (colour plate VIII) of 1505.[60]

Dawson Turner himself undertook some research into the provenance of this altarpiece and in many ways this first entry in the catalogue stands as typical of his methodology. He recounts how he has checked through catalogues in his possession to establish its recent history:

> This picture was the property of a well-known collector of his time, Mr Edward Coxe, of Hampstead, brother to two men of greater notoriety, Archdeacon Coxe, the traveller, and Peter Coxe, the auctioneer, author of the poem, entitled 'The Social Day'. Of Mr Edward Coxe's paintings there were two sales by auction; the first by his brother in 1807; the other eight years subsequently, by Squib. In the catalogue of the former I find this piece (no. 56, of the first day's sale) described as follows: '*Saints adoring the Saviour in the arms of the Virgin*; richly colored and attentively executed throughout. Titian, in his famous picture of the Cornaro Family, has evidently studied this picture, dated 1505. From the [John] Purling Collection: originally belonged to the Pembroke Family.' It passed into my hands in the autumn of 1814, when it was brought to Yarmouth, with forty-four others, by Mr William Carey, a man whose zeal and ability in the cause of British art – picture-dealer as he was, and consequently interested in the productions of the ancient masters – have not been exceeded by any individual within my knowledge.

Turner comments upon Carey's assessment of the altarpiece in his catalogue of the paintings he brought to Great Yarmouth. He agrees with his reference to the influence of the Umbrian artist Pietro Perugino (died 1523) in the two standing figures, but points out that 'he must surely be mistaken in supposing the kneeling figure to be designed for Lorenzo de' Medici, who died in 1492.' He cannot think that the kneeling figure is 'any other than the Donatore; the same for whom it was originally executed'. He suggests that it might also be the same member of the Pesaro family whom Titian painted in his celebrated altarpiece in the Pesaro Chapel, in the Frari Church, Venice, a comment based upon an engraving after the Pesaro altarpiece by Lefevre. Such scholarship is not without its hazards. The identity of the donor has continued to be a matter for conjecture and the early circumstances of the commission remain unclear. Turner's assessment of his painting was admirable for the period: it was rare for the early Italian masters to receive any attention from earlier British collectors.

A manuscript survives in the family collection that shows that Dawson Turner meticulously recorded the opinions of visitors to Bank House. He presumably used an earlier version of this when compiling his catalogue entries for the *Outlines*.[61] He particularly valued and recorded the opinions of artists, picture dealers and connoisseurs and among the former were the Royal Academicians Sir William Beechey RA (1753-1839);[62] William Redmore Bigg RA (1755-1828); family friend Thomas Phillips RA (1770-1845); James Ward RA (1769-1859) and Henry William Pickersgill RA (1782-1875).

Other visitors who proffered opinions included Poussin Hazzard Nursey, whose father Perry, an amateur artist and collector based in Suffolk, had named three of his sons after famous painters.[63] On one occasion father and son visited together and added their comments to the long list of those who had considered the authorship of the painting *View in the Campagna di Roma*: 'The sky and right hand are quite Gaspar; and I have no doubt of its being his. One of the figures is quite the counterpart of one in your large picture. I have seen other pictures by his hand equally finished.'[64] Further visitors included the dealers William Buchanan, J. Smith of Bond Street, Delahante and Thomas Moore Slade and also the dealer and artist Henry Walton. Norfolk-connected connoisseurs included the celebrated botanist James Edward Smith (1759-1828) and Mr Andrew Fountaine (1808-73) of Narford Hall. The printseller 'Graves' was presumably Henry Graves (1806-92), brother of engraver Robert Graves, while the artist John Seguier (1785-1856), superintendent of the British Institution and younger brother of William Seguier, first Keeper of the National Gallery, also visited. Antiquaries included the Rev Thomas Kerrich (1748-1828) and Sir Robert Harry Inglis (1786-1855). The auctioneer and antiquary James Christie (1773-1831), the son of the auctioneer James Christie, is recorded just once: in his opinion *Titian and his Mistress* was painted by '*Cavaliere Liberi*'.[65]

Among the Norfolk artists who visited was of course John Sell Cotman, but others included Robert Ladbrooke (1769-1842), Thomas Charles Wageman (1787-1863), Joseph Geldart (1808-82) and his friend 'Mr Moore'. The latter visited on 7 July 1842 and their comments are given some attention. Geldart had visited on a number of occasions, including the previous year when he called Turner's *The Rape of Europa* attributed to Titian 'the best picture in Norfolk'.[66] This time he commented on Jan Steen's *The Christening* (fig.26): 'The best Jan Steen I ever saw, & a very remarkable one, in wanting the fat oily surface so common with him. It is on that very account far more like Titian, which is what Jan Steen aimed at … I should almost have taken it for a Venetian picture.' Geldart's friend Mr Moore supported his previous judgement in proclaiming that the *Martyrdom of St Catherine* was indeed a sketch by Van Dyck.[67] Some

26 *Jan Steen,* The Christening Feast. *Reproduced by kind permission of the Trustees of The Wallace Collection, London.*

visitors were quite frank in giving their comments: John Sell Cotman, for example, made a last visit before taking up his teaching post in Kings College School, London and simply said of the *View in the Campagna, Rome*: 'One of the most beautiful specimens of nature I ever saw: I care nothing who did it' (23 January 1834). Dawson Turner remained keen to record new opinions, continuing after the *Outlines* had been printed. On 12 February 1841 Andrew Fountaine (fig.27) of Narford commented of this same painting: 'Really a very beautiful picture and I should think it by Orizonte.' Mr Fountaine's opinions were perceptive but he was surprisingly unaware of John Crome's work. Of Crome's *View on the River near Yarmouth,* he commented: 'That picture is just midway between Wilson & Rembrandt. The man that painted it (I never saw any of his works before) was a giant' (22 February 1841).

Turner's most prestigious visitor in the field of art history studies and the tricky question of attributions was the celebrated German art

27 *Andrew Fountaine (1808-74), by Alfred Edward Chalon (1780-1866). Watercolour and body colour on paper. (Private collection.)*

historian Dr Gustav Friedrich Waagen (1797-1868), who came to Bank House on 2 October 1850 and was later to publish his travels in *Treasures of Art in Great Britain.*[68] Waagen's opinions are recorded in a rather extraordinary manner, as the manuscript attempts to give something of the flavour of the cadences of the visiting scholar's accent with phonetically spelt direct quotes. By the time Waagen's work was published in 1854 Turner's collection had been sold and so Waagen never actually published his report on Turner's collection. Instead he penned a brief description of Turner himself: 'I admired the unresting activity and discrimination with which this already aged gentleman has collected materials for the history and antiquities of Norfolk, which amount to more than sixty volumes. The numerous drawings and etchings with which this work is illustrated proceed from the hands of the late Mrs Dawson Turner and her daughters, displaying great talents and unwearied industry. Mr Dawson Turner's interesting collection of pictures has since been sold at Christie's rooms.'[69]

The manuscript record of Waagen's unpublished opinions takes on an increased importance as he saw the collection in its entirety. Waagen's consideration of Gaspar Poussin's *View in Tivoli* is positively relished: 'Ah! Ah! A … h! Magnificent. Magnifique! Shuberb! shuberb! Dat is shuberb pickter! Vir faine! Extreme faine! Createst power. Arranged too mit so creat taste. Te best taste: te haighest – one feels tat pickter: 'tis all his best style, excellent, ma foi – excellent.' By contrast, when finding himself in front of the three small paintings all optimistically attributed to David Teniers the record shows: 'A very cursory glance at all of them; & not a syllable'. When shown the *St John Preaching in the Wilderness,* attributed to Annibale Carracci, Waagen evidently struggles: 'Thrice interrogated. Not a word. At last – "who dat is by? Tat vone?"' One can almost feel the silence hanging in the air as Waagen struggles not to cause the collector any offence.

Perry Nursey would have been pleased to hear Waagen's praise of his friend Wilkie's *The Harvest Field*: 'Might be a Rembrandt for power,' while Thomas Phillips too would have been pleased to learn that his portrait[70] of Lady Palgrave (née Elizabeth Turner) and her sister Mary Anne Turner was admired: 'Vone of te best Phillips I ever see. Vir' clever, & vir' clear.' Waagen strenuously endorsed the quality of many of the paintings, notably the Bellini. He relished the painting of the head of St Peter in particular, which still stands as the area of the painting most demonstrably the work of Titian himself rather than by studio assistants. Cuyp's *A Man Giving Provender to a Horse* was also much admired as a 'nice Coyp', while there was 'not the slightest doubt' about *Old Woman and Goose* by Dou. Jan Fyt's *Dog and Hare* also received high praise, as did Guido Reni's *Virgin with the Infant Christ and St John*.[71] Turner's *Fruit Piece* by de Heem also won the art historian's admiration, although as by Jan David and not Cornelis: 'of de greatest power. Not possible to see a finer vone. Arranged mit so ver' great taste.' He also admired Turner's Hobbema as more 'poetical' than most and paused to consider the painting that had always caused so much discussion, *Christ Among the Doctors* attributed to Mazzolino, finding it a puzzle: 'interesting & rich little pikter'. He did not question Turner's sketch relating to Rubens' Banqueting House ceiling painting of *Peace and Plenty*, considered Jan Steen's *The Gossiping* 'ver' faine' and had 'not the smallest doubt' concerning Titian's *The Rape of Europa* as being in his 'Tintoret style'. All in all the family must have been well pleased with the great man's verdicts, even if his heavily Germanic accent did cause some amusement.

Dawson Turner was willing to lend his paintings to exhibitions, being pleased to demonstrate just how the collections of Great Yarmouth provided an example for contemporary artists to follow. Two exhibitions of Old Master paintings were organised by the Norfolk and Suffolk Institution for the Promotion of the Fine Arts in Norwich, in 1828 and 1829, in emulation of similar exhibitions arranged at the British Institution in London. Contemporary artists were encouraged to draw inspiration from the masters of the past, with a view to improving their contribution to the 'British' School, a paternalistic view of artistic encouragement typical of the period. It was John Sell Cotman who corresponded with Dawson Turner over his four loans from Bank House, one of which was Bellini's *Madonna and Child with Saints and a Donor*. On Saturday, 17 October 1829, Cotman wrote that 'I have great pleasure to say your pictures arrived here all perfectly safe.' Presumably to put Turner's mind at rest, Cotman went on to explain the placing of his pictures in the display, drawing a plan of the space and marking their positions. The Bellini was placed directly opposite the entrance to the exhibition, in a corner position 'on a level with the eye', quite possibly on an easel that would have given it a visual prominence in the display. Cotman reassured Turner that 'Every attention has been paid to the Yarmouth Pictures.'

The critic for the *Norwich Mercury* duly regarded Turner's Bellini, together with his *Landscape* by Gaspar Dughet, as holding:

> very prominent situations within this blaze of art ... the [Bellini] is a very fine specimen of early Venetian art, and is one mass of light and splendid colouring. By the date on the picture it should appear that it was painted when Bellini was 83 [*sic*] years old, and is one of his best pictures. Although Titian and Giorgione were his pupils, he was not too proud to profit in his latter years by their style of colouring, and the consequence became that his last efforts were his greatest. The kneeling figure is said to be a portrait of Lorenzo di Medicis; the two standing saints are a close imitation of nature, and display great force and fidelity.[72]

We know from surviving watercolours of the interior of Bank House, two of which are now in the collection of Norwich Castle Museum & Art Gallery and Trinity College, Cambridge (colour plates IX, X), that Dawson Turner hung some of the most prized examples from his collection in the drawing room. Possibly by Elizabeth Turner, the watercolours provide clear evidence concerning Turner's collection and its arrangement on the walls.[73] His Bellini can clearly be seen hanging in the centre of one wall (colour plate X), above his set of three small pictures attributed to Teniers, and flanked on either side by his *Fruit Piece* attributed to De Heem and *Our Lady of the Fish*, attributed to the Spanish painter Del Mazo (*c.*1612-67). All the paintings shown in these drawings are catalogued in William Druery's record of the collection published in 1826, except the Del Mazo, which suggests that this was a later addition to the collection and that the watercolours postdate 1826. Thomas Phillips's portrait of *Elizabeth and Mary Turner,*[74] which can be seen hanging on the centre of the wall adjacent to the De Heem, was painted and exhibited at the Royal Academy in 1825.

It is in this room that we see the coming together of Dawson Turner's artistic interests; where music was played, the Turner ladies studied and created works of art in their own right, and the finest of Turner's art collection was hung. It was here that Hannah Sarah and Mary Anne divided up the task of producing the outlines in lithography to illustrate the catalogue. It appears a subtle tribute to their work that Dawson Turner entitled his catalogue after their illustrations rather than his own catalogue discussions. In addition, a key component of each entry was the initial description penned by Mrs Mary Turner. To complete the family enterprise, the dedication of this privately circulated book was to Turner's only son Gurney, at that time serving as a surgeon in the East India Company. Dawson Turner's dedication was signed off on 1 May 1840.

Conclusion

Dawson Turner effectively rewrites the job description for the role of patron of the arts for the mercantile class of gentleman in the early 19th century. At the heart of business in Great Yarmouth during these years, he was also a practising collector and connoisseur, endlessly seeking self-improvement while supporting local artists, promoting collections in the vicinity and befriending artists and collectors in London and throughout Britain.

Turner's *Outlines in Lithography* stands as an original and informed contribution to the history of collecting in Britain in the first half of the 19th century, researched, written and created as it is by the collector himself with the help of his immediate family. In this respect he was engaged upon a task that mirrored that of Horace Walpole just over a century earlier when compiling his catalogue of his father Sir Robert Walpole's collection at Houghton Hall in Norfolk. Nevertheless in that instance, although a family production, neither the resultant catalogue, *Aedes Walpolianae*, nor arguably even the collection was the work of the collector himself. His own assessment of his collection and of the accompanying *Outlines in Lithography* comes in the entry for one of the few paintings in the collection not to bear an attribution. Although charmingly self-effacing in accordance with the fashion in such moments of published self-encomium, much that Turner says reveals the nature of the man, as patron, connoisseur and collector:

> And thus I close a work, the preparing of which, if it has cost me a considerable portion of time, has afforded me at least an equivalent portion of gratification. It has brought me into more intimate, and, if I may use the expression, into more confidential acquaintance with objects, that have, for the last thirty years, been a source to me of daily pleasure. It has caused me to strive to obtain a greater knowledge of one of the arts most calculated to smooth the mind and correct the taste; and it has given me the opportunity of recording several anecdotes that I have been glad to be thus enabled to preserve, connected with interesting events in my own life, or, still more, with deceased friends ... Many of the opinions advanced in it will, I know, be disputed: some will most probably be found erroneous: to all considerations of that description I am indifferent: it is the lot of man and what proceeds from him. But I hope and trust that what I have brought together, may give pleasure to my family and my friends, and to the very few judges and patrons of art, to whom alone it is my intention that it should be submitted; and I shall be glad if any of the latter should be induced by it to do the same for pictures of a higher class and of more pretensions.[75]

To find a parallel in the history of art one should perhaps turn to an earlier figure, the renowned connoisseur and collector Cassiano dal Pozzo (1588-1657), one of the most important art patrons in 17th-century Italy. A patron of Poussin and friend of Galileo, he was admired for his learning in the fields of natural history and antiquities. Cassiano conceived the ambitious project of employing artists to make copies of all surviving examples of Roman antiquity. These works were classified thematically in his 'Paper Museum', to record as complete a picture as possible of ancient civilisation. At the same time he commissioned a comparable number of natural history drawings, including geological specimens, which were similarly classified. Scholars and dilettanti throughout Europe consulted these and Cassiano dal Pozzo's 'Paper Museum' came to represent the finest imperative to acquire knowledge in the joint fields of art and science. While Cassiano's achievement towers above that of so many collectors and patrons in the history of art, his approach does provide a touchstone to the nature of Dawson Turner's magisterial presence in a subsequent time – albeit in a regional context. In the changing field of early 19th-century cultural endeavour among the mercantile, scholastic and antiquarian classes in Britain, Turner held a unique place in the modern search for meaning in art patronage, connoisseurship and collecting.

The breadth of Turner's interests informs his connoisseurship and his relations with those he patronised. His 'manufactory' of artistic family endeavour created at Bank House also stands as a memorial to his extraordinary and inclusive approach to antiquarian, scientific and cultural pursuits. The sometimes-acerbic remarks he attracted from visitors bemused by the industry they witnessed may be seen quite simply as a reflection of the originality of his energetic approach. The memorable bewilderment of Benjamin Robert Haydon when confronted by 'one incessant scene of fact collecting' was only the tip of a prodigious paper mountain for which it was no small feat for Turner to be that 'immense, living index'. The family's engagement with artists and natural scientists, connoisseurs and collectors, family and friends ensured that this was no world of arid bookishness. Turner's passionate relationship with a widow 35 years younger than himself after the death of Mary Turner in 1850 is another indicator of the passionate nature that Turner applied to all aspects of life. This unique and indomitable extended household could hardly continue at such a pitch without their mentor. The subsequent family estrangements are a further reflection of the impassioned success of Bank House and its *pater familias* in their prime.

ANDREW MOORE

CHAPTER THREE

Nature's Treasures: Dawson Turner's Botanical Collections

As Britain's long war with France came to an end in March 1814, followed by Napoleon's exile to Elba and a peace settlement in May, Dawson Turner took the earliest opportunity to visit Paris.[1] Accompanied by his wife Mary, his two eldest daughters Maria and Elizabeth, his future son-in-law William Hooker and his friend Charles Lyell, Turner, an acclaimed botanist with an international reputation, travelled, in effect, with a botanical party of extraordinary expertise. While Maria and Elizabeth may have been studying botany in earnest for only three years (and Mary Turner's interest had been curbed by family cares), Hooker, Lyell and Turner were renowned in the difficult study of the non-flowering plants such as mosses, lichens and algae. The level of their competence marked them as different from other travellers but their interest was not untypical. Nor was their lack of professional scientific positions. Lyell in particular, a staunch Tory for whom science was a gentlemanly attainment, did not support the idea of science as a career. Natural history, and especially botany, was considered part of, rather than distinct from, polite English culture well into the 19th century. Such pursuits merged with other activities such as landscape art, gardening, travel and antiquarianism, and were as avidly pursued by women as by men. In particular, forming collections of natural objects became immensely popular, even fashionable, and the ability to acquire choice specimens could be used not only to promote an understanding of nature but also as the means to achieve social distinction. This was especially the case in Britain where, apart from a few holders of university posts, botany was largely carried out by private independent individuals scattered across the country, often with little or no access to the few public collections of note. The surprising news Turner had to report on his return, therefore, was that:

> all the Botanists & all the men of science in France are collected in Paris … & everything public. They do not seem able to comprehend how it is with us, that both in arts & sciences individuals possess such treasures & many of those who have cultivated them with most success reside far from London.[2]

Turner's linking the possession of 'treasures' with the successful cultivation of science is indicative of the work and purpose of botany in this period. Collections were essential to the main aim of botany, namely the classification of plants. To establish the order of nature botanists required as many specimens as possible. In the practice of the science, therefore, collectors and finders of plants were as valuable as those who compiled and catalogued them. As Turner indicated, this was especially the case in England where few collections of note were public. When in Paris, Turner did concede that public collections in which objects were gathered together in one place possessed the great utility of making it easy for the scholar to 'compare as well as observe'. Nonetheless, in comparing public French collections with private English ones, Turner concluded that while 'more splendor is in France' there was 'more enjoyment in England'.[3] For naturalists such as Turner this enjoyment consisted partly in the pleasure of possession. In this respect, passion and desire were just as important in making collections designed to produce scientific knowledge as in any other form of collecting.[4] Indeed, what characterises early 19th-century scientific experts is their love of collecting, without which it is unlikely that the discipline and labour involved in accumulating and maintaining a natural history collection could be sustained.

Naturalists not only had to keep their collections in a good state of order and preservation within the home, but also had to add to them. Since no one individual could travel enough or collect enough, a major part of the work of botanists was to cultivate correspondents in order to acquire specimens and information through exchange. Finding sufficient time and energy for this could present problems for busy botanists like Turner, who explained his situation to a valuable correspondent he was fearful of losing: 'when I tell you that I live here the only resident partner of a large Banking establishment, that I have no small botanical correspondence, & have also on my hands a great part of the education of my little girls, you will scarcely think me unreasonable if I intreat of you not to be too scrupulous in exacting an answer to every letter before you oblige me with a second.'[5] Despite the effort involved, the mutual dependence of all botanists on others for specimens – and the immense quantity of correspondence this generated – reveals yet another form of pleasure: the social bonds and friendships resulting from such exchanges.

In order for an exchange to be useful, however, correspondents had to be able to supply what the other most wanted: experts, for example, did not appreciate being offered common plants. Learned botanists who wanted to take advantage of the widespread popularity of natural history to encourage more participation in this way had therefore to ensure that collectors could recognise whether plants were new or rare and thus worthy of being sent to an expert. Towards this end, Turner collaborated with the Swansea porcelain manufacturer and botanist Lewis Weston Dillwyn to publish *The Botanist's Guide Through England and Wales* in 1805. By listing all the plants of note according to the counties in which they were found, Turner and Dillwyn aimed to entice novices to become contributors to botanical science as well as to direct the traveller in 'his researches'.[6] This union of polite culture and scientific botany was most explicit in Thomas Walford's *The Scientific Tourist* (1818), which directed travellers to 'the principal objects of Antiquity, Art, Science, & the Picturesque, including the Minerals, Fossils, Rare Plants, and other Subjects of Natural History', and recommended to the lover of plants 'that valuable little work, the Botanist's Guide, by Dawson Turner, esq. where he will find the cryptogamous plants of each county'.[7]

If tourists, who had long succumbed to the charms of flowering plants, were now interested in cryptogamic plants this, indeed, owed much to the efforts of Turner. The popularity of botany in Britain from the late 18th century was due to the relative ease with which Linnaeus's system of classification allowed plants to be identified. The scientific names of plants, consisting of genus and species, reflected Linnaeus's view of the order of nature in which related species were grouped into larger family units or genera. Based upon the reproductive parts of plants – flowers and fruits – his classification came to be known as the sexual system. The difficulty of understanding the non-flowering plants, however, was writ in the very name Linnaeus gave them: cryptogamia, or 'hidden sex', in the expectation that sexual reproduction would eventually be found in them. While the *Botanist's Guide* helped those eager to collect cryptogams, it was Turner's early work on seaweeds and mosses that stimulated interest while making clear the difficulties involved.

Turner's own enthusiasm for these plants – especially his first and abiding interest in seaweeds – was most likely due to his growing up in Great Yarmouth on the Norfolk coast and, in particular, the practical instruction in observing seaweeds that he received from Lilly Wigg, a local shoemaker turned schoolmaster, whose accuracy of observation and strenuous autodidactism may well have accounted for Turner's later encouragement of novices in this difficult area of botany.[8] Wigg's keen observational skills enabled him to detect new and rare seaweeds, whose value was enhanced by the fact that Turner could observe them in a fresh state. This was of crucial importance because while all plants faded and suffered change when pressed and preserved as dried specimens, some marine algae were particularly susceptible to pressure and in drying were often altered beyond recognition. Even though others did possess the property of recovering their natural forms if immersed in water, Turner emphasised that only those observers who had seen the plants in their places of growth or in a recent state should be trusted.[9]

Turner's study of mosses highlights further difficulties in the study of cryptogams: not only did Turner know from experience that distinctions between mosses could be made only by those who had seen them growing in nature, he also recognised that aspects of the accepted classification devised by the Leipzig physician and botanist Johan Hedwig were practically too difficult for most botanists. Hedwig had made remarkable improvements to his microscope that allowed him to detect extremely minute 'male flowers' that characterised some of his genera. However, the expense of such a good microscope made Hedwig's observations difficult to replicate, leading the Reverend Samuel Goodenough to express reservations, believing that 'he will fail whoever thinks to form a system on such minute discriminations'.[10] In 1805, therefore, Turner proposed rejecting the use of hard-to-detect male flowers in favour of more obvious characters. Although Turner thereby reduced dependence on powerful microscopes, he did concede that complaints that Hedwig's system was founded on 'parts too inconspicuous to be easily examined ... goes rather against the study of mosses in general, than against any particular arrangement; for, among individuals themselves so small, it necessarily follows, that the parts connected with the fructification, on which alone generic distinctions can properly be founded, must be often exceedingly minute'.[11]

The classification of seaweeds also depended upon the use of a microscope and this, together with the need to observe freshly collected materials, placed a special emphasis on drawings of specimens. Such drawings not only captured characteristics that were lost once specimens had dried, but also – more importantly – provided the means by which botanists could compare the magnified details of different species, which was essential for the purposes of classification. Turner was therefore always on the look out for those who could provide him with drawings as well as fresh specimens. Once he embarked upon his ambitious study of seaweeds in 1807, Turner relied almost exclusively on the artistic skills of Hooker, who lived in Norwich. Having him so close was invaluable: when Amelia Griffiths sent recently collected seaweeds from Devon, Hooker aimed to be at Turner's house when the plants arrived so 'that they may be drawn fresh'.[12] It was, however, a distant correspondent who most clearly revealed the value of drawings. When Ellen Hutchins of Bantry Bay, Ireland sent Turner specimens of her remarkable discovery of the fruit of *Fucus tomentosus*, being aware of the changes the dried specimen would undergo, she also sent a drawing of the plant as observed in a fresh state. Turner, who was already deeply impressed by the new discoveries Hutchins was making

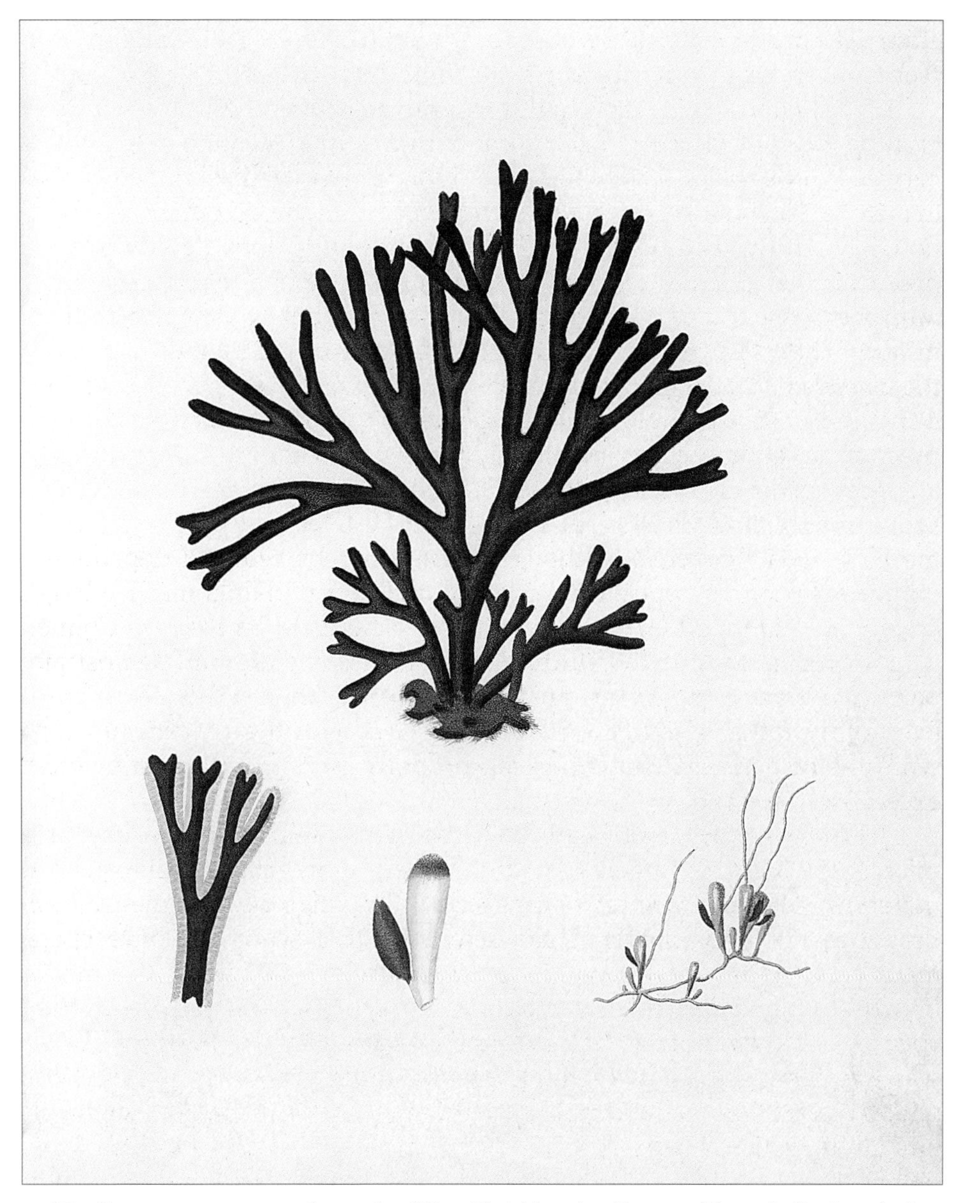

28 Fucus tomentosus *drawn by Ellen Hutchins for Dawson Turner's* Fuci, *vol. 3 (1811), plate 135.*

and by the quality of the specimens he received from her, requested that her drawing be included in his work (fig.28). So valuable were accurate observations of seaweeds that Turner warned Hutchins: 'While you send me such drawings as these I shall go on eternally begging, & shall cease to ask you for plants.' His only regret was that Hutchins' microscope was 'not one of the best'.[13]

Turner's efforts to obtain specimens, information and drawings were enhanced by his being socially and scientifically well connected. Elected a Fellow of the Linnean Society of London in 1797 and of the Royal Society in 1802, Turner was part of the scientific élite. In particular, the Linnean Society, founded in 1788 by James Edward Smith, a Norwich botanist who had purchased Linnaeus's collections, served to bring together botanists of means who could attend meetings in London and contribute papers to its *Transactions*. Such activities, however, represented only a small part of the practice of botany and, as already indicated, unlike the all-male membership of the Linnean Society, correspondence networks reveal that botany was not confined to gentlemen: it could and did involve contributors of a low social status and was one of the sciences to which women made important contributions.[14]

The fact that those who contributed to botany in this way were private individuals scattered across the country means that, when looking at how experts acquired the collections upon which they based their publications, we need to consider why collectors were willing to send specimens to botanists like Turner. The answer to this is most clear in the 36 volumes of James Sowerby and J.E. Smith's *English Botany*. Started in 1790, this work, consisting of illustrations and descriptions of each plant, and designed as a complete record of the flora of Britain, was highly dependent upon specimens supplied by local collectors. In its production over the next two-and-a-half decades, readers of this work would easily have seen that, in the case of rare or new plants, the name of the discoverer was prominent. When the war with France made travel beyond Britain difficult, contributing to this grand undertaking greatly increased the enthusiasm for botanical collecting, and even eminent and learned botanists, such as Lyell, made their reputation through the *English Botany* without ever publishing themselves. When the work came to a close in 1814, Sowerby declared that it was 'now so nearly completed as ... to make it a perfect National Flora'. Moreover, by containing the names of those individuals who assisted in the work, *English Botany* 'will hand down to posterity a list of nearly all the British Botanists of its time, with the date of their flourishing in the scientific world'.[15]

In 1814, therefore, with the completion of the *English Botany*, many botanists lost one of the main inspirations for collecting unless they happened to be interested in a particular group of plants being described by an expert. For seaweed enthusiasts, Turner's study of the genus *Fucus* (which included almost all seaweeds at that time) provided a spur to collecting, since their reputations could be made through his publication. By 1814, however, with botanists bemoaning the completion of *English Botany*, Turner's rate of production had slowed down alarmingly.

Delay

By the time of his Paris trip, Turner had produced three of the four volumes of his magnificent monograph on the *Fuci*, but was well behind the initial projected date of completion of the work, which had been based on the monthly appearance of the parts that comprised the volumes.[16] Encompassing descriptions and figures of species of seaweeds from as many different places as he could obtain, Turner's work was highly dependent upon information and specimens from botanists in other parts of the world. The peace of 1814 was therefore perceived to be of great consequence for botany, and for the completion of undertakings such as the *Fuci*. Dillwyn, co-author of *The Botanist's Guide*, told Turner how delighted he was to hear that 'this wondrous & glorious turn which has taken place in foreign affairs, has already enabled you to resume your Continental Correspondence, & thereby served to revive your botanical ardor.'[17] To the disappointment of fellow botanists, however, whatever botanical zeal had been ignited in Turner at this stage appeared diminished rather than increased by the trip to Paris despite his examination of marine plants in the impressive herbarium at the Muséum.[18] By August, Dillwyn was expressing concern that Turner had 'deserted nature in favor of the Arts', or at least found the latter 'more attractive'.[19]

The appeal of Paris, however, had always been more than just the renewal of botanical contacts, as Lyell had pointed out as soon as the end of war looked likely:

> I am wishing ardently for the restoration of the Bourbons, because (among better reasons) we could loiter at Paris without any fear of transportation to Verdun; & I hope the march to Paris will be unnecessary to the Allies, lest the Goths & Vandals in the intoxication of Victory should avenge the burning of Moscow by that of Paris, with all its Museums of stolen treasure![20]

It was this stolen treasure that attracted the travellers and, although Turner did visit Paris's scientific museums, it was the paintings in the Louvre and the lure of buying prints that proved to be the highlights of the 1814 tour, and the main purpose of Turner's visit to Paris the following year.

The first Hooker heard of this second trip in autumn 1815 was on his return from his honeymoon. He lost no time in writing to his father-in-law. 'I had really hoped that Botany & Botanists would have been more the objects of your pursuit this time than when you were last at Paris,' Hooker pointedly wrote, before stating how very 'vexed' he would be if Turner did not visit those botanists who had assisted his work, and above all if he did not call on the great traveller and naturalist Alexander von Humboldt.[21] In the event, Turner had already visited his 'botanical friends', and had admired the splendid scientific collections at the 'Great

Museum at the Jardin des Plantes', many of which contained the spoils of war. In the same way as pictures in the Louvre were being repatriated, in the shell collection Turner found a commissioner from the King of the Netherlands 'busily employed in reclaiming the property stolen from his Sovereign, the quantity of which, to judge from the number of specimens to which strips of blue paper are attached, was prodigious'.[22] Despite Turner's enjoyment of these sumptuous displays, it was the stultification of French science that struck him in 1815, making Paris even less of a spur to his scientific activity than the visit of the previous year. Most of the botanists, oppressed by the Prussian occupation and often denied their salaries, were 'doing nothing': the 'fatal influence' of the present times, Turner concluded, 'pervades & taints & palsies every thing, even Botany'.[23] Moreover, those naturalists who were still producing work could find no publisher. The fact that even the great Humboldt could not persuade a 'bookseller to edit' the account of his travels in South America 'tho' unquestionably one of the most interesting ever given to the world', put, in Turner's opinion, 'the present wretched state of literature in France in a stronger light than almost any thing else'.[24]

Notwithstanding the discouraging state of French botany, Paris perhaps could not revive Turner's botanical ardour because lack of contact with Continental botanists was not the reason for the delay in completing his monograph. Although Turner had complained about not being able to acquire specimens of a particular species for his 1802 *Synopsis of British Fuci* because most of them 'are natives of the Mediterranean and Adriatic, whence our opportunities of procuring them are always small; and, from the lately perturbed state of Europe, have been for some time totally destroyed', this was not the problem he faced in 1814. Directly after completing the separately published numbers that made up the third volume of his *Fuci* in 1811, Turner had determined that there would be one more volume 'for which I have nearly a sufficiency of materials, & I have promised, both for my own sake & the publisher's, to let them appear regularly every month'.[25]

Those studying seaweeds within Britain were impatient for the completion of Turner's work on two counts. First, it would provide a through-going study of the group and, second, it would release all the specimens being borrowed and hoarded by Turner, restoring them to their owners' collections and making them available to others. By 1814 Samuel Goodenough, algologist and Bishop of Carlisle, had clearly had enough: 'Pray what is D. Turner about?', he enquired of Turner's Norwich friend James Edward Smith,

> I will tell you what all his friends are about – *complaining*. Sir Joseph's collection is detained with him – his correspondents can get no answers from him – The excellent Mrs. Griffiths is out of heart, & I fear, that her ardour

> has been cooled by it. The Indefatigable Miss Hill sent him years ago series of Plants to elucidate difficult species, & cannot get them back from him, nor even the smallest acknowledgement about them, or answers of any sort – Miss Hutchins is in the same story – & all his friends are complaining that not one Number has appeared for nearly a twelve-month.[26]

When the elderly botanist the Reverend Hugh Davies heard that Turner and Hooker had visited Paris that summer, and that Turner had become a 'a conisieur [*sic*] in old prints and pictures', his response is telling: 'I wish the Parisians would give M^r^. Turner & M^r^. Hooker a good flogging each, and send them home to complete their engagements to the public.'[27] Even though botany was pursued by private individuals, many of whom, like Turner, were employed in business, the expectation was that the declaration of an undertaking (especially one involving subscribers) would be both inspired by and fulfilled for the public good. Not least, since priority for the discovery of a plant was established by the publication of its description, the prestige of collectors who found new seaweeds depended upon Turner's getting his work into print before these plants were found and published by foreign botanists. Delays such as Turner's thus affected the entire botanical community.

Complaints had, in fact, started as early as 1812, and Smith had tried to deflect criticism of his friend, explaining that 'Turner is very busy about banking, visiting, educating his daughters, & being all things to all men & women – & still botanizes – He is printing a Lichenographia Britannica with Borrer – the latter *most author* – Turner *most editor* — but he is a man of extraordinary talents & activity.'[28] Smith was in a good position to comment on Turner's work on lichens, having just looked over proof sheets of this collaborative work with the independently wealthy Sussex botanist William Borrer. Despite Turner having encouraged this ambitious undertaking, his belief that a book describing the lichens would be 'the best botanical work ever published', his admiration of Borrer's skills, and the first sheets being printed, this project also stagnated, with mutual accusations of lack of commitment. A disappointed Turner (who had hoped that Borrer would find the confidence to take the project over completely) was both frank about his collaborator's enviable state of independence, and open about his own failings: 'Were you an indolent man; were you in the habit of breaking your word intentionally; were you, like me, continually engaging in some new project or other when you haven't half time to finish those already in hand; or were your days and nights occupied in business; I should in none of these cases wonder at your delay.'[29]

Turner's botanical friends, however, were destined to wonder at *his* delay for several more years. It is clear that business concerns preoccupied him more than usual: in the summer of 1815 Lyell hoped that Turner's botanical zeal would 'blaze forth' once he found a banking partner in whom he could place 'implicit confidence'.[30] By 1816, however, the economic depression following the end of the Napoleonic Wars forced Turner to give even more attention to business. The dangers of not doing so were all too clear: Turner's friend William Roscoe, Liverpool patron of the arts, historian, and founder of the city's botanic garden, was forced to sell his home, magnificent library and collection of paintings when his bank collapsed.[31] Despite these concerns, Turner not only managed any business difficulties, but clearly did so to such an extent that he was able to afford expensive travel to France and to indulge his new passion for prints and books. Given Turner's relatively secure financial status as measured by these activities, and his earlier claim that he already had all the materials he needed to complete the *Fuci* in 1811, why were the remaining numbers produced so slowly that it was not finished for another eight years?

Arrangement

At the start of his work on seaweeds Turner had hoped that, by describing and figuring all the specimens of *fucus* he could obtain, he would be able 'to throw as much light as lies in my power upon the division of the submersed Algae into new genera'.[32] By the early 19th century the number of species that had come to be defined as *fuci* had increased to such an extent that botanists held that, rather than being seen as a single genus, the group should be regarded more like a natural family, containing several genera. Turner's aim therefore was to determine the characteristics that united certain species while making them distinct from others. The difficulties he had to contend with, however, were great. The first problem was deciding whether particular plants *were* seaweeds, and on what basis they could be distinguished from sponges, lichens or other forms of algae. It was the complexity of establishing the differences and similarities between the different groups of cryptogamic plants that made Turner so keen to encourage and engage in work on the lichens and especially on the different types of submersed algae.[33] In 1802 he had stated that, to come to a new arrangement, all these plants should be thrown into a general mass, 'paying no respect to the genera as they now exist, all of which comprise plants of the most anomalous nature'.[34]

Apart from their systematic complexity, investigation of the 'submersed algae' presented other challenges. In the late 18th century these plants were almost as strange and foreign to most botanists as Joseph Banks's Australian flora, for the sea and its productions were largely unexplored. 'Why should it be thought impossible that the sub-marine plants, like the animals of that element, should have powers and properties new, original, and peculiar to themselves?' inquired Samuel Goodenough and Thomas Jenkinson Woodward in 1795. Botanists studying seaweeds were warned of the necessity of laying aside 'all comparisons and ideas of analogy taken from plants growing on land', for the marine algae presented a baffling series of transformations in their modes of existence for which it was 'not easy to account on philosophical principles'.[35] Above all, however, in a science of observation like botany, the knowledge of seaweeds had to be built up from partial glimpses – sometimes of only battered, hard to recognise specimens picked up on beaches among the 'rejectamenta' of the sea.

Given Turner's grand systematic aims, from the outset the monograph became a record of his doubts and difficulties in classifying seaweeds. One of the most problematic was *Fucus natans*, the name given to the seaweed found in almost every sea floating about in vast quantities. Turner believed, however, that had he a better range of fresh specimens, all the types now labelled *F. natans* would prove to be numerous different species and varieties. He presented the description and figure of the specimen he had selected as the true *F. natans* (fig.29), while observing that had he 'considered it right to be guided altogether by my own inclination in the arrangement of the different species of *Fuci* for publication, I should certainly have been tempted rather to have reserved the present for the conclusion of this work, than to have given it a place at the very commencement'.[36]

In the same year, Turner privately admitted to Hutchins that the specimens she was sending to him were so superior to some of those he had already figured that it made him regret 'that I had the folly to set about such a work as this till I had procured more materials, or even that I had the vanity ever to undertake it at all. I am got so far as to feel my own ignorance completely'.[37] A year later, as Turner worked on the numbers for the third volume of *Fuci*, his indebtedness to Hutchins became more apparent. This volume opens with Hutchins' figure of *Fucus tomentosus*, which Turner described as a species 'so peculiar, that its place in the system has been repeatedly called in question; and almost all the older botanists concurred in removing it from the Fuci to the Sponges, thus virtually, if not intentionally, declaring their opinion, that it belonged more properly to the animal than to the vegetable kingdom' (fig.28). Although this natural object had been established as a plant, in the summer of 1808 Hutchins was the very first observer to detect its fruit.[38]

Turner's increasing dependence upon Hutchins was most apparent in their correspondence. By 1810, Turner was exasperated on the one hand by several very puzzling species that showed that 'Nature sets at defiance all our puny attempts at arrangement,' and on the other hand by the eminent botanist Robert Brown urging him to publish

29 Fucus natans *drawn by William Jackson Hooker for Dawson Turner's* Fuci, *vol. 1 (1808), plate 46.*

his ideas on the genera of the submersed algae 'without delay'. The complexity of deciding exactly which features of algae would provide the basis for dividing up the species into genera and establishing a new systematic arrangement made Turner wish 'to put it off as long as I can', convinced as he was of his own inability to do it satisfactorily, and sceptical that genera had any existence in nature. The pressure from botanists eager for his views on arrangement led him to pay Hutchins a great compliment. Clearly impressed by her acute observational skills, Turner asked whether she had ever turned her attention to this subject. 'If you have,' he confessed, 'you will in the highest degree oblige & serve me by a communication of your ideas. Tell me how to distribute the British species, & I shall have such a foundation as I can easily build my system upon.'[39]

Hutchins had indeed thought about the subject, telling Turner that she used to amuse herself 'with conjecturing what your future arrangement may be'. Although she admitted that she 'found it a subject greatly beyond my powers of seeing into & that one day's experience generally contradicted that of the former', she did send a detailed account of her views in response to Turner's request.[40] However, emboldened perhaps by hearing that Turner agreed with her opinions, Hutchins herself began to add to the pressure on Turner to produce his arrangement of the marine algae. Once the final volume of *Fuci* was underway, she was 'impertinent' enough to tell Turner how often she wished that at the end of his monograph he would give plates illustrating each genus not published in the work 'for I imagine you will arrange all the submersed algae'.[41]

Turner could be in no doubt that this new arrangement was what the botanical world was waiting for. 'I long to see your concluding fasciculus, w^{h}. will, of course, contain your ideas on the subdivision of this overgrown genus,' wrote Robert Brown after Turner's trip to Paris in 1815.[42] It may well have been Turner's need to tackle this task that made Hooker so eager for him to meet the French botanists who had proposed divisions of the genus *Fucus* based on a different classificatory framework. Although Turner would later describe the new arrangement by Jean-Vincent-Félix Lamouroux as 'ingenious' and 'comprehensive',[43] his reason for not endorsing it is possibly revealed in the account of his meeting with Lamouroux in Paris. What the two botanists discussed is not known, but Turner did record his opinion that, like the French in general, Lamouroux 'is rapid in conception & manner, inclined to build theories upon weak foundations, & in his opinions somewhat positive'.[44]

In contrast, Turner remained cautious, his empiricism leading to both disappointment and satisfaction. When the *Fuci* was eventually finished in 1819, it was 'painful' for Turner to acknowledge that it was incomplete, owing to the great mass of species continually being discovered. Moreover, until all the species could be brought under one view, Turner's grand aim of 'reducing the Marine Algae in general under natural families, in a well organized system' was, he declared, impossible.[45] His readers could not have been surprised. As the numbers making up the final volume slowly appeared, Turner had already admitted that he was unable to return the family of plants formerly all 'confounded' under the name *Fucus natans* as he had 'almost promised', since the specimens he required from all the world's oceans 'can only be casually procured through the kindness of friends'. No length of time, in his view, would have enabled him to finish the work as he had wished.[46] Turner did, however, feel satisfaction in taking leave of his readers knowing that he had, as a botanical author,

> laid before them a set of figures, upon the accuracy of which they may rely; and which, as representations of things that are, will, through every change of human opinions, retain an undiminished value; while they may serve, in the hands of some more able, and more fortunate successor, as the ground-work of that which he had hoped to have accomplished himself.[47]

Despite Turner's failure to subdivide the *Fuci* into new genera, his achievement was significant. By the end of the 19th century, his work, which described many unknown species collected by travellers, was heralded as the 'best of all the early books'; while at mid-century his careful investigations were believed to have done much to dispel 'the primitive chaos which existed at the time when Turner began his history of *Fuci*'.[48] In an article on '*Fuci*' written in 1815 the *Edinburgh Encyclopaedia* discussed the work of 'that most scrupulously exact naturalist Mr Turner of Yarmouth'. Drawing attention to the beauty of Hooker's drawings, the number of distinguished botanists and travellers who had contributed specimens and Turner's 'ample and luminous' descriptions in both Latin and English, the *Edinburgh Encyclopaedia* declared that in 'no botanical production was there ever greater attention paid to minute accuracy'. And there, in print, is forever held out the great promise of Turner's careful researches:

> Every classification of fuci must, in the present state of our knowledge of them, be to a certain extent artificial; but from this author, as near an approach to a natural arrangement as possible, may confidently be expected.[49]

The fact that a new arrangement eluded Turner should not cast a shadow over the whole of his botanical work; in fact, the impatient anticipation of the conclusion of the *Fuci* reflects his high standing among his contemporaries.

Friends

In the unsettled time of the French Revolution and the Napoleonic Wars, botany had provided Turner with a sense of identity and had provided a way of serving the public interest. By 1820, however, his decision to give it up was perhaps promoted not only by his changing intellectual interests but also by changes in the botanical community itself. The publication of works of sumptuous plates in which Turner took so much pleasure was no longer viable, and botanists like Hooker had begun to challenge other aesthetic values by publishing more compact books in English and not Latin.[50] Turner also regretted how the completion of Sowerby and Smith's *English Botany* had 'sadly broken the chain of connection among us British Naturalists who live far from London'.[51] Moreover, the untimely deaths of several of his younger correspondents greatly affected Turner. But two other losses in particular are likely to have made him feel that it was time to draw his botanical days to a close. In 1820, Turner lost the easy face-to-face familial contact with his closest botanical companion when Hooker moved to Glasgow to take up a university chair and, in the same year, Sir Joseph Banks, who had dominated science since 1778, died. Turner's sense of belonging to a past botanical era while at the same time expressing his faith in the future of botany was most clearly encapsulated in his gift of his magnificent collection of plants to Hooker on his departure.

Turner, whose journals, correspondence and botanical works reveal that he classified everything and everyone, made a second gift to Hooker at this time: his extensive collection of portraits of botanists.[52] Although the disposal of his herbarium marked the end of Turner's active work in botany, the removal of the likenesses of those who produced botanical knowledge did not extinguish Turner's fascination with their lives, and the later expression of his botanical interests consisted more in the description of men than of plants. In 1833 he began preparing a second edition of Richard Pulteney's *Historical and Biographical Sketches of the Progress of Botany in England* of 1790 (intending to add 41 accounts of notable botanists), and also started work on a projected three-volume biography of Joseph Banks. Despite his admiration of Banks's 'extraordinary penetration', 'liberality', 'acuteness', and willingness to put 'his life in jeopardy, for the sake of promoting the interests of science & mankind', Turner gave up on the task after spending 12 years transcribing Banks's extensive correspondence.[53] What we have lost by this is less an account of Banks's life than the perception of this life by one of his contemporaries who shared many of the values of what by the 1830s had come to be regarded as the scientific old regime. Banks, who became one of the most powerful men of British science through the links he forged with the political establishment, had used his great wealth to accompany James Cook on the *Endeavour* voyage in quest of the southern continent (Australia), and then to maintain the collections he amassed on this and other voyages, which he made available to scholars in his London home. He had survived the ravages of tropical disease when most of his shipmates died, but failed to publish his great floral discoveries, and was an authoritarian and often controversial President of the Royal Society of London from 1778 to 1820.[54] In the absence of a biography, Turner's tribute

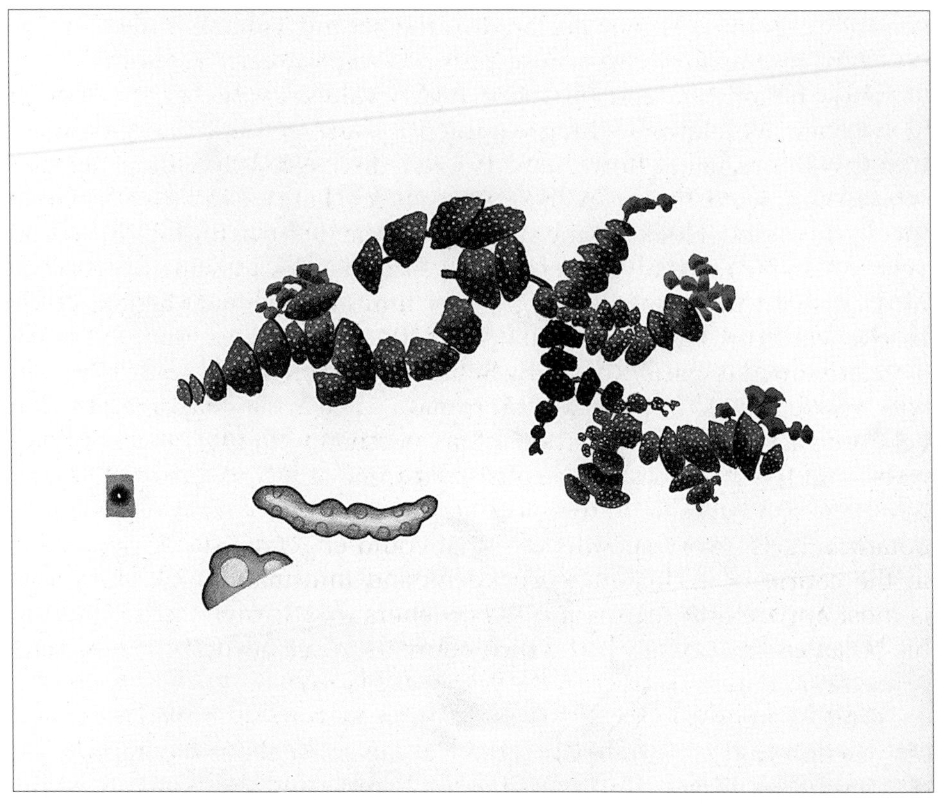

30 Fucus banksii *drawn by William Jackson Hooker for Dawson Turner's* Fuci, *vol. 1 (1808), plate 1.*

to Banks remained his *Fuci*. This work, dedicated to Banks as 'The Patron of Science', contained numerous references to the Banksian collections and opened with the description of a new seaweed named *Fucus Banksii* in honour of Banks (fig.30). With perhaps more insight into character than he realised, Turner proclaimed *'F. Banksii* is altogether a plant *sui generis*, and differs from every other species yet known. Its substance is so extraordinarily tough that it almost resembles a piece of leather.'[55]

Turner's monograph on *Fucus* commemorated many of his friends, with new species carefully chosen so as to be appropriate to those whose names they bore. Those specimens that Turner deemed most beautiful were usually allocated to the aristocrats or political figures that had enabled him to receive seaweeds from far-flung places and, occasionally, to honour a fellow botanist such as Aylmer Bourke Lambert, who was not an algologist himself (colour plate XI). More surprising to the modern reader (though not to those in the period when the sciences had yet to acquire professional status and had not been formulated as disciplines) Turner's monograph can also be read as an account of early 19th-century sociability. Botany, Turner declared in the second volume, unites 'in the bonds of friendship those whose pursuits were already the same'.[56]

These botanical friendships were highly valued by Turner who tended to cultivate his interests with great intensity, and perhaps did not always find this appreciated. Borrer and Hooker discovered this to be the case when, on a Scottish tour in 1808, they visited James Brodie with whom the Turners and Hooker had stayed the year before. Brodie 'likes you very well', Borrer told Turner, 'but was best pleased with Mrs Turner, for y^{r}. conversation was too *scientific* for him', while a note tagged on by Hooker confirmed that Brodie liked 'M^{rs}. T … better than either you or me – we are much too scientific'.[57] Even among the keenest botanists, Turner was referred to as 'our intellectual friend'.[58] The artist Benjamin Haydon believed that Turner approached all his pursuits with the 'habits of Botanists', and that his life was 'one incessant scene of fact collecting'.[59] It was, however, precisely one of the most important means employed to collect botanical facts – correspondence – that could engender deep friendships in the course of exchanging specimens and information. Although this is most apparent in the great mass of letters that Turner accrued during his botanical researches, and which allow us to see beyond the mere fact collector, it is also clear from the pages of his *Fuci*.

While Turner celebrated his association with many botanists, it was his reaction to the loss of friends that reveals most about the importance of friendships forged through shared interests and the ways in which natural history united people. Readers consulting the entry on *Fucus longifolius* in the second volume of *Fuci* are interrupted, as was Turner in the course of preparing the description of this seaweed, by news of the death of Daniel Mohr, a young professor whose 'immoderate zeal' for natural history had worn out his 'tender' and 'delicate' frame. 'I speak feelingly upon the subject of his death,' Turner told his readers, 'for I lament in him one of the kindest, most liberal, and most instructive of correspondents'.[60] Although Turner praised Mohr as one of the foremost seaweed experts, the tone of his eulogy is overwhelmingly personal, revealing the importance of the emotional economy that sustained the practice of natural history in this period. Turner's grief overflowed into his letters: 'Cryptogamic Botany has lost her most ardent & most able votary in my poor friend Mohr,' he told Brown, while Hutchins heard how 'Botany has lost her most zealous, most profound, & most useful student, & I one of my best friends, tho' we were known to each other only by our letters.'[61]

When the botanist the Reverend James Dalton heard news of Mohr's death from Hooker he sent condolences to Turner, knowing how deeply his 'kind hearted friend' would feel such a loss.[62] At times of distress, botany provided both occupation and consolation; after his young son had been burnt to death in 1806, Turner had found that botanising brought comfort 'when I walk out alone'. But more valuable than this was the sympathy of botanical friends, for this spoke to his heart and reminded him of his social duties.[63] Many years later, while sorting through his letters, Turner realised that more than ten of his correspondents had died. 'I do not know when I have felt so painful a chill', he admitted, lamenting the decrease in the number of friends to whom 'it is possible fully and freely to open our minds'.[64] One of those to whom he had opened both his mind and his heart was Ellen Hutchins, and in their friendship we can see that Turner's botany did not exist in some isolatable and abstract scientific realm, but was crucially connected with religious, social and emotional issues.

It was in 1807 that Turner had opened the correspondence with Hutchins that was to inspire and sustain her for the remainder of her life. Through Turner, Hutchins gained a formidable reputation among early 19th-century men of science for her capacity to find cryptogamic plants, her beautifully preserved specimens and her skilful botanical drawings, despite suffering from poor health and a troubled domestic life in the isolation of Bantry Bay. The youngest daughter and second-youngest child of 21 children (of whom only six survived into adulthood), she devoted much of her time to caring for her brother Thomas, paralysed following an accident, and to nursing her elderly mother. Hutchins' troubles became acute in 1813 when she and her mother moved to Bandon, 30 miles from Bantry Bay, after her oldest brother Emanuel took possession of the family home and drove them out. In Bandon Hutchins became desperately ill and barely able to care for her mother who died in early 1814. As her illness worsened – due, she believed, to her family disputes – she relied increasingly on Turner's friendship, claiming that their correspondence was the one source of happiness in her life. She died on 9 February 1815, shortly before her 30th birthday.

Although they never met, Turner expressed deep and abiding sorrow at Hutchins' death in the concluding volume of his *Fuci*. Here, at the very end of a work to which she had contributed so much, he paid tribute to her. Bringing together their shared love of botany and poetry, he lamented his loss and praised her qualities by quoting some lines of verse (fig.33). The fact that the quotation bears no attribution indicates that these lines were so well known in the early 19th century that Turner expected his readers to recognise them as part of James Hurdis's 'exquisite' *Tears of affection; a Poem Occasioned by the Death of a Sister Tenderly Beloved*.[65]

Family

Although the quotation from Hurdis was used to celebrate Hutchins' virtues, the choice of this poem, written in remembrance of strong familial bonds, reflects the way in which Turner had justified the increasing

152 258.—FUCUS CORNUTUS.

Fucus cornutus, frond cartilaginous, flat, nerveless, seldom branched, beset with distichous, alternate, patent, subulate ramuli, some simple, others pectinate, bearing on their inner side subulate incurved capsules.

Cape of Good Hope. *Mr. Burchell.*

ROOT, composed of numerous, compressed, closely interwoven fibres, of the same color and substance as the frond, and spreading in wide patches over shells and other submarine bodies.

FRONDS, numerous from the same root, growing in tufts, between flat and compressed, preserving from the base to the summit an everywhere equal width of less than a line, wholly devoid of midrib or veins, generally once or twice irregularly forked, and, except near the root, beset throughout their whole length with distichous, alternate, patent *ramuli*, standing at very short distances from each other, scarcely two lines in length, some simple, others bearing at their sides two or three others, which are still smaller, are subulate, subcylindrical, set so close as to touch each other, and are between erect and patent, yet slightly incurved: all of them are quite entire at their margins: of the larger, some appear as if it were likely they would lengthen into branches.

FRUCTIFICATION, situated upon the ramuli in their inner side, consisting of three or four extremely small, subulato-setaceous, incurved *capsules;* but these in my specimens were so young that it was impossible to discover the contents.

COLOR, a bright red, like that of bricks, in the recent plant; fading to a pale orange, from being kept long in fresh water.

SUBSTANCE, between cartilaginous and membranaceous.

Specimens of this Fucus were sent me some years ago by Professor Mertens; but I have lately received it in a more perfect state from my friend, Mr. Burchell, whose recent return from the Cape of Good Hope is likely to form an important epoch in our knowledge of the Natural History of Southern Africa; loaded as he is come with the various treasures, which an expedition for five continued years, through countries scarcely ever trodden by Europeans, has enabled a man of his activity and knowledge to collect. For my own part I can only lament that he did not return sooner: this work might otherwise have received material assistance from his kindness. But to regrets of this nature there would never be an end, whatever number of years might be allotted to the publication. The length of time already bestowed upon it has given rise to other and more serious sources of regret: among them none is so great as the loss of my friends, whose communications have chiefly enabled me to render it what it is; and among these friends there is assuredly none whom I have in every point of view so much reason to lament as Miss Hutchins. That I have by her untimely death been deprived of a most able assistant, and that Botany has lost a votary, as indefatigable as she was acute, and as successful as she was indefatigable, this work bears abundant testimony; and the *Lichenographia Britannica*, should it ever be published, will do so no less unequivocally. But few, if any, except myself, can appreciate her many amiable qualities; her liberality, her pleasure in communicating knowledge, her delight in being useful, the rapture she felt in tracing the works of the divine hand, and the union in her of those virtues which embellish and improve mankind. Three years have now elapsed since she died, and every succeeding year makes me more deeply feel what I have lost, and how with her is gone a great part of the pleasure I derived from these pursuits.

" In every season of the beauteous year
" Her eye was open, and with studious love
" Read the divine Creator in his works.
" Chiefly in thee, sweet spring, when every nook
" Some latent beauty to her wakeful search
" Presented, some sweet flower, some virtual plant.
" In every native of the hill and vale
" She found attraction, and, where beauty fail'd,
" Applauded odour or commended use."

a. *F. cornutus*, nat. size.
b. *branch*, magnified - - 6.
c. *part of the same* - - - 3.

31 *Dawson Turner's tribute to Ellen Hutchins, with a quotation from James Hurdis's 'Tears of affection; a Poem Occasioned by the Death of a Sister Tenderly Beloved', in* Fuci, *vol. 4 (1819), p.152.*

intimacy of their friendship. By the late 18th century the family had come to be seen as both a social and a natural moral unit within which love and intimacy was allowed, and whose boundaries clearly demarcated illicit relations. While friendship between males was highly valued outside the family, intense friendships between men and women, even if generated by shared interests, required some device whereby they could be sanctioned.[66] Turner appears to have resolved his desire to deepen his friendship with Hutchins by finding a way to make her part of his family. This occurred just after Turner had admitted his difficulties with arranging the seaweeds and had sought Hutchins' advice; a time made all the more difficult by the illness and subsequent death of his infant daughter Katherine, which followed that of his previous child, a son. When Mary Turner gave birth to another girl a few months later, Turner wrote to Hutchins the following day, stating that as the nurse assured him that this child was to be the 'flower' of the family, he proposed 'to call her Ellen after yourself'. Moreover, he hoped that Hutchins would be godmother to the child, as he knew 'no female in the world whom I sh^{d} so earnestly wish a child of mine to emulate'.[67] Hutchins was overwhelmed by feelings of 'tenderness & gratitude', and told Turner 'how glad I sh^{d} feel to be God Mother to the little babe & thus be in some sort connected with your family'.[68]

Although the focus of their correspondence remained botany, from this point on letters from Turner continued the discussions of art, books and family news he had already begun to include, while Hutchins responded in kind and was always eager for news of 'my little child'. As Hutchins' health deteriorated, and delays in the production of *Fuci* increased, they continued to correspond, despite warnings from Hutchins' physician and concern on Turner's part. Although Turner prayed repeatedly for the preservation of Hutchins' life, it was also imperative, he stressed to her, not to be 'wanting in efforts on your own part to second His goodness'. Rather than writing to him, therefore, she should obey her religious duty and do all in her power to prolong her life, even though Turner had found in her correspondence 'a pleasure that I declare to Heaven I never yet found in that of any other individual, excepting those of this house', and also knew that 'if deprived of that pleasure' he 'would long ago have sunk into … apathy & indolence'.[69]

This debt was not trivial. For figures like Turner who stressed not only private religious feeling but also an active and useful life in society, indolence was anathema. His reaction to untimely deaths was due in part to recognition of his own mortality and the necessity of not wasting whatever time was allotted to him. In this, Turner was not untypical: it was the period when making good use of time could be proclaimed the 'true source of happiness'.[70] During the unsettled period of the wars with France, pressure for a renewed commitment to religious and moral principle was often expressed through attitudes to nature and the family.[71] Losing oneself in the wonder of nature was thought to counteract selfish individualism, while maintaining the home as a place of tranquillity, comfort and regularity encouraged contemplation. It was the perception of order in this world that was held to be the first step in perceiving a grander order, and the primary place where this occurred was in the family, which was taken to be a microcosm of society as a whole. Like societies, families required a framework of discipline, usually upheld by the male head of the household. We have already seen that Turner took an active interest in the education of his children; in addition he ensured that the activity of the household included regular contemplation of God's word by reading a chapter from the Bible '& notes' after breakfast.[72]

In the Turner home, moreover, nature and family came together in a direct way for this was where Turner carried out his botanical researches and kept his natural history collections. We tend to assume that natural history objects are essentially isolatable *because* they are scientific, but when scientific practices were conducted in the home, the study of nature through ordered collections also served to shape relationships within the family, including those involving women and children.[73] Mary Turner had been as 'ardent' a botanist as Ellen Hutchins and, even though her 'care of a family' had 'given a different turn to her thoughts', she was no less fond of botany.[74] It was in the context of the home that Maria and Elizabeth developed their interest in botany and where Turner taught them their 'Botanical A.B.C.'[75] The religious, social and emotional issues contained in works like the *Fuci* were not, therefore, irrelevant to the quest to produce a scientific arrangement of seaweeds, but in fact part of the purpose of botanical learning in this period. The importance of the home in fostering the values Turner held about nature and family may lie behind his reluctance for Hooker to engage in dangerous foreign travel, and in his inability to understand why Hooker's 'restless mind will not suffer him to be at peace, tho' he is surrounded at home by all the comforts that affluence, refined society, & the attachment of his friends can afford'.[76]

The fact that, except for the accident of his father's unexpected death, Turner would have been a clergyman and not a banker, may help us understand more clearly not only his disappointment at not producing order in the seaweeds, but also his caution. Establishing the *correct* order in nature was paramount, for it reflected God's purpose in the world. This may well be why Turner liked the mosses 'better than any other branch of Botany'.[77] With their 'highly beautiful & simple' systematic arrangement revealed by the microscope, mosses clearly exhilarated Turner: 'Can any thing be more wonderful, or are the traces of the hand of the Deity anywhere more visible? I shall never forget the emotions I felt on the first day that I examined & determined to study Mosses.'[78] Though Turner had intended to return to the mosses, by the time the *Fuci* was completed in 1819, Hooker had already produced not only his monograph on liverworts, but also a work on British mosses and the start of one on exotic species.[79] Since, however, it was Turner who had encouraged Hooker to take up the mosses as consolation for giving up foreign travel, we can see that facilitating and organising the work of others was as important to Turner as his own efforts in striving to achieve botanical order.[80] Turner may have failed to reduce the families of seaweeds to a 'well-organised system' but the same could not be said of his own family and those he included within it.

Despite the strict regularity of the Turner household, visitors, whether scientific or not, enjoyed their visits to Turner's home and remembered above all the family's hospitality and happiness. Moreover, this was not a family in which daughters were seen but not heard, nor one in which 'boisterous spirits' were quelled.[81] Lyell, who frequently recalled his visits to the Louvre with Turner in 1814, would also fondly remember the fun he had on the trip with those 'saucy girls' Elizabeth and Maria Turner.[82] And while Lyell's son, seeing Mrs Turner and her daughters etching at 6.30 in the morning, considered their industry far greater than the effort he expended at schoolwork, it is striking that Turner's daughter chose to depict her mother lounging on a sofa reading a newspaper (fig.46).[83]

After 1819 Turner published very little more on botany but it remained an active interest for him and his family, not least through the marriage of his daughter Maria to Hooker in 1815. Turner warmly supported Hooker's botanical career, penning the Latin inaugural lecture that Hooker was expected to deliver on taking up the botany chair at Glasgow but was incapable of writing, and then involving himself in the political negotiations surrounding Hooker's appointment as Director of the Royal Botanic Gardens at Kew in 1840.[84] However, the way in which botany was embedded as an enjoyable activity within the family – beginning with Turner's being 'prodigiously' happy in 1811 'from the inclination my two eldest girls have recently expressed to become botanists' – is best caught in a later informal sketch by one of these daughters, Elizabeth, showing her two sons receiving 'a lesson of botany' from her younger sister Ellen (fig.32).[85] But these two grandsons did not continue the family line in botany. Instead it was Turner's grandson Joseph Hooker, Maria and William's son, who was to become the botanist of that generation, ultimately acquiring a pre-eminent position within the international scientific community.

Turner, however, for whom family was so important and intimately connected with botany, threatened this botanical dynasty just at a point when Joseph's career was teetering on the brink of a new and insecure form of professional science.[86] Turner's elopement in September 1851 with a woman much younger than himself and of humble social origins had consequences not only for his own family but also for the worldwide community of botanists. For the few in the know, the gossip circulated via botanical correspondence networks with as much potency as news of

32 *Elizabeth Palgrave's sketch of her two sons, Francis Turner Palgrave and William Gifford Palgrave, receiving a botany lesson in 1835 from her younger sister Ellen Turner, from her sketch book of 'Drawings of the Turner family,'.*

a scientific discovery. 'I heard all about D. Turner from Joe Hooker,' wrote Dublin botanist William Harvey to Jane Loring Gray in Massachussetts. 'It is much worse than I had supposed & nearly as bad as it can be. It will make a very serious difference to Sir Wms income & the future prospects of the family – more's the pity.'[87]

In the event, Joseph Hooker went on to have a successful career in the context of the new professional science of the later 19th century. His position as a paid botanist contrasts with his grandfather's pursuit of botany as part of polite culture and religious sensibility.[88] In this respect, Turner's botanical researches are important not only for their contributions to the development of botanical knowledge but also for the way in which they reveal the social structure of British science at the start of the 19th century. Investigating the little-studied groups of cryptogams in a period before science was a professional discipline, Turner, although engaged in daily business as a banker, came to be regarded not as a solitary provincial amateur but as one of Britain's foremost botanists. His reputation was acquired not only through his researches in a difficult area of botany but also through the way in which he recognised the importance of establishing and maintaining a community of naturalists. This required a shared idea of the public good; a notion that is often associated with the emergence of professional science supported by government, but which was shaped within the British context by the fact that the private collector and private collections remained of central importance to the progress of natural history well into the 19th century. The investigation of Turner's botanical work has therefore required exploration of how he articulated the processes of making collections and producing knowledge, and how the practice of these ideals was reflected in his published botanical works, his strong friendships, his religious views, the financial costs of his scientific pursuits and the organisation of his own household.

ANNE SECORD

Acknowledgements

For permission to quote from manuscripts I thank the Master and Fellows, Trinity College, Cambridge; the Trustees of the Royal Botanic Gardens, Kew; the British Library; Norwich Castle Museum & Art Gallery; and the Royal Society of Medicine Library.

Where references to the correspondence between Dawson Turner and Ellen Hutchins are followed by an asterisk, this indicates that transcriptions of those letters can be found in M.E. Mitchell, ed., *Early Observations on the Flora of Southwest Ireland: Selected Letters of Ellen Hutchins and Dawson Turner 1807-1814* (Dublin, 1999).

CHAPTER FOUR

Dawson Turner and Book Collecting

Ten years ago, the reputation of Dawson Turner as a collector of books and manuscripts seemed secure. Those who had consulted his voluminous surviving correspondence found a man clearly much liked, with extensive connections in the worlds of botany and of antiquarianism, with friends among artists and in literary circles, a collector able to keep peace even with the irascible Sir Thomas Phillipps and in contact with collectors of books, manuscripts and autograph letters across a wide social spectrum, in England and on the continent. His status as a book and manuscript collector was established. The British Museum Library had acquired his celebrated extra-illustrated large-paper copy of the second edition of Blomefield's *History of Norfolk*, its original 11 volumes multiplied with several thousand prints, drawings and watercolours illustrating the topography, antiquities and more general history of the county. During his lifetime, the museum had bought from him for £1,000 one of the centrepieces of his collection, five volumes of manuscripts relating to the history of Britain, including a long series of royal letters and two volumes concerned mainly with Mary Queen of Scots and James V and VI.[1] At the auction of his manuscripts in 1859 the museum had also been an assiduous and determined bidder, acquiring more lots than anyone else. In his employment as a banker,[2] as a botanist and as a collector and amateur, here was a person of exemplary qualities. As the late A.N.L. Munby concluded in the only extended study of him as collector of manuscripts and autograph letters,

> Anyone who makes a study of the lives of book collectors soon discovers that they are not necessarily agreeable men. It may be that the singleness of purpose – ruthlessness is perhaps not too strong a word – which really great collectors require is generally incompatible with sensitivity to the comfort and convenience of the collector's family: and certainly many collectors have been less than scrupulous about the means which they have employed to achieve the coveted end of acquisition. To these trends Dawson Turner provides a most happy exception.[3]

'This friendly, aimiable and industrious man.'[4] The family picture of the early 19th century remains unchallenged: a tight-knit group of mother and six daughters, all but one of whom possessed more than average artistic talent, annotating, copying, drawing and putting in order the assortment of information that flowed in abundance across the tables in the house at Great Yarmouth: his two sons had different duties in their education, and one became a successful schoolmaster.[5] The house became filled with his collections. Pictures hung not just in the main reception rooms, but also in passages and spare space everywhere. At the back was a laundry that doubled as a children's playroom, and latterly became a store for Turner's ever-growing collection of autographs.[6] Admittedly the artist Benjamin Robert Haydon expressed some alarm on witnessing the scene of domestic industry when he visited the family for three weeks in 1817, but Turner's evident fondness for his domestic circle outweighed anxiety.

> Turner by his regular habits had managed the whole House like a school. The children knew not Idleness from their infancy, tho incessantly occupied with business – a magistrate & a banker, he educated all & often listened to his youngest child & corrected her lesson while he shaved ... After Breakfast was over, he read a chapter in the bible, & notes, and then all arose, Mrs Turner taking the tea caddie in her hand for the drawing room, the children following her, Turner to the bank, and I joining the Children. One seized a drawing, another a French grammar, a third her spelling book, a fourth her etching needle; all knew their duties and all were employed as if they had an appetite to gratify.[7]

Not a moment of the day was to be wasted. In 1834, Turner's second daughter Elizabeth noted of her own nine-year-old son and his younger brother that the two boys had had a three-week spring holiday in which they had learned the first book of the *Aeneid* and worked on Xenophon and Sallust. In the summer she reproached herself for the 'idleness & follies of my own childhood' now (in her view) evident in her children as she vainly tried to make them 'avoid having the same cause for self reproach, by urging them to greater application & zeal than their mother shewed'.[8]

However, there now hang over Turner questions respecting his judgement in the means by which he obtained some of the most valuable papers in his collection, and the extent to which he was willing to protect a source of materials that to some people outside his immediate circle seemed at least suspect. In 1997, Janet Ing Freeman demonstrated that many of the papers in Turner's collection had been removed without consent from the possession of the Tollemache family, either from Helmingham Hall in Suffolk or from Ham House, near Richmond in Surrey.[9] The person responsible for their removal, William Fitch, was one of Turner's

33 The Library at the Bank House with the family portrait by Thomas Phillips RA above the fireplace. Drawing by one of the Turner girls. (Trinity College Library.)

most loyal correspondents, his letters stretching over the years 1819 to at least 1851. Thanks to his marriage to Rachel Alexander, protégée of the elderly and increasingly infirm Countess of Dysart, Fitch had easy and privileged access to the libraries and papers of both houses. By the time that Turner sold the Scottish royal letters to the British Museum in 1853, the fact that they had been taken by Fitch from Ham House in the mid-1820s had almost passed into history.[10]

Yet even in 1825 it would have been difficult for Turner not to suspect their origin. In 1840, the death of Lady Dysart left Fitch disappointed in his hopes for a significant bequest, and it also brought an end to his profitable rummaging. But he still had another source. Besides his activities at Helmingham and Ham, he also acquired – whether by removing them himself or by acquiring them from an intermediary is not clear – papers from the town archives at Ipswich. This archive was in so bad a state of disorganisation that in 1835 it was remarked by the Royal Commission on Municipal Corporations.[11] But it was Fitch who claimed ownership in passing several portions of it to Turner, and who, after acquiring from the archive the 16th-century manuscript of John Bale's play *Kynge Johan*, arranged, with the help of Turner, to sell it to the Duke of Devonshire. Naturally, Fitch did not mention to Turner the exact origin of the papers from Lady Dysart. Of *Kynge Johan* he readily admitted to Turner in 1832 that it had been removed 'with a large quantity of loose papers' from the Corporation Chest at Ipswich.[12] If Turner preferred to hear and see no evil, others were less shy. John Holmes, bookseller and then assistant in the Manuscripts Department of the British Museum, shared his anxieties concerning Fitch and Ham House with Turner in 1829.[13] Some years later, Sir Frederic Madden, Keeper of Manuscripts in the British Museum, who had been consulted about *Kynge Johan*, noted in his diary, 'A pretty sort of scoundrel this Mr Fitch must be! his name should be *Filch*.'[14]

Fitch's long association and friendship with Turner, formed on the basis of their shared antiquarian interests, developed into a mutually profitable business relationship as Turner time and again took the bait offered. The largest body of evidence of Fitch's depredations is in his letters to Turner. If Turner was to remain innocent, he had also to remain ignorant. Whether, and how far, he remained ignorant, or chose to ignore unpalatable facts, is at best a matter for speculation. The ordinary gossip of social intercourse (and the gregarious Turner was well informed on all manner of subjects) can hardly have protected him from rumour.

If Turner is no longer the unblemished figure that Munby saw, he is nonetheless worthy of attention as a prime example of a kind of collecting that characterised the middle years of the 19th century. His exceptionally well-documented life takes us beyond the names that dominate histories of collecting during what Seymour de Ricci called the 'Dibdinian age', which in his view terminated with the sales of Richard Heber's several libraries in the 1830s.[15] Turner lived for a further 20 years, and the sales of his own collections in their turn helped shape those of the late 19th century. Tirelessly welcoming, possessing collections of manuscripts in particular that were of value to a growing number of antiquaries, a sympathetic friend and supporter to those in need, often to the extent of lending them money, Turner is central to understanding the history of book and manuscript collecting in England between the Napoleonic wars and the 1850s. He also epitomises the ways in which social structures and hierarchies could be broken down by shared interests. He had no family connections with the aristocracy, and he could claim no privilege through high positions in the armed services or the Church. But he won the respect of many members of the aristocracy through mutual passions for books and manuscripts, his readiness to share knowledge and the sound advice that he was often in a position to provide. He won his position by knowledge.

Munby's sympathetic portrait of Turner as a collector of autograph letters remains the fullest account of the development of his interests and priorities in this field. A pupil of the collector William Upcott (1779-1845), for many years sub-librarian of the London Institution and with whom he was in correspondence by 1816, Turner lived to see Upcott need to sell important parts of his collection.[16] An interest that began haphazardly (it was Upcott who made him organise his own collection, though neither man could have foreseen Turner's assiduity in this) was transformed in 1821 by the joint purchase with Hudson Gurney, his exact contemporary in the bank, of the collection assembled by the 18th-century Suffolk antiquary Cox Macro. This brought a few medieval manuscripts. More significantly, it brought whole series of letters from the 17th century and since; and it demonstrated to Turner the importance not just of single autographs, but also of groups. The lesson was to be amply vindicated when his own collection in turn came to be auctioned in 1859, such archives being just the kind of lot that most attracted the historical and documentary instincts of Sir Frederic Madden for the British Museum.[17]

Turner did not restrict himself to Britain. At various times his agents included Giuseppe Molini and Giuseppe Vallardi in Italy,[18] Jules Renouard in Paris and Samuel Hamilton in Washington D.C. But his central interests were in Norfolk, in British history and literature and, for most of his life, in botany. He did not become a national figure as a book and manuscript collector until he was in his fifties. The scale of his collecting, of books and of pictures, dominated his home town, but he was not alone. The local history published in 1826 mentioned half a dozen other collectors of paintings and the topographical and historical libraries of J.F. Ranney and of Robert Cory, former mayor.[19] Turner himself had been a Fellow of the Linnean Society since 1797, and of the Royal Society since he was twenty-six. But though he was also elected to the Society of Antiquaries and, though after his retirement from Yarmouth he moved to south-west London, there underlies his correspondence a sense of distance in more than a geographical way. By the late 1820s he was enrolled also in societies and academies from Göttingen and Leipzig to Dublin, from Stockholm and Edinburgh to Rouen and Caen.

As was reflected in his immense and detailed correspondence, Yarmouth was still remote. Until the 1840s, links with London were by coach or by sea. The first railway line between Yarmouth and Norwich was built only in 1844, and Norwich was connected by rail with the rest of the country only after that, when a line through Thetford linked with Ely and Cambridge. The town developed from a port and minor watering place into a fashionable seaside resort in the early 1850s. Until then, its overland connections with the rest of the country did not encourage crowds. A more direct railway route between Yarmouth and London via Ipswich was proposed in 1845, and Turner was one of the bankers for it. That year, trains to London via Norwich, Ely and Cambridge took seven hours. Though there were two daily mail coaches to London in the 1840s (their number had not changed for years), many people still found ships preferable to the road: steam packets sailed twice a week in the 1840s, and sailing ships took a little longer. For large parcels, sea was the ordinary route.[20] It was also possible to meet the steamers passing out at sea, in Yarmouth Roads.[21] When in 1834 Turner's daughter Elizabeth wrote from Hampstead about a forthcoming visit, she anticipated coming by the Edinburgh steamer.[22] As for other parts of the country, although letters could be moved quite speedily, anything heavier might take considerably longer. In 1817, the quickest way for a parcel to be sent from Liverpool to Yarmouth was by road via London. The alternative route by sea, depending on infrequent direct sailings, could take two months, as Turner discovered when he sent a parcel in the other direction.[23]

Locality was not just important to Turner and to other collectors like him. It was difficult to escape, unless there was also a London town house and regular need to spend prolonged periods there. Although Turner and his family made several trips abroad, there was never a sense either of cosmopolitanism or of metropolitanism. In these circumstances, correspondence was all the more important. Turner kept up his interest in the Royal Society and some of its internal politics, though he seems to have taken less interest in the Society of Antiquaries. Local antiquarian societies were another matter, and he published many papers in *Norfolk Archaeology* from the first volume in 1847 onwards. In transferring his affection from the *Gentleman's Magazine*, where he had previously placed papers on Norfolk topics, he was one of many who, by preferring a local publication and supporting a local society, contributed to the decline of the older periodical.

For many of his friends, he was almost synonymous with eastern Norfolk. The art dealer George Buchanan looked to him for introductions and information, and confided in him when the collapse of the market for paintings in the early 1850s was putting him in great difficulty: in 1852, Buchanan was declared bankrupt.[24] So did the Sothebys, for the world of books and manuscripts. The fashionable London bookbinder Charles Hering sought his recommendation to other collectors in Yarmouth.[25] Before the introduction of the penny post in 1840, it was common practice to send out parcels of letters or other papers such as prospectuses, to be posted locally and thus more cheaply. Turner was ideally placed to act as an agent in such matters. In 1838, for example, the London bookseller Joseph Lilly sent him a packet of catalogues to distribute among his friends.[26]

It was also Turner who seems to have introduced Dibdin and Richard Heber to the great library at Blickling, north of Norwich. And though Lord Spencer had described to Dibdin some of the bibliographical excitements at Holkham when he visited the house in 1812,[27] Dibdin still had not seen the library when he wrote his *Bibliographical Decameron*. Turner was, thus, all the more eager to mend matters a little later:

> Next week it is my intention to pass with Mr Coke at Holkham, when I wish I could have any prospect of meeting you. Mr Coke would, I know, be delighted to see you, & I could safely promise you a very rich treat in his library, which is almost wholly unexplored, & contains such a treasure of early editions as I never saw in any other. Many of them, unfortunately, are in a bad state, from there being no librarian or other person appointed to take care of them. ... I am sorry my own library is not of a kind to enable me to hold out any temptations to you to come down to Yarmouth.[28]

At Holkham, he both introduced visitors[29] and also played a central role in trying to bring to publication the catalogue of manuscripts in the collection inherited by Thomas Coke. He was pivotal in encouraging Frederic Madden to revise the task after William Roscoe had been obliged to retire. But, as costs mounted, even he could not persuade Coke of the need to make a survey available to the public, let alone with the series of coloured plates that he envisaged. Roscoe's and Madden's work remained unprinted and unpublished. Instead, Turner made himself responsible for having engraved and printed, in an edition limited to 50 copies, a series of plates that was to have accompanied the catalogue. Despite various hopes in the book trade, the plates likewise remained unpublished.[30]

The following pages are not primarily concerned with Turner's autographs, which were Munby's principal focus. Like many other collectors, he regarded letters as integral to historical understanding, to be set beside portraits (painted, drawn or printed), relevant topography and other biographical detail. Printed books had to be placed and seen in their human contexts. The inter-relationships of manuscript and print – in all their forms – were crucial to him. For these reasons, it is impossible to treat Turner simply as a collector of discrete kinds of document, printed or manuscript, book or letter, drawing or etching, lithograph or engraving. Even some of his botanical specimens were preserved amongst his general correspondence, where it may be safely assumed that he considered them to be most usefully placed and classified. For him, each kind of document, like each part of a document, supplemented and supported others. Each was critical to the way in which he viewed and treated his books. In no parts of his library was this more apparent than in the tens of thousands of letters, portraits, newspaper cuttings and other matter that he inserted in these books. In 1817, Haydon described him as 'an immense, living Index',[31] a term that suggests a certain mechanical doggedness. Turner was more than this. While his life was (until his last unhappy years following the death of his first wife) highly organised, in his enquiries, in his correspondence and in his collecting, he was valued as much for his hospitality, his generosity and his sociability.

For a private individual, owning no estate to administer and with no public career to speak of, his surviving correspondence is prodigious. The nine packed shelves in Trinity College, Cambridge, containing perhaps 16,000 letters arranged in chronological order, do not do justice to the size of his incoming mail. They contain nothing on the banking business, only a small part of his exchanges with booksellers, few book invoices, and little correspondence with bookbinders or with the printers of his many books and pamphlets. His family wrote frequently and profusely to each other, but their letters are kept separately and many are still in the possession of his descendants. His main chronological file of correspondence, in French, German, Italian and Latin as well as English, is rich in the details of natural history collecting; with antiquaries and people all over the country seeking subscribers for their privately published works; with good causes of all kinds; with learned societies; with local and national politics; about his pictures; with promoters of local improvements; with engravers and artists; with autograph collectors; and with other book collectors. Yet, even where it is strong, it is not comprehensive. A glance at the summary descriptions of his books in the auction catalogues of his library[32] shows how he was in the habit of slipping letters by authors of books into copies of their own works, with a portrait if possible. Though he did so on many occasions, he did not invariably make a copy of that letter for his own files of incoming correspondence. Besides this series, he also maintained other ones of autographs of people usually of some public standing in their own sphere, whether politics, the Church, literature or other activities. Most of these have since been dispersed. There were further collections, likewise carefully sorted, relating to family matters, particularly where these could not be fitted into the general series. Another series consisted of local affairs and of his business interests other than the bank.[33]

Turner's reputation as a collector rests on pursuits having different emphases at different periods in his life, but all of which retained his attention to some degree. Unlike some collectors, he did not entirely cease in one area on taking up another. It is important always to remember that for many years he followed his various collecting interests more or less simultaneously. In spring 1814, when he first made the acquaintance of Thomas Dibdin, buying from him a copy of the newly published *Bibliotheca Spenceriana*, much of Turner's surviving non-family correspondence is concerned with natural history, and much of it was with people overseas. But he was also collecting paintings. A list of pictures bought by him from James Poole in Norwich that year includes works by or attributed to Guido Reni, Annibale Carracci and Velasquez.[34] Nevertheless, and setting aside his interest in paintings and botanical specimens, circumstances have combined to emphasise his collecting of manuscripts and autographs over his collecting of printed books or of prints. In practice, all of these different categories were likewise parts of a single activity.

His first affections were for botany, and in particular mosses, lichens and seaweeds. Plenty of examples were to be found locally, and his summary local flora was included in Druery's *History of Yarmouth* published in 1826.[35] He was assiduous in acquiring the best copies of books on the subject, and if possible the manuscripts – original source material, transcripts and authors' correspondence — that made up the books. He owned both Francis Bauer's coloured engravings of plants reared at Kew and a collection of Bauer's original drawings. The drawings of Franz Carl Mertens, of Bremen, whose kindred interest in algae made him a welcome correspondent, he regarded as the work of a man who deserved better of public memory.[36] His copies of books such as Knight's *Pomona Herefordiensis* (1819) and Lambert's *Description of the Genus Pinus* (1803-24) were carefully chosen: the latter was of particular interest because it consisted of the plates still uncoloured, and marked for correction by Dryander. He had expensive books such as Bauer's *Illustrationes Florae Novae Hollandiae* (1813-16), and part (only) of Sibthorp's *Flora Graeca* (1806); and he treated his best botanical books as he did the rest of his library, inserting specimen letters from their authors so as to enhance the interest of particular copies. But he seems to have taken little interest in collecting the history of botany: there was, for example, no Fuchs, though he could point on his shelves to William Turner's *New Herball* printed at London in 1551 and bound up with the second part printed at Cologne.

He assembled, not surprisingly, a comprehensive collection of the works of Sir William Jackson Hooker, who married his eldest daughter in 1815.[37] But much of the depth of his botanical library was to be measured in the privately printed works, or works of which only part was ever issued even to a few friends. Robert Brown's *Prodromus Florae Novae Hollandiae et Insulae Van-Dieman* (1810) was withdrawn by its author, and only a few copies of the first volume ever circulated. Sir Thomas Cullum's *Florae Anglicae Specimen* [1774?] dealt with a subject nearer home, in Suffolk, but was never formally published. Nor were the works of Lewis Dillwyn, MP, Sheriff of Glamorganshire and three years Turner's junior, on the flora of Swansea and its neighbourhood. Some books were presentation copies: from Relhan in Cambridge, from H.A. Schrader in Göttingen, from Jo. Flüggé in Hamburg. Sir Joseph Banks gave him a copy of his privately printed plates after Engelbert Kaempfer's 17th-century drawings (now in the Sloane collection in the British Museum) of plants growing in Japan.[38] The King of Denmark gave him Lyngbye's *Tentamen Hydrophytologiae Danicae* (Copenhagen, 1819). Dillwyn dedicated to him his *magnum opus*, the *British Confervae* (1809), choosing to address him as 'Member of the Imperial Acad. Nat. Curiosorum and of the Göttengen [sic] Physical Society'. The copies of Alexander von Humboldt's publications arising from his voyage to Central and South America carried with them a friendship struck up in Paris by Turner and his wife.[39] Mrs Atkins's privately issued cyanotype photographs of *British Algae* (1843-) dated from after an astonishing period in botanical publication, and marked the beginning of new techniques in the subject.[40]

For many of these books, published either with or without colouring, merely to be coloured was not enough. Natural history works such as *Curtis's Botanical Magazine*, Hooker's *Botany of the Antarctic Voyage* (*Flora Antarctica*) (1844-7), or the *Conchologia Iconica* were available either coloured or uncoloured: individual parts of the *Flora Antarctica*, for example, cost either 5s. or 8s. But colouring by hand was an unpredictable process, and Turner was always anxious to be reassured that he had the best available: in this he had much in common with his contemporary bibliophiles. Because subscribers tended (or so it was claimed) to receive the best copies, picked by the publishers, and the ordinary trade was left to take what was left, without choice, the relationship between a collector and his supplier was of some importance. As Reeve Brothers, in London, explained when there was a difficulty over Turner's copy of the *Flora Antarctica*,

> In a work which passes through so many hands, particularly colourers, the only chance we have of getting together an unblemished copy is by selecting it from the monthly delivery as it comes in from the binder.[41]

Foreign books were as important as English ones, but they were not always easy to discover. On the one hand Frederick Bush, a local bookseller in Yarmouth, was able in 1794 to supply copies of La Fontaine and Rousseau, and the 15-volume collected edition of the works of Frederick the Great, besides Bayle's dictionary; on the other, some new books presented problems. In the late 1790s, Turner relied on Henry Escher, one of the immigrant booksellers in London, for German books, asking for poetry and drama as well as for a quantity of botanical works. In order to keep abreast of German publishing, for a while he subscribed to the *Allgemeine Literatur-Zeitung*, and Escher also sent many books on approval: Turner kept most of them.[42]

Turner's own taste for particular kinds of books was nowhere more evident than in those that he published himself, or which he subsidised others to publish for him. When his own heavily illustrated four-volume royal folio *magnum opus* on seaweeds, *Fuci*, was published in parts on commission by John and Arthur Arch in London in 1808-19, he arranged to have 25 copies printed on large paper, in folio. Of the total edition of 275, 52 copies in quarto, and 11 in folio, had their plates coloured initially.[43] The letterpress was by John M'Creery, who had made his reputation for fine work before he moved from Liverpool to London in 1805 and there quickly proved himself to be one of the most reputable printers in the capital: as printer of the second edition of Dibdin's *Bibliomania* in 1811, he came to the attention of a large bibliophile audience. As became his habit with his illustrated books, Turner gathered together the copies of the unfinished plates, besides the original drawings, and arranged for them to be bound up.

In retrospect, publication of the *Fuci*, involving different sizes of hot-pressed paper, choices of retail price and coloured or uncoloured copies, can be seen to have been a critical part of Turner's education as a bibliophile. But it was rooted in his English experience however much he also drew on his overseas correspondents. With the defeat of France in 1814 he could spread his wings and travel. France and Italy were

34 *Elizabeth Palgrave drawing (1832) of her children, Inglis age 5 and Reginald age 3, from her sketch book 'Drawings of the Turner Family'. (Private collection.)*

again accessible to tourists. For a few months, access to the continental mainland became easier, and that summer he went with members of his family to Paris. Much of the journal that he compiled on this occasion was taken up with details of pictures and sculptures, with visits to the main museums and with the habits of the French. Turner was always interested in food, but he also remarked on people's clothes, the frequent lack of street paving and the lack of gutters to take away rainwater. Night after night was spent at the theatre. Not having any introduction to the Bibliothèque Royale in the rue Richelieu, he was limited there in what he could see, though he was much helped by the experienced Théodore-Edme Mionnet of the Cabinet des Médailles. But he did glimpse the copy of the Valdarfer Boccaccio (1471), and thus reflected on the astonishing price paid in England so recently by the Marquess of Blandford in the belief that the Roxburghe copy was unique.[44] He noticed, too, how traces of Napoleon were everywhere being removed – even to the extent of abstracting his portraits from the printsellers' shops.

Bookshops were another matter, and his summary reveals a mixture of disappointment and discovery:

> Booksellers' shops abound on the quays to the south of the Seine, particularly those opposite to the Louvre. Like the other shops in Paris, they are dirty & small compared with ours in England. Even the best of them make little show; tho' some, as De Bure, Treuttel & Wurz, Pichard, & a few others, keep considerable stocks. The number of those who print catalogues is small: even De Bure had published none since 1806, Pichard since 1810, or Treuttel since 1812, a circumstance, which, added to the inconsiderable number of books in the possession of the largest among them, places in the strongest point of view the present state of Literature in Paris. All agreed in the same story, that little or nothing new is at this time going on; but all expressed hope that things would shortly mend … Contrary, too, to what La Ballardière had yesterday led me to expect, they were unanimous in their praise of Napoléon as a patron of letters; 'ah', said old Pichard, & he was only the echo of what had been said by the others, "*si cet homme là avait resté il auroît porté tout au plus haut degré. Il faisait travailler les ouvriers et encourageait les talens. Il fit tant de quais, de rues: à la vérité nous n'étions pas malheureux sous son regne: mais la guerre étoit son fléau et l'expédition à la Russie achevoit de le détruire.*" What is to be seen in the booksellers' shops is almost exclusively French literature; & of this the prices are not so materially different from those of books in England as I had expected: an 8vo. vol. of moderate size without plates usually sells for about 6 francs, & a 4to. vol. for double that sum. Barrois is almost the only bookseller in Paris who keeps any assortment of foreign books: they are nearly at the same price as with us. Specimens of early printing are very rare: the first, however, that I saw, were not so costly as to lead to the inference that the black letter part of the bibliomania exists in France as in England, except indeed as to books with prints, – Missals I could scarcely find away.[45]

Invoices from Paris bookshops show him exploring new fields of bibliophily. From Pichard he bought for 1,000 francs (the equivalent of just over £40) a large paper copy in red morocco and bound in 15 volumes of the *Cérémonies et Coûtumes Réligieuses de tous les Peuples du Monde*, with its renowned plates by Picart. From Paravicin he bought a manuscript *Horae* for 360 francs, together with three printed *Horae* for a total of 44 francs. Nepoeu, with whom he was to have many more dealings, produced a trio of early Books of Hours, including one on vellum printed by Hardouin, with miniatures finished in gold and colours, the whole bound up in green velvet, for 72 francs,[46] and another in quarto, with 30 miniatures and bound in red morocco, for 150 francs. A few months later, Nepoeu sold him two very different manuscripts, an illuminated *Roman de la Rose, 'exemplaire qui a appartenu au Président de Thou, et qui vient du Chalet de Soubise'*, at 200 francs,[47] and a mid-15th-century manuscript of the *Pélérinage de la Vie Humaine*, with its illumination only partially finished, for 500 francs.[48]

After the battle of Waterloo he returned to France. By September 1815 he was in Paris, in the company of his friend the artist Thomas Phillips. They found a city clearly in the hands of a victorious army, and witnessed the repacking of works of art for return to Italy: 'We saw it as left by Napoleon in its glory; we saw it in the confusion of Christie's auction room the day after a sale; & we saw it in its desolation.'[49] It was on this trip that he met Dominique-Vivant Denon in the Louvre, Aubin-Louis Millin in the Bibliothèque du Roi, and Humboldt, and thus gained a perspective informed by private knowledge of individual sentiments.[50] His understanding was developed further in his correspondence with the picture-dealer Alexis Delahante. In 1815 he also made his first visit to Normandy; he was there again in 1818 with his family and John Sell Cotman, and in 1819.[51] At Rouen he found the library much richer in manuscripts than in printed books, and at Caen he was disappointed to find little by way of either manuscripts or early printing.[52] He thought both libraries under-funded; and in his subsequent account of Rouen he found an excuse to insert remarks critical of the British copyright legislation requiring the deposit of new books in the university libraries – a view he shared with his friend the antiquary John Britton.[53]

Book-buying concerning what he had seen continued when he was back in Britain, as Treuttel & Würtz in London supplied books on Normandy. He was buying books again at Paris in 1819.[54] He went to Italy in 1825-6 in the company of the painters Thomas Phillips and William Hilton.[55] In both countries he sought out the bookshops (particularly those having stocks of illustrated books), printsellers and dealers in works of art. Another family journey in 1833 took him to Bruges, Ghent, Brussels, Mechelen, Antwerp and Leuven, and to the towns on the Rhine. Ever energetic, and wasting not an hour, he sought out all the main buildings and public collections of pictures, besides the major libraries. In Brussels, the keeper of the manuscripts in the Burgundian library, Joseph Marchal, produced a fine group of illuminated manuscripts for his visitors. The missal decorated in Florence by Attavante de Attavantibus in the 1480s, which had belonged to Matthias Corvinus, reminded Turner of Leonardo da Vinci.[56] Marchal's selection also included the Chronicles of Hainaut and the Breviary of Philip the Good,[57] and Turner was proud to note that when his daughter saw a copy of Horace she observed that it differed from the received text.[58]

Though he flirted with them at Paris in 1814-15, medieval illuminated manuscripts seem to have held only very limited attraction for him as a collector. He had obtained the mid-15th-century Flemish Book of Hours now in the Huntington Library by 1832.[59] Experimenting again, in 1825 he also obtained a group of Chinese drawings dating from the 1660s and illustrative of costume and modes of life. Both they and his Persian manuscripts of a *History of the World* and of Ferushta's *Hindostan* were to appear as oddities in the auction of his library after his death.[60]

By the late 1820s his interests had become more or less settled. Like so many others of his generation, Turner fell under the spell of Thomas Frognall Dibdin, whose untidily extrovert handwriting sprawling across deluges of letters spoke of a man unstoppable in his enthusiasms. The earliest surviving letter from Dibdin to Turner dates from April 1814, and is concerned with a confusion over Turner's wish for a large-paper copy of the *Bibliotheca Spenceriana*.[61] Dibdin's *Bibliographical Decameron* was published in three volumes, on large and ordinary paper, in late autumn 1817, after many delays (no unusual thing for Dibdin). Ever attentive to detail, even to the point sometimes of fussiness, at the end of October he was writing to

> all my bibliomaniacal friends to have their copies bound, in the first instance, out of sheets, by Lewis. They will in consequence have a larger, cleaner, & more beautiful book: as the plates are not beaten, & every care is taken, by the insertion of silver paper between every leaf, to prevent the ink from stirring. Lewis has already 80 copies, large & small, in hand, of the *first two volumes*. The binding will not retard the delivery of the volume a *week*. Of your *two* copies, L.P., perhaps you will make the experiment with one — morocco or russia — The charge being the same – 30s. per vol: which considering the size & intricacy of the tomes is not extravagant.[62]

Whether or not he appreciated Dibdin's advice for the binding on this occasion, Turner followed fashion and Dibdin in developing a taste for fine printing, always wishing to be assured that if he was buying prints they were either specially selected, or were the best of their kind. He spent heavily on binding, usually with a favoured group in Great Yarmouth but never seeking ostentatious – and expensive – ornament. On the other hand, books printed on vellum or other special materials held their own attractions. One copy of his *Account of a Tour in Normandy* (2 vols, 1820, again published with the help of J. and A. Arch) was printed on vellum, and was retained by Turner himself. Apart from the ordinary copies, there were large paper copies, copies with proof plates, and one copy on India paper. Again in 1822, Cotman's *Architectural Antiquities of Normandy*, with a text by Turner and published with the help of the same booksellers,[63] was printed in a choice of various special copies, and a single copy on vellum. The habit of printing a copy on vellum of most of his publications remained with him still in 1848, in his survey of the monuments in St Nicholas's Church, Great Yarmouth.[64] The taste for special copies affected his choice in purchasing. Vellum copies of La Fontaine's *Fables*, printed by Didot in 1799, and Parini's *Odi*, printed by Bodoni in 1791, both came from the collection of the Maréchal Junot, Duc d'Abrantès, one of several French libraries auctioned at London in 1816-18.[65]

The continental trade remained essential to him for as long as he collected. By the end of the 1790s he had been buying not just books on natural history, and books in German. With the help of London booksellers, especially Henry Escher and Dulau, he was also turning his attention increasingly to parts of the bibliophile market. By the 1820s his regular London suppliers of new books further included C.F. Molini, J.H. Bohte, and the firm expanded to Treuttel & Würtz, Treuttel jr & Richter. The 1830s brought dealings with Bossange, with Barthès and Lowell, and with David Nutt. These were leavened with occasional dealings direct with foreign booksellers including Molini and Gamba in Italy.

Years before, he had become a practised buyer at the major London auctions. The Woodford sale at Leigh & Sotheby in 1809 produced a crop of books by Thomas Pennant, besides copies of Schaeffer's *Fungorum Bavariae et Palatinatus Icones* (4 vols, Ratisbon, 1762-74) at £14 10s. and Chardin's *Voyages à Perse* (4 vols, Amsterdam, 1724) for £16.[66] The same sale provided a *papier vélin* copy of Desfontaines' *Flora Atlantica* (Paris, 1798), illustrated by Redouté and others, and a presentation copy to Woodford himself. At the Benjamin Heath sale in the following year, and bidding again through Arch, Turner concentrated on the ancient world, acquiring Brunck's edition of Aristophanes (Strasbourg, 1783) and Gronovius's Aelian (Leiden, 1731-44), both on large paper, and paying £17 10s. for the celebrated Amsterdam 1763 edition of Herodotus in a Russia leather binding by Kalthoeber.[67]

At the same time he was also buying through the ordinary retail trade. His purchases in 1810 from Arch included a fine copy of the Naples edition of Hamilton's *Campi Phlegraei* for £26, and a set of Bayardi's *Antichità di Ercolano* for £47 5s., one of the highest prices Turner was ever to pay for a printed work. As soon as it appeared, he bought his first volume of Dibdin's edition of Ames's *Typographical Antiquities* from the publisher William Miller, in Albemarle Street: his name was not, however, among the printed list of subscribers. The sale of Colonel Thomas Stanley's books in 1813 produced the five-volume Dante printed at Venice in 1757 under the patronage of Catherine, Empress of Russia: acting again through Arch, Turner thus obtained, for £37 16s., one of the special copies on large paper with the plates printed in different coloured inks. But in many respects the Stanley sale was a disappointment. Prices were high – twice those in the retail trade according to Arch – and Turner succeeded only with three bids: he also acquired a copy of Butler's *Hudibras* with the Hogarth plates inserted and in Walther's best blue morocco binding, and the five volumes of Jorge and Antonio de Ulloa's *Relacion Historica del Viage a la America Meridional* (Madrid, 1748). Other books passed over his head, or eluded him. Even though the copy of De Bry's voyages, a work of unique bibliographical complexity, did not answer the gushing description in the catalogue, the Duke of Devonshire still paid heavily for it. The copy of Monstrelet's *Chroniques de France* (Paris, 1572) was fought over by William Beckford and Sir Mark Masterman Sykes, before being bought by the latter for £136 10s. At more modest levels, Mouradja d'O'hsson's folio *Tableau Général de l'Empire Othoman* (Paris, 1787 etc.), bound by Walther, sold for £29 8s., where Arch claimed to have a copy of equal quality in the shop for £24, and Heineken's *Idée Générale d'une Collection d'Estampes* sold for £5 12s. 6d., where Arch had one for three guineas. Offered just nine months after the Roxburghe auction, the Stanley books provided the first opportunity to bid on books of a kind comparable with what had appeared in what had immediately been recognised as a landmark sale. The mania of July 1812 still held. At both the top and the bottom of the market, prices were high, sometimes seemingly exorbitant. Turner's own choice, here as on other occasions, was eclectic, often ambitious; and like most collectors he lived in hope of a bargain. Though he was still strong in botanical books and in illustrated books, there always remained an unexpected element in his buying.

The sale of Ralph Willett's library and botanical drawings in December 1813 brought only four purchases, a mixture of French history and visual stimulus: if the reproductions of Carracci's frescoes in the Palazzo Farnese (Rome, 1757) was an ordinary book, his choice of Canaletto's series of etched views of Venice was of more interest, while he strengthened his French holdings with Hellyot and Bullot's *Histoire des Ordres Monastiques* (1714-19) and, most expensively at £44 2s. (42 guineas), Montfaucon's *Monumens de la Monarchie Françoise* on large paper. Hand in hand with the more unusual books that he found in Paris went his purchases in London booksellers and auction-houses. His Walton Polyglot Bible arrived from the Duke of Grafton's sale in 1815, and his copy of Scheuchzer's *Physica Sacra* (Vienna, 1731-5) came from the library of the Duke of Devonshire.[68] In the same year he was buying prints by Piranesi and Wierix, the six-volume *Museum Florentinum* (1731-42) and – for just three guineas – Robert Adam's *Ruins of the Palace of the Emperor Diocletian at Spalatro* (1764).

The large paper copy of *Gerusalemme Liberata* printed at Venice in 1745 under the patronage of the Empress Maria Theresa and illustrated by Piazzetta held obvious attractions for a purchaser of Italian 18th-century illustrated books. His copy of the *Ibarra Sallust* (Madrid, 1772), another collector's *sine qua non*, was bound by Derôme. In his vellum copy of the collection of plates engraved by Rosaspina after Correggio's paintings in the convent of San Paolo at Parma, with letterpress by Bodoni (Parma, 1800), his tastes for pictures and for fine printing came together.

These were equally evident in his relations with his contemporaries, in his patronage of a small group of artists and the acquaintance that he sought with others. John Crome and John Sell Cotman are discussed elsewhere in this volume.[69] Turner's long friendship with, and patronage of Cotman, who as travelling companion and drawing master to most of his household became almost a member of the family, allowed privileged access to his work. Of many plates Turner possessed multiple copies. The unique copy on drawing paper of *Engravings of the Sepulchral Brasses in Norfolk and Suffolk* (Great Yarmouth, 1819) was extra-illustrated with plates by Turner's wife. Of the *Architectural Antiquities of Normandy* (1822) he possessed unique copies on vellum and on thick large paper, the latter with proofs of the plates at their different stages, besides a copy from the more regular large paper edition with plates on India paper. These three were all included in the sale of Turner's books when he left Yarmouth; but he retained to the end of his life his copy of Cotman's early work, the *Collection of Etchings, Consisting of Picturesque Specimens of Saxon, Norman and Gothic Architecture* (1811), including a proof of Cotman's very first etched plate. Turner was determined to gain a comprehensive record of his work.

His friendship with the engraver Charles Heath brought proofs and presents. His copy of J.M.W. Turner's *Liber Studiorum* was obtained from the artist himself,[70] and he was careful to obtain the best impressions of the *Picturesque Views of the Southern Coast* (1826) and the later *Views in England and Wales* (1832). Collections of prints by Sir Robert Strange (1725-92), Thomas Kerrich (the volume was said to have inspired C.A. Stothard[71]), Stothard's *Monumental Effigies of Great Britain* (1811-), Denon (a collection of 72 plates presented by the artist to Mrs Turner, who etched his portrait), Willam Camden Edwards of Bungay (for whom Turner had a particularly high regard[72]) all spoke not just of Turner's visual and antiquarian sense, but also of his friends and of the close connections in his mind between the print trade and book publishing. As with his books, Turner made a habit of embellishing his files of prints and drawings wherever he could. The volume containing about two hundred of Captain Baillie's prints, copied from Rembrandt and other mainly Dutch artists, was, for example, enriched with a copy of Rembrandt's own plate of *The Gold Weigher* along with a few further plates and an autograph note by Baillie.

His knowledge of Thomas Bewick, whom he met in Newcastle in 1809,[73] was no more than that of an acquaintance, but he still chose the histories of *Quadrupeds* and *British Birds* on imperial paper, Bewick himself selecting the copies – as no doubt he did for others as well in a market that was so particular.[74] Turner also subscribed to the *Fables* of Aesop in 1818 – choosing a copy on the largest, imperial, paper. But on the whole, and notwithstanding Bewick, whose delicate work had its own appeal, he seems to have preferred the engraved or etched line to the woodcut or wood-engraving. Inevitably for one so interested in illustration, Turner became aware of the work of William Blake. He noted a copy of Blair's *Grave* with Blake's designs (1808) in 1817, in the stock of Lackington, at a price that he thought attractively cheap. Once acquired, he inserted in it not only a letter from Blake, but also a copy of Schiavonetti's engraved portrait of Blake after Thomas Phillips, perhaps his greatest friend in London's artist circles.[75] Though he later enquired after other work by Blake, who sent him a list of his illuminated books for sale, any that Turner may have bought are not now recorded. However, Blake's letter to him of 9 June 1818 provides the most convenient summary in existence of Blake's stock at that time, ranging from 10 guineas for *Milton* and five guineas each for *America* and *Europe* to three guineas each for the *Songs of Innocence* and the *Songs of Experience*, and two guineas for the *Book of Thel*. The large colour prints made in the early 1790s were priced at five guineas each. As Blake was careful to explain, he printed his work as the orders required, and there was no stock. But though Turner later also acquired the *Book of Job* (1825) from Joseph Lilly, he seems not to have taken matters any further in 1818.[76]

Dürer, rediscovered by German romantics at the end of the 18th century, and the subject of further interest in the wake of publication of his designs for the prayer book of Maximilian I, was no more than an incidental interest. Turner's copy of the *Little Passion* was bound up with Aldegrever's four evangelists, and was a present in 1813 from the Norwich picture-dealer and an old school friend, Captain James Poole – 'a name,' noted Turner, 'well-known in the annals of art'.[77] For many years he claimed not to be interested in collecting prints, but this claim requires some modification. In 1813, the same year in which Poole gave him the volume of Dürer and Aldegrever, he also bought a volume of

1 The Turner Family, *1814, by Thomas Phillips RA. Dawson Turner stands over his wife Mary and their elder daughters, Maria who married Sir William Jackson Hooker, and, seated on the ground, Elizabeth who married Sir Francis Palgrave. (Reproduced by kind permission of Rupert Goodman.)*

II *Albert Cuyp,* A man giving provender to a horse, *watercolour copy by Elizabeth Palgrave of a painting in Dawson Turner's collection.*

III *Cornelius de Heem,* Fruit Piece, *watercolour copy by Elizabeth Palgrave of a painting in the collection of Dawson Turner.*

IV *Gaspar Dughet, called Poussin,* View of Tivoli, *watercolour copy by Mary Anne Turner of the original which was in the collection of Dawson Turner.*

V *Meindert Hobbema,* Road-side Inn, *watercolour copy by Hannah Sarah Turner of an original which was in the collection of Dawson Turner.*

VI *Pierre Mignard,* Madame de Maintenon and her Niece, *watercolour copy by Hannah Sarah Turner of a painting which was in the collection of Dawson Turner.*

VII The Two Sisters, *Elizabeth (left) and Mary Anne Turner, by Thomas Phillips RA, 1824. (Photographed by Stephen Bates.)*

VIII *Giovanni Bellini,* Madonna and Child Enthroned with St Peter and St Paul and a Donor, *1505. (Reproduced by kind permission of Birmingham Museums & Art Gallery.)*

IX *Drawing Room at the Bank House showing the* Christening Feast *by Jan Steen above the fireplace and the* View of Tivoli *by Poussin to the right of it. Watercolour by Elizabeth Turner. Norwich Castle Museum and Art Gallery.*

X *Drawing Room at the Bank House showing paintings of the Two Sisters by Thomas Phillips on the left hand wall and the* Virgin Enthroned with Child *and Saints by Giovanni Bellini on the right hand wall. Watercolour by one of the Turner girls. (Reproduced by kind permission of Trinity College Library.)*

XI Fucus Lambertii *drawn by William Jackson Hooker for Dawson Turner's* Fuci, *vol. 4 (1819), plate 237.*

etchings by Sandby at Lord Gainsborough's sale.[78] He seems to have made little effort at a systematic collection of earlier prints of any kind: anyone seeking materials before the mid-18th century in his auction sales will have found scant encouragement. Examples of earlier work in the catalogues of his library are piecemeal, though like other collectors he used Bryan's *Dictionary* of painters and engravers as a file in which to collect relevant examples. Copies of much of the older work discussed in this and the other standard books were increasingly difficult to find, and Turner did not have the same dedicated curiosity about them as did, for example, his friend Francis Douce.[79] Though the sale of his printed books in 1859 concluded with a long section of prints, there was no sign of sustained interest in collecting older examples. The Antwerp engraver Hieronymus Wierix was represented by a copy of Natalis's *Evangelicae Historiae Imagines* published at Antwerp in 1593,[80] and Adrien Collaert by his contributions for the plates in the *Vita, Passio et Resurrectio Jesu Christi* (Antwerp, *c.*1598).

In his taste for extra-illustrated books Turner was at one with his contemporaries. They were a means to both historical and personal ends. To a mind that was so attuned to gathering, evaluating and arranging knowledge, whether in botany or art, manuscripts or printed books, the pages of books, set between their covers, offered filing systems of their own. If extra-illustration was made popular and renamed in the wake of James Granger's *Biographical History of England,* first published in 1769-74,[81] it could also trace its roots at least back to the late middle ages. In Turner's hands it became more than a fashionable pursuit. It became an essential means of organising the mass of information contained in his library. Furthermore, like his files of correspondence, the books were also used as indexes to his own social life and that of his family. Here were not just the obvious books, but, often, special copies. His copy of Granger, revised and extended by Mark Noble (1804-6), was on large paper and bulked out from seven volumes to ten. It had belonged to the publisher and dealer William Richardson himself, whose own series of 160 engravings of heads was the foundation of many a more ordinary copy of this standard exercise in modern bibliophily. Clarendon's *History of the Rebellion* was another established target, Turner's copy of the six volumes of the 1810 edition, on imperial paper, being fattened up to 10 with 650 portraits. His Boswell was more ambitious. Two sets of four volumes each were mounted into six large imperial folio volumes, and furnished with about 1,700 portraits, views of places mentioned and assorted newspaper cuttings, along with a few autographs.

Extra-illustrated books, like autographs, required method in their organisation. Turner was always keen to hear how others arranged their collections, and in return for token gifts of engravings or lithographs drawn, whether in choice of subject or in scale. Booksellers, printsellers and others who supplied the matter for such collections could not help but notice the unequal demands for different parts of their stocks. The extra-illustrated books in his library were not all of Turner's making. Anxious to meet the requirements of a taste that set so much store by the conjunction of text and illustration, booksellers and publishers were also eager to provide their own ready-made goods. In 1837, the Glasgow publishers Blackie & Sons offered to make up a copy of Robert Wodrow's *History of the Sufferings of the Church of Scotland* to Turner's taste.[85] James Boaden's *Memoirs of Mrs Inchbald* (1833), illustrated with an assortment of autographs, portraits, stage scenes and newspaper cuttings, had belonged to his friend and fellow-autograph-collector William Upcott,[86] and in 1837 Upcott offered his help to Turner in making up other books.[87] His copy of Henry Swinden's *History of Great Yarmouth* (1772) had belonged to the local antiquary John Ives (d.1776), who had inserted various additions. But the extra-illustration of dozens of works was thanks to the labours of Turner, his wife and his daughters. Autograph letters were added, but so too were the portraits drawn or copied in his own house.

The most celebrated of all his extra-illustrated books, and one that is unique in its scale among British topographical literature, is the copy of the revised edition of Blomefield's *History of Norfolk* (1805-10), now in the British Library. By the time Turner and his family ceased work on it, the series stretched to 58 volumes, together with 12 boxes of deeds and seals.[88] But he also possessed a second copy, the 11 volumes of the original extended to just 40 with manuscript additions, plates by Mrs Turner, tracings and assorted cuttings. At the sale in 1859 it was bought for £21.

The long friendship between Turner and Dibdin brought its own bibliographical consequences. Etchings by Mrs Turner were inserted into many of the books written by the latter. Turner also came to own Dibdin's marked proofs of *Book Rarities* (1811), devoted mostly to Lord Spencer's library. His copy of the second edition of *Bibliomania* (1811) was not only provided with a manuscript key to the characters mentioned, but was also specially bound by Hering in Russia leather, with silk linings, and further ornamented with a fore-edge view of Strawberry Hill.[89] The prize, however, was the first volume (of four) of the *Typographical Antiquities* (1810), of which the sale description at the auction in 1859 provided a suitably imposing description:

> Illustrated with numerous autograph letters, addressed to the author during the progress of the work, embracing nearly all the celebrated Book Collectors in the palmy days of *Bibliomania;* also the original Drawings made for the plates, and impressions of most of the latter in different stages, with sketches of many other subjects originally intended for the work, but not so used; a considerable number of original Documents, which are either reprinted in

> the work, or introduced in facsimile amongst them, two original leaves from the press of CAXTON, referred to at page 354; portrait of Dr Dibdin, a private etching by Mrs Dawson Turner, etc. The total number of Illustrations is one hundred and eighty-six.

The volume appears to have been presented by Dr Dibdin to Mr Dawson Turner, who remarks concerning it — 'There are few more curious or interesting volumes to be found upon the shelves of my library.'[90]

If such a volume represented *in parvo* a particular kind of bibliomania, it was not the last of Turner's interest in special copies of his friend's books. Dibdin repaid the compliment, expatiating on Turner's library over several pages in his *Reminiscences* in 1836 and lauding his ability to follow business and 'bibliomancy' in equal measure.[91]

Turner's own view of the relationships of the different parts of his library are to a large extent to be discovered in the ways in which he arranged his manuscripts and other loose matter into volumes and then the volumes into series. But these could take no account of printed books, and for these he has left the clearest of all statements of another kind. At different times in his life he prepared catalogues of his library. That of 1816 represented a collection still in its early stages, only a few months after his trip to Paris following the allied victory at Waterloo.[92] Other catalogues devoted to particular aspects followed; of the pamphlets,[93] and of the printed catalogues in 1838.[94] The principal catalogue of his manuscripts was begun in 1834, and a few copies of part of it were printed off for friends at that time.[95] After reflection, Turner abandoned it, and in his last years began a more detailed account in 1854. A yet further catalogue, extending to five volumes and dating at least partly from the 1830s, was sold in his manuscripts sale in 1859, and passed into the hands of Sir Thomas Phillipps.[96] In some ways the most original was a catalogue of the printed books drafted in 1839 and then set out more neatly from 1843 onwards.[97] These five volumes were divided into four sections that portray the mind of a bibliophile, with tastes at once quite separate from, and yet inevitably overlapping, that of an antiquary. They demonstrate more concisely than any other document the spirit in which Turner approached the task of book collecting. The volumes of this catalogue were arranged as follows:

1 Books privately printed.
2 Books privately printed.
3 Those printed in small number, or rendered rare by accident.
4 Works of art, and books printed on vellum or on India paper or coloured paper.
5 Illustrated books, books with remarkable autographs, and sundries.[98]

As was remarked when the series came to be auctioned, there was much in the list of privately printed books that supplemented the standard work on the subject by John Martin.[99] If this was one extreme of bibliophily, the other was surely the often despised and rejected detritus of time-sensitive cheap printing. The importance he set on his collections of handbills, prospectuses, advertisements, newspaper cuttings and lottery bills was made very clear by their description in the fifth volume. Some of this material was supplied by Thomas and Frederick Strong, print-dealers in Long Acre in London who specialised in making up themed collections of newspaper cuttings, mostly of a topographical kind but also on other subjects, and whose advertisements could for a time be found prominently on the cover of the *Gentleman's Magazine*. Besides these, he also saved notices of meetings, pasting them in with his correspondence along with specimens of printing including an early Christmas card and an example from the first impression of penny black stamps, sent to him by Henry Cole.[100] Turner was by no means the first person to collect seriously what now tend to be termed printed ephemera but, as in all that he did, he ensured that even this recalcitrant material was organised and bound up so that it could be easily referred to.

Turner's own notes to this series are of especial interest, as they take us closer still to the mind of this highly organised collector:

> Much, it is obvious, might be written upon the contents of each of these Sections: but the nature of a catalogue like the present forbids the entering into such particulars except for the sake of explanation. I will, therefore, only say of the last, whose title is indefinite, that it is principally composed of Miscellanies of various kinds, — advertisements, handbills, lottery-puffs, cuttings from newspapers, prospectuses, etc. 'id genus omne' — articles which are commonly thrown away, but which acquire an interest, and sometimes a remarkable one, from juxta-position. Every separate book here enumerated is described at some length; their rarity seemed to entitle them to this; and the task was one of great pleasure to me, inasmuch as the performing of it appeared like discharging a debt of gratitude for the amusement and instruction they had afforded.

To some of his contemporaries, not the least remarkable aspect of his collecting was his insistence on binding up as much of his collection as possible. He was proud of the bookbinders in Yarmouth: 'I think I could convince you … that Yarmouth yields only to London in the excellence of its binders', he wrote to Dibdin in 1815.[101] The November 1820 bill from his most regular binder, John Shalders of Yarmouth, included the binding of 23 volumes of letters at 5s. apiece.[102] By the beginning of 1821 he was arranging to have bound the third series of autographs, some 1,324 letters gathered into six Russia leather volumes. In 1822 it was the turn of another local binder, G. Hazard, who was employed to bind up volumes of private correspondence. Other money was spent with Shalders on mounting papers in albums. A decade later most of the binding of autographs was in the hands of William Smith, also of Yarmouth. All this was in calf. Turner's preferred material for his better books was Russia leather and he resisted suggestions for novelty when, in 1846, Reeve Brothers of King William Street in London suggested to him that it would be appropriate to bind an expensive flora in the caoutchouc method, 'very strong and lasting', and used by Reeve even for large folios. Turner insisted on conventional structures and materials, despite the cost: in light of the rapidity with which caoutchouc bindings disintegrate he was prudent to resist Reeve's proposal.[103] His aim was usually neat and practical sturdiness. It was nonetheless evidently with some satisfaction that he noted one of his copies of his *Synopsis of British Fuci* (1802) had been bound by his friend the printer and bookbinder John Dawson Downes of Yarmouth, 'who invented, and seems alone to have practised, the art of stamping upon the cover impressions of the plants themselves', adding also that he thought Downes had never bound more than four copies in this manner.[104]

Turner's earliest published work, in 1800, was as a botanist; and it was as a botanist that he was elected a Fellow of the Royal Society in 1802.[105] It was not until almost thirty years later that the first of what were to prove several volumes drawn from his manuscript collection was to appear. The *Literary Correspondence of John Pinkerton*, antiquary, literary forger and historian of Scotland, was published by Colburn and Bentley in 1830, in London.[106] Two years afterwards, Turner issued privately a pamphlet, *Catalogue of the Works of Art in the Possession of Sir Peter Paul Rubens at the Time of his Decease*, printed from a manuscript at that stage still in the possession of Fitch.[107] The *Thirteen letters from Sir Isaac Newton* (1848), printed initially in an edition of just 50 copies for friends and then reprinted for a wider audience in *Norfolk Archaeology* in 1849, made a more considerable stir; and the *Descriptive Index of the Contents of Five Manuscript Volumes, Illustrative of the History of Great Britain* (1843; reprinted 1851) proved a prelude not to the intended printed catalogue of his manuscripts, but to the sale of these volumes to the British Museum in 1853.[108]

These privately printed pamphlets and books, like the etchings and lithographs by his wife and daughters, had a dual purpose. Each was a means of distributing scholarship, but each also enabled Turner to offer presents – sometimes but by no means always – in return for favours whether of information, or a book or manuscript. When in 1847 he offered a copy of his wife's etchings to the bookseller H.G. Bohn in exchange for some books, he was speedily rebuffed.[109] For amateurs it was different. The ability of collectors to exchange gifts among themselves was an important activity. Living in a fishing town, Turner also occasionally sent barrels of herrings to his friends who might appreciate these rather than books or papers. But the world of autograph collecting in particular depended to a considerable extent on exchange, where individual items might have a low commercial value, or where there would be embarrassment in selling letters by a living person.[110] The prints made by members of his family provided Turner with an ideal stock on which to draw for presents to all kinds of people, be they bibliophiles, antiquaries or botanists: the plates were not available in the trade and they were self-evidently rare. He was in the unusually fortunate position of having a talented family of artists. Some others, such as Turner's occasional correspondent Francis Wrangham,[111] maintained their own programmes of private printing. Sir Thomas Phillipps, with whom Turner was in correspondence for twenty-odd years, used the publications from his Middle Hill Press in similar ways, his most favoured correspondents receiving successive pages of the catalogues of his manuscripts as they were gradually set and printed.[112] Phillipps wooed Turner over several years with books in what he hoped would lead to an exchange for the early 14th-century Glastonbury cartulary that Turner had acquired among the Cox Macro collection in 1820: it was, for Phillipps, the chief attraction of his library. In 1833 Turner declined an offer from Phillipps of £100 – in Phillipps's words 'very nearly the price of £1 for each leaf'[113] – but he never succeeded in stemming Phillipps's persistence, and 11 years later refused £150.[114] If a cash offer would not work, perhaps gifts would both avoid Phillipps's ceaseless shortage of money and also be socially more appropriate. The cartulary remained in Turner's possession at his death.

While Phillipps was in a class by himself, there were also many others clamouring for attention. Turner published parts of his collection, and he dealt as he could with requests such as that from Agnes Strickland, who in 1841 enquired,

> Have you in your celebrated collection of Autographs any original letters from Plantagenet & Tudor Queens of England, calculated to give interest to the memoirs of those Princesses, in case you should feel disposed to favor me with copies or extracts for my present undertaking, 'The Lives of the Queens of England'? Perhaps you will … oblige me with a list.[115]

He acquired the letters of the poet Thomas Gray to Norton Nicholls as a gift from Thomas Mathias, to whom they had been bequeathed by Gray himself. But though he allowed John Mitford to read them when he was preparing his collection of Gray's poems for Pickering's octavo series of British poets in 1837, he was unwilling at that time for them to be published. Mitford's explicit appeal to Turner, in the preface to his edition, exposed to readers questions of private ownership and public interest on which Turner was usually inclined to be generous. 'It is much to be desired, that this gentleman should add to the obligations he has already conferred upon the public, by permitting them to be acquainted with a correspondence which will afford more than all the rest, a familiar acquaintance with the character of Gray.'[116] By 1843 Mitford had succeeded, with the publication that year by Pickering of the Gray-Nicholls correspondence. Again it was an octavo – modest enough in size but with opportunities for just the kind of individualities that Turner so enjoyed in his own publications. Mitford had already published with Pickering four volumes of Gray's works. This further volume was to contain, besides the letters owned by Turner, material drawn from manuscripts bought by Mitford at the Strawberry Hill sale in the spring.[117] But to do so, Mitford had to draw Turner into a position of collaboration: Mitford remained the editor, while Turner was allowed a subsidiary role – suggesting, for example, that the volume should be dedicated to Samuel Rogers (to whom Mitford had already dedicated previous work by Gray). Writing in August mostly in the first person plural, Mitford was anxious that Turner should feel well rewarded, and turned to his own negotiations:

> I mentioned to Pickering that I wishd he would print some copies for you especially, in a manner distinguishd from others: and if you would like 20 copies of Large Paper, or thick, or colord Paper, he has promisd me that no one else, neither himself nor myself, should have any impression. This should be exclusively yours; but if you wishd any impressions distinguishd from the rest in any different way from this, he will feel happy in meeting your Wishes, & whatever you choose, you may depend on no one else having.[118]

Turner took a dozen copies on tinted paper.[119]

In some fields as a collector Turner has strong claims to be a pioneer, and sometimes an innovator. His attention to ephemera has already been mentioned. To a modern eye, some of the most interesting features of Turner's collecting are not in the fine or the extra-illustrated copies, or in the emphasis on individuality. Rather, they are in what was once most common of all: the ephemera of everyday life, the newspapers and the advertisements that he collected so painstakingly.[120] Italian chap books, last dying speeches, railway prospectuses, shop bills and playbills all had their place in his interests and, as they were bound up into volumes, in his collecting. A series of lottery notices dating from between 1802 and 1826 was bound up in half-Russia:[121] his bindings were not necessarily cheap even for this kind of material. Another series of large albums contained hundreds of printed papers of all kinds relating to Great Yarmouth since 1732, each volume arranged in approximately chronological order.[122] Old newspapers from the 17th century onwards were all of interest. He kept not just British newspapers, London and provincial, but also examples from the United States, South America and Australia. The radical MP Joseph Hume, whose country home was at

East Somerton, north of Yarmouth,[123] helped with the latter. The complete set of William Cobbett's American newspaper, *Porcupine's Gazette*, had been gathered up with some difficulty by the British Ambassador to the United States. William Upcott supplied him with specimens of early English examples, and offered to send the first numbers of new London titles in the 1830s.[124] Newspaper cuttings could also be of interest. Some he pasted at appropriate places into his correspondence files. From Joseph Haslewood's library, sold in 1833, he obtained a collection on literary and book trade matters reaching from 1695 to 1832, and he possessed several other volumes of similar nature. From the London bookseller John Wilson he obtained two large albums of book trade notices.

His interest in catalogues – trade, private, exhibition – was shared with Dibdin, whose own auction sale in June 1817 revealed something of the reference library that had supported his voluminous and generally well-informed writings. Turner went further, and further also than Upcott, in assembling a supporting reference library. The collection of catalogues of libraries and from booksellers occupied lots 1,732 to 2,182, the whole of the seventh day, of the sale of his printed books in 1859. Much of the eighth and final day was taken up with catalogues of pictures, for sale, at exhibitions or in private or public collections. But simply in terms of bulk, the catalogues of books were more noticeable. Since many of the lots for these were of multiple titles, the total of auction catalogues alone was over 1,500. In some ways most remarkable was the accumulation of booksellers' catalogues, English and foreign, that Puttick & Simpson thought worth putting up for auction in 1859. Here there were fewer early catalogues: none before Robert Scott's landmark catalogue of 1674 and only a handful from the 18th century. But seventy or eighty booksellers who had dealt or sought to deal with Turner were represented – some, including Lackington, Longman, Nattali, Payne & Foss, and Thorpe, in long runs. One lot, of English and foreign booksellers' catalogues from almost two hundred firms and dating between 1772 and 1854, was bound into 145 volumes. This was quite apart from other lots containing series of catalogues from the major London booksellers. Turner also took care to have at hand details of new publications. Not many private owners retained, as he did, a set of the *Publishers' Circular*; and though he stored many prospectuses among his correspondence he also had bound up what eventually amounted to eight volumes of them issued between the late 18th century and 1850, besides a parcel containing the equivalent of two more. These he arranged not in chronological order, but by subject, supporting evidence elsewhere in his albums that there was a concentration on listing and sorting his collections in the early 1850s.[125] 'A volume of Prospectuses is very much a volume of intentions of what men have meant to do, not what they have fulfilled,' wrote

Turner in this collection. 'I have said enough, I hope, to satisfy the most fastidious, that such a collection, far from being a childish one, is not without considerable interest.'

By the 1850s there was already some market for old auction and booksellers' catalogues. As Puttick & Simpson noted in describing Turner's copies of these books, Dibdin's large paper copy of the auction catalogue of the library of James Edwards (1815), including the Bedford Missal, had sold for the high price of £2 3s., and his priced copy of the Ratcliffe catalogue (1776) had gone for £2 8s.[126] Private vanity had for at least a century[127] combined with commercial interest to encourage the issuing of a few copies of some auction catalogues on fine or large paper. Turner's collection of English auction catalogues began with the first printed one of all, the Lazarus Seaman sale of 1676, and he treated many of the catalogues as he did the rest of his books, inserting letters and notes either for reference or as enhancements. Into all three of his copies of the Upcott catalogue (1846) he inserted a copy of his memoir written for the *Gentleman's Magazine*, with a copy of his daughter's lithograph portrait of Upcott. For years, he employed Thomas Gregory, of the London Institution, to add details of prices realised to his auction catalogues.[128] Companions within the same covers of some of his volumes often revealed something of Turner's ways of thinking. However, it is not clear why a copy of the Dibdin catalogue (with a note that only 24 copies had been printed with the headline 'Bibliotheca Rosicrusiana') should have been bound up with the William Hayley sale (1821), that of Queen Charlotte's books and prints (1819), a collection of Napoleon medals (1819) and the autographs of John Thane (1819). The emphasis was firmly on English sales, though there were some unusual foreign ones, such as J.G. Graevius's interleaved and annotated copy of the Nicolaas Heinsius sale (Leiden, 1683). The two copies of the great sale organised by De Bure in 1819 of the books of Aubin-Louis Millin, *conservateur* in the Cabinet des Médailles in the Bibliothèque du Roi and friend, adviser and supplier to Turner, were relics of a principal link with the Paris trade.

Finally, and outside the trade, were the catalogues of private libraries, contemporary and earlier. The compiler of the 1859 sale catalogue of Turner's books did not lose the opportunity to flatter Sir Thomas Phillipps when he came to the copy of the Middle Hill catalogue. Like others, he could not forbear to remark on the absence of order in this most disorderly of productions; on the other hand, the library showed its possessor 'to be gifted with the spirit of a Bodley, a Cotton, or a Harley, and, in his pursuits, to be deserving, like those eminent men, of the respect and gratitude of his country'. A few readers at least may have reflected that each of these heroes was now fastened either by name or by collection to a national library: the eventual fate of Phillipps's collection was already, in 1859, a matter for public concern.

Even the sale catalogue of Dibdin's books in 1817, when he was obliged to sell the best of his personal reference library, did not list so many catalogues. But by the 1840s there were many more auction sales each year than there had been during the Napoleonic wars and previously. The release of private and institutional libraries onto the European market following the French Revolution had created an abundance in the British trade. This in turn was reflected in the modish circles of bibliomania so colourfully encouraged in the writing of Dibdin, and so misleadingly promoted in the trade by reminders of the high prices fetched by some books on particular occasions. It also had its effect in book collecting more generally. Not everyone could buy 'fifteeners' (that is, books printed before 1501), or medieval manuscripts; but many people could afford to accumulate libraries that would have at least a representative number of books from the fashionable presses of the past or recent past, such as Aldus, Bodoni or Didot, copies of well-known illustrated books, or a selection of standard history and literature. Turner retained the resulting auction catalogues, and thus by his death had created what was, in effect, an archive.

Dibdin's was at once a more select and a more profound collection. Though both possessed large collections of catalogues, Turner's interest was perhaps more often in them as catalogues than as bibliographical records. Where Dibdin had also collected the older literature concerning the history of printing, authorship and book collecting, Turner had very little of this nature. Turner's interests were in the present; Dibdin's were in the past. If such a summary generalisation is fair to neither, it does reflect the priorities of each man. And, whatever their differences in attitude or in emphasis, they were friends whose frequent correspondence speaks of mutual respect and sympathy.

Turner's name is not among the buyers at the Dibdin sale in June 1817, and hardly any correspondence survives in his papers at Trinity College for the second half of that month. Although at this time his principal interests were still in botany, he was fast developing into a serious book collector. 'You are bibliomaniacal gallantry itself,' wrote Dibdin in November, in response to an invitation to Great Yarmouth, adding that he found Turner's 'anti-bibliopegistic' reasoning unanswerable.[129] In due course, Turner acquired not just special copies of Dibdin's publications, but also the files of correspondence and other papers related to them.[130]

As a banker, he had a professional interest in forgery and in banknotes. Here, however, were not just the works of W.H. Ireland, whose notoriety as a Shakespeare forger gained him a valued place in many libraries: Turner possessed one of the rare collections of engraved facsimiles of the supposed documents, published in 1795 and of which only two similar copies were said to exist, in the libraries of the Duke of Marlborough and of John Dent.[131] The case of the engraver W.W. Ryland was a very different affair, in that his conviction and hanging for issuing forged bills were based on poor evidence.[132] Turner also kept collections of banknotes printed by the new process of siderography, a method of making multiple steel engravings invented by Jacob Perkins and most familiar in the background of the penny black stamp.[133] A few other experiments in combating counterfeits were preserved among his correspondence. As an inveterate publisher of books and pamphlets relating to his collections, he learned the need for at least a smattering of printers' vocabulary. The *Specimens of Types* in Moyes's printing office in London (1831), addressed to 'professional gentlemen requiring works splendidly executed', conveniently encapsulated the principal typefaces and names of founders likely to be met in ordinary work; but this slim book was not enough.[134] He had not just the standard modern works on printing by Caleb Stower and by William Savage (he subscribed to Savage's *Practical Hints on Decorative Printing*), but also half a shelf of type specimens from the foundries of Caslon, Fry, Figgins and Wilson. By 1838-9, when he was contemplating the printing of a catalogue of his manuscripts, he did not go automatically to his customary printer, Charles Sloman in Yarmouth, but instead sought quotations from three firms including Josiah Fletcher in Norwich, who sent him a specimen of the type proposed.[135]

Although he possessed several early printed books, Turner could not be accounted a serious collector of them. He had little interest in the black-letter books idolised by Dibdin and a generation of collectors who supported their high prices in the salerooms. Apart from a handful of printed books of hours, he possessed a German *Speculum Humanae Salvationis* printed at Basel in 1476 (a late acquisition, bought from Joseph Lilly in 1847[136]), an Ovid *Metamorphoses* printed at Venice and a few others. He possessed his copy of the Nuremberg Chronicle by 1803, when he had it rebound by Downes in Yarmouth.[137] His copy of Brandt's *Stultifera Navis* (Lyon, '1488', i.e. 1498) came from Payne & Foss in 1813, when he was still to some degree experimenting in his buying, and is now at Harvard.[138] His solitary Caxton, an imperfect copy of the *Doctrynal of Sapyence* (1489) bought from Joseph Lilly for 10 guineas in 1837,[139] though with a highly respectable provenance, was likewise isolated in a collection where the emphasis was so much on manuscripts and ideals of bibliophily other than any insisting on incunabula. When in 1844 Lilly sought to tempt him with a copy of a considerably rarer Caxton, the *Book of Divers Ghostly Matters*, Turner took it on approval, but then returned it even though the price was reduced from 10 guineas to nine. Lilly had done his best with a book that he described openly as 'generally imperfect' but also one of only three copies known to him.[140] Of only slighter later date, Henry VIII's *Assertio Septem Sacramentorum* was from the library of Richard Farmer, with his characteristic bibliographical notes. Coverdale's *Certain Most Godly, Fruitful and Comfortable Letters*, a collection of letters partly written by the English martyrs and printed by John Day in 1564, was also a rarity of its kind in the library, as was the copy of the *Portiforium*, or breviary, printed for the English market during the short Roman Catholic interlude in the mid-16th century.[141] In general, Turner had few very early printed books, and few of a theological (as distinct from antiquarian or ecclesiological) nature.

The copy of Cicero's *De Officiis* (Lyon, 1502) that had belonged to Henry VIII as a boy was of much greater interest to him on account of the note inside ('Thys Boke Is Myne Prynce Henry') than on account just of its age.[142] The same principle was true of the copy of the printed *Livre des Statuts et Ordonnances de l'Ordre et Milice du Benoist Sainct Esprit* (Paris, 1578) in which Henri III had written prayers and other religious notes.

Turner watched, listened, advised and sympathised as some of his most frequent correspondents considered the future of their libraries. In 1819 he had cleared some of his own shelves with an auction through Simon Wilkin in Norwich.[143] Like many collectors, he considered sales during his lifetime as space in his house ran out. Of his friends, Upcott, Roscoe, Sotheby and Dibdin were among several others who were obliged to dispose of all or part of their collections through financial need. For almost all his life, Turner managed to avoid such necessity. His need was domestic, and he contemplated a sale for some years, seeking advice from trusted members of the trade. Among them in 1839 was the Quaker John Arch, who had proved a staunch ally in publishing Turner's books many years before. In a letter not least interesting for the insights it offers on the London book trade, Arch now wrote with his usual idiosyncrasies of spelling and punctuation:

> Dear friend,
> I duly rec'd thy favour dated June 29 relative to the most desirable mode of disposing of thy library or a considerable portion of it. Before I proceed to the consideration of that subject I must say that I am gratified by the assurance that I possess so much of thy good opinion & regard, after our acquaintance extended through so large a portion of our lives
>
> I am aware that thy collection of Books is a large one, containing among other literature the principal Works published in England during the last 30 to 40 years, many of them upon largest paper with additional Illustrations &c, and must have cost a large sum of money. It is needless for me to say how much works of this description are depreciated when brought into the market without especial recommendation. The celebrity & taste of the proprietor of this Collection, will doubtless insure prices much above those obtained usually of late, if brought before the public in a favourable manner, but how this is to be done is the difficulty, as thou

hast justly observed, & it is not a small sum, for if brought to public sale, it is not recommendable to make much reserve, as it would be perceived & proclaimed by the Booksellers, & operate injuriously. In the disposal of our Stock, I sold considerable quantities at Evans's Hodgsons & Southgate but being advised by some Booksellers & some of our Friends to make a sale of the remainder of our Books, & near the City, I put them into the hands of Southgate, who is a respectable active & punctual man, & pretty well acquainted with modern Books. He took a good deal of pains, but made an indifferent catalogue of 6. days. He had what he considered a good Copy & a good Sale, in which some things sold pretty well, some moderately & the larger portion at low prices, from which when Duty & commission (15pc) were deducted, I considered it to be an impoverishing operation – Besides the Auctioneers I have mentioned, there are Christie & Manson & Sotheby – the former are respectable but I do not think them to have a great acquaintance with Books in the Booksellers sense the latter has not recovered the station which the House once had — Evans is in my opinion the best qualified by knowledge & experience but of late times has not had much occupation, I fear from want of confidence in his punctuality, could he find security, I should prefer him.

There are some Booksellers, who would buy large Lots of Books but in thy case, I think that a public Sale is the preferable as by that means the proprietor may reap the advantage of his own Character & of competition, more completely.

For the sale of such property, it appears to me that the months of April & May are the best time, when Gentlemen from all parts of the Kingdom & Foreigners are in town. The Trade will of course be found where their Game abounds – perhaps it might be most advantageous to have 2 Sales (not very distant from each other) which I am not able to judge, as it would in measure depend upon the Booksellers having large stocks of similar Books upon hand or not – I have not for the year past paid much attention to sales – Since the decease of my Brother in April, the care of his affairs, with daily attention to some Business in which I am interested at Smith Elder & Co of 65 Cornhill (where some of our Customers have by my solicitation removed their accounts, upon which we receive a commission). For part of the Bargain I am accommodated with a Desk &c at their House, free of charge & where I attend most days from 10 to 1/2 past 2/, with the winding up of a Business of 45 years, tho' all in a small way, have occupied me completely. Much of what I have above communicated is I believe pretty well known to those having considerable intercourse with Booksellers. I believe that Payne & Foss could give a good opinion upon most of the points involved in the subject, & are very honourable people –- so could H.G.Bohn, James Bohn & some others, but I do not think that their standing is equal – the acting upon safe ground, if attainable in these times, tho' it may be more expensive, is most satisfactory with process, & I believe pays best in the end. I should apologise for giving these opinions to one, whose experience in general is much greater than my own.

I should have accpted thy obliging invitation to pay thee a visiting conference at Yarmouth on this occasion, which would also have been a visit of much pleasure to myself were I not so circumstanced personally, that I cannot travel without inconvenience especially long Journeys; in consequence of which I have gone to a distance, only among my relations, of late years, & for this reason I am not able to comply with thy proposal, for which I feel most obliged, & consider it to be a proof of thy friendship.[144]

For years, Turner was more than a customer at the main London auction houses, and he often found himself in the position of confidant. With both Samuel Sotheby, who died in 1842, and his son Samuel Leigh he enjoyed a correspondence that went far beyond ordinary business, as the Sothebys pursued their studies of early printing and in the wake of the Kloss sale of 1835 Samuel Leigh became fascinated by the books supposed to have belonged to Melanchthon. After the elder Sotheby's bankruptcy in autumn 1836, Turner lent money to enable work on the history of printing.[145] The question of sale seemed to come finally to a head in spring 1841, when Leigh Sotheby sent a printed list of the season's forthcoming sales, and proposed to Turner the exact wording for an addendum stating that he had 'received instructions to announce for sale by auction in May The Principal Portion of the Magnificent & well known Library of Dawson Turner.' This was too much, and brought Turner back with a bump. He kept Sotheby's draft advertisement in his customary correspondence files, but added a note of his own to the word 'principal': 'No – thank God.'[146]

As his library's archival value increased, questions as to the future became of greater importance. By the end of the 1840s there was a new seriousness in the question. John Britton, querulous and always insecure, but endlessly learned as an antiquary, suggested that a public fund should be raised to buy the collections, and give them to the city of Norwich.[147] The Liverpool collector Joseph Mayer, beside whose omnivorousness Turner seemed almost unambitious, hoped that at least the autographs would go to the British Museum.[148] Mayer's letter was followed a month later by one from the London bookseller Charles F. Molini: his Italian trade was falling off, but he was still able to write of an impending sale of Turner's collections.[149] Turner well knew the importance of promoting any sale well before it happened, so as to arouse widespread and strong interest, and gossip could do its work. In 1851, Turner consulted with Puttick & Simpson on their charges in sales of manuscripts.

In the end, it was a combination of two crises, one financial and one family, that precipitated a sale not of the manuscripts, but of the printed books. His wife Mary died on 17 March 1851, aged seventy-six. Increasingly lame, Turner was left in a house no longer vibrant with a large family. The letters from antiquaries, booksellers, picture dealers and friends continued to arrive, but the mechanisms, the busy help that had enabled him to enjoy such correspondence, no longer existed. In autumn 1851 he arranged for more of his albums to be bound up, as usual, by the local binder Joseph Diboll. When Diboll submitted his account at the beginning of November, it also included a charge of £7 15s. 9d. for two weeks' work, the second half of October, in packing and removing the library.[150] Arrangements were made by Turner's lawyer to insure the pictures and plate still at Bank House (for a total of £2,400) and the books sent to the local bookseller Charles Sloman (for £6,000).[151]

Perhaps the changes in Yarmouth, as the fishing town in which he had grown up was turned into a holiday resort for city-dwellers, added further to Turner's melancholy. His financial affairs were in disorder. He had always been generous with his time and money; and he had also borrowed. The loan of £4,200 from his son-in-law Sir William Jackson Hooker had been paid off,[152] but his principal assets were in his collections: of books, manuscripts, prints and paintings.

In most accounts of collectors, stress is naturally laid on accumulation: on the mixture of personal interests, enthusiasms, financial resources, opportunities, market trends and social circles that contribute to the mass formed within contexts of place and time. The post-mortem dispersal of collections accordingly occupies another chapter, with different concerns and priorities. Turner falls into the smaller category of those who choose or need to relinquish important parts of their possessions near the end of their own lifetime. He did so partly out of necessity and partly as a result of his deliberate withdrawal from the social life that he had known. The orderly files of his bound correspondence now in Trinity College cease in 1851.

The idea of a sale had nothing to recommend itself to those who cared for him most deeply. One of his oldest friends, Hudson Gurney,[153] pointed out the need for the companionship of collections as one aged:

> I have heard it reported that you have some intention of selling your books and collections – which I hope much you will not do – We are now both of us come to such an age, that communication with the world must of necessity be very much foreshortened.

Gurney wrote from experience, after a prolonged period of illness when he had had to rely on his own considerable library at Keswick Hall, just outside Norwich, to keep his mind from stagnation and depression. But he was also alert to Turner's own habits of thought, and he was prepared to be frank:

> I am well aware of the truth of what you have always said, that loose reading was the idlest of occupations, & that your habits have been of constant occupation & activity – But under the diminished power of age this must cease – & the being in possession of objects to fall back upon is a mercy hardly to be overestimated.[154]

The whole of Turner's career, the whole of his family and household arrangements, had been driven not merely by bibliomania, the disease of which Dibdin was so skilled a delineator. Though he mingled with people whose collecting of books, of autographs or of medieval manuscripts consumed much of their energy, and though he pursued his collecting with a very similar constant excitement, Turner was not to be counted among them in the same way. Gurney, only a few months older than Turner, had known him throughout his adult life, as fellow-banker, as fellow-antiquary, and as confidant and friend. No-one was in a better position to dissect Turner's motivations, or to understand the import of what he said, while Gurney's own self-confessed inclination to indolence made him all the more aware of the contrast with his friend. And Gurney was clear: that there was in Turner's collecting not just a sense of moral responsibility but a sense of moral duty, what others might term a gospel of work. Idleness was not merely boring; it was corrupting. With that in mind, it is easier to understand the household in Great Yarmouth, with its constant activities of sorting and copying, of writing and drawing, which so struck visitors such as Haydon.

Turner's second marriage caused consternation amongst his family, his friends and the partners in the bank. It was hurried, it took place in Scotland rather than in England, and it was socially well beneath him. The collections that had brought him status and given him entry into houses and families on terms far above any that might have been accorded a straightforward country banker, were of no personal value in such circumstances. Turner was spurned by his married daughters and for the most part by their husbands. Sir Francis Palgrave, married to his daughter Elizabeth, brought opprobrium on himself as he tried to reconcile the various parties: for a time after Turner's removal to London with his new wife he was the only visitor. Elizabeth died in 1852, thus leaving Palgrave an independence in the matter not available to his brothers-in-law. Eventually, in March 1853 Turner moved to the suburbs, and settled in Castelnau, between Barnes and Hammersmith Bridge in south-west London, in an estate recently developed by a member of the Boileau family: the family was based in Norfolk, and this may have been an attraction.[155] To Turner's son-in-law, viewing matters from distant Hampstead, it was an area where 'you get an indescribable conviction, that the reality is well adapted for couples who would rather not care to have much enquiry made about their marriage certificates'.[156] Turner had demeaned himself further.

Unable to introduce his new wife in society, he had deliberately cut himself off, not even visiting his old West End haunts in the Athenaeum, the Royal Society, the Linnean Society or the Society of Antiquaries. Palgrave was blunt, as usual: in his view Turner was managed by his footman ('a sharp fellow') and by 'a lecherous old toad, who was a species of housekeeper to my late mother in law – and his wife'.[157] Matters were made no easier by the fact that Turner's new step-son was considered a ne'er do well, and in Palgrave's mind there was even some doubt concerning the apparent attacks of insanity that his new wife suffered in June 1852. But whatever the difficulties in London, Palgrave could not approve of the actions of the bank, back in Yarmouth, where Turner was still a partner.[158] Justifiably apprehensive of how he would be treated, and aware by March 1852 that the partners wished to eject him by the end of the year, Turner still refused to go and face them himself.[159] The bad temper and resentment that fuelled his wish for retirement was not in his interests financially. Furthermore, although so far he had kept up payments on the post-obituary covenants and marriage settlements he had made for his children, there hung over him a debt of £43,000 from these quarters alone.[160]

35 *Dawson William Turner, aged 19, reading in the Library at the Bank House. Pencil Sketch. (Private collection.)*

In London, Turner began to plan the sale of his library and other collections. First to go were some of the paintings, sold in 1852 for £2,000, where Turner had valued them at £3,000.[161] Palgrave urged him not to part with his books or prints, believing that he would not receive anything near their true worth and, like Gurney, knowing that he would be deprived of one of the few pleasures left to him. But Turner was adamant. Sotheby's planned sale for the summer had to be postponed, as the general election in July distracted the attentions of possible customers. Then it was postponed again as Parliament lurched through a series of government crises. Lord Derby resigned and Lord Aberdeen became Prime Minister in a coalition government in December. Meanwhile, Turner was worrying about his extra-illustrated Blomefield, whether to include it in the auction or to give it to the British Museum. Ever anxious to preserve matters from too much haste, Palgrave was against both courses. In the museum it would be 'of no use or interest – where no body will come for it': as Deputy Keeper of Public Records he clearly had a low opinion of his colleagues in Bloomsbury. Suggestions that it should pass either to Turner's son and namesake, or be given to Norwich Public Library, were equally unwelcome.[162]

The catalogue of his books eventually offered at auction by Sotheby & Wilkinson in March 1853 portrays only part of Turner's library. Much of it was left stored in boxes in Yarmouth. He could not resist arranging for a few copies of the catalogue to be printed on large paper.[163] The title page called it the 'principal part', invitation enough to those interested: the sale occupied 7 March and the following five days, and then 17 March and the six following days, a total of 3,238 lots, many of them made up of multiple items, spread over 13 days in all. 'I believe I never saw a collection of equal extent with so small a quantity of trash,' wrote Sir Francis Palgrave to Gurney.[164] For Sotheby, the sale fell in a season that had included A.W.N. Pugin's books at the end of January. It was midway between a sale of autograph letters from the Congregationalist historian Sir John Bickerton Williams (d.1855) on 5 March and an anonymous sale including Nelson correspondence at the end of the month. But the market was flat, and even so well-known a name, and so large a sale, could not guarantee success.

Palgrave's cautious assessment, that Turner would recoup £3,000 for the £10,000 he estimated the collection had cost, proved to be all too realistic.[165] Many of the lots were bought in and, after his death on 20 June 1858, there were further auctions at which the same books reappeared. Turner's sole Caxton, a copy of the *Doctrinal of Sapience,* with a distinguished provenance including William Herbert, Richard Farmer, John Towneley and the Duke of Devonshire (who had removed two leaves in order to perfect his other copy), failed to sell in 1853: perhaps the fact that this same copy had fetched £83 in the Towneley sale led Sotheby to placing too high a reserve.[166] Six years later, when it was put up again, it fetched a mere £22. His copy of the Nuremberg Chronicle (1493), 'of unusually large dimensions', also left unsold, was to fetch only £8 5s. six years later. Other lots that failed to attract sufficient interest in 1853 included a Grangerised Clarendon, and a Grangerised Lodge *Portraits of Illustrious Personages of Great Britain* on large paper (1779), bought in in 1853 and sold in 1859 for £42.[167] The copy of Bassandyne and Arbuthnot's Bible of 1576-9 (the first to be printed in Scotland), better described as to its defects six years later, sold finally for £75. Henry VIII's copy of Cicero sold in 1859, having been bought in earlier. Even some specially prepared bibliophile copies were left unsold in 1853, including James Christie's *Disquisition on Etruscan Vases,* with an unpublished manuscript by Christie on the Circensian games, and the copy of Dibdin's *Bibliomania* (1811) with a fore-edge view of Strawberry Hill. The copy on vellum of Cotman's *Architectural Antiquities of Normandy* sold only in 1859, for £13 10s. – less than a special copy on large paper with several additional plates.[168] To be left at the end of the 1853 sale with almost 200 volumes of the *Gentleman's Magazine* from the beginning and with 28 volumes of Sowerby's *English Botany* was a misfortune if space was at a premium. Turner had bought the former, previously the property of Joseph Goodall, Provost of Eton, from Thorpe in 1840, for just £31 3s., and it was to reach only £26 10s. when it was re-offered in 1859.[169] In the case of the latter, his custom of inserting extra plates and correspondence was in the end justified here too: the Sowerby, with plates by Mrs Turner, fetched a respectable £32 in 1859. Quaritch offered books from the library in 1853, including a group of French works concerning Normandy, and a printed Book of Hours (Paris, 1508) for a modest £3 18s.[170]

* * *

In October 1853 Turner suffered a stroke, and he never fully recovered. He died at Brompton, aged eighty-three. The family retained some of his books and pictures, as well as most of the personal correspondence that had formed so important a part of his life. Most of the rest of his collection was allowed to go to auction. The sales of April and May 1859 were both organised by Puttick & Simpson. First came the printed books, described as the 'remaining portion' of the library and occupying eight days. They realised £2,380 5s. 6d., a fraction of what Turner had paid over the years. But if the 1859 post-mortem sale of printed books was on the whole more successful than the removal sale of six years earlier, there were still many disappointments. The six volumes of the Daniells' elephant folio *Views of Oriental Scenery* (1798-1800), of which the subscription price had been £180, sold for just £21 10s. despite a puff in the catalogue. Prices were poor, though that did not prevent booksellers like Lilly subsequently seeking much higher ones in the ordinary trade. A few books were given away before the sale, but members of the family also either bought at the sale or withdrew about forty lots. In this way Hooker regained his own drawings for the *Fuci* and his drawings of Iceland; Sir Francis Palgrave regained a group of his late wife's drawings including her portrait of Crome; and his son Francis Turner Palgrave obtained the series of soft-ground etchings made by Cotman in 1814-17 and believed to be unique. William Jacobson, a son-in-law, regained the unique copy on large paper of his *Patres Apostolici* (Oxford, 1838); Dawson W. Turner regained the unique series in five volumes of 667 etchings and sketches made in the house at Yarmouth between 1812 and 1824; and Mary Turner rescued the portfolio of topographical drawings including the early work of her mother. Money mattered, but sentiment mattered more.

Much more important, and dominating the manuscript sales of the season, the manuscripts were sold in a five-day sale beginning on 6 June. A yet further, minor, sale followed of autographs, on 3 April 1860.[171]

36 *Children at work in the Bank House 1822, Ellen aged 11, Dawson William aged 6, and Gurney aged 9. Sketch by Elizabeth Turner. (Private collection.)*

The sale of June 1859 brought to an end any thoughts of Turner's manuscripts passing *en bloc* into the British Museum. Copies of the catalogue were printed both on ordinary paper (at 2s. 6d.) and on better paper, with plates, at 7s. 6d. Private collectors were active, including John Forster, whose purchases eventually passed to the Victoria & Albert Museum, and the Duc d'Aumale, whose anxiety to obtain the best of the French manuscripts and autographs was a matter of some concern to Frederic Madden in the British Museum.[172] Besides those for the museum, the London bookseller William Boone also held commissions for the Duc d'Aumale and for the Duke of Newcastle, so there was some pre-sale negotiation. The Bodleian Library and Cambridge University Library bid through Stewart, their customary London agent. The obvious absentee was Sir Thomas Phillipps, who restricted himself to placing a modest (and, as it proved, unsuccessful) bid on the Glastonbury cartulary. He had been far more active at the sale of Libri's manuscripts in March, where he had spent heavily.[173] His inactivity at the Turner sale meant that prices remained mostly moderate. No-one was more anxious than Madden, who compiled a long shopping list and bid through Boone. He was generally successful, managing to carry off for the British Museum most of the important series of correspondence, besides the Lauderdale papers supplied to Turner by Fitch:[174] Madden took a generally historical perspective, and the long series of letters and papers concerning Richard Heber, whose affairs had been so much the concern of Dibdin, were allowed to go elsewhere.[175] He had also wanted the French early 15th-century Bible epitome and Apocalypse, with over a hundred large miniatures (lot 42),[176] but was forced to stand aside and let the Duc d'Aumale buy it through Boone for £48 6s., so as to avoid competition from Boone for d'Aumale over lot 221, Guillaume de Guilleville's illuminated *Pelérinage de la Vie Humaine*: this was bought for the museum for £52.[177] The Glastonbury cartulary, about which Phillipps had importuned Turner for so many years, was secured for the museum.[178] The museum's failure to buy the manuscript of Defoe's *Compleat English Gentleman*, a rare appearance of a Defoe autograph in the market, was a rebuff: Madden authorised bidding up to £55, but it went to Bumstead, on commission for the Manchester collector James Crossley, and the museum finally acquired it at Crossley's sale in 1885.[179] The supposed Milton autograph of his contract with Samuel Simmons for payment of £5 for the copyright of *Paradise Lost* was easily dismissed, Madden remarking that Milton was by 1669 quite blind.[180]

There were other minor irritants. Madden was determined to buy the correspondence of the 17th-century Orientalist and historian of the Greek church John Covel, but he found himself bidding against Stewart, the Cambridge library's agent, and so the price was higher than he wished. 'I think,' he drily noted in his diary, 'the Cambridge people have acted ill in not stopping the bidding of their agent after I had given up to them the other MSS. they wanted.' He was referring partly to the letters from John Strype, bought for the university library for a modest £25, but perhaps also to the letters from Isaac Newton that Turner had removed from the Covel correspondence and published privately in 1848; they were bought for Trinity College Library for £93 9s., a quite exceptional figure for the college to find for its library at that time. On the other hand, the price for the George Vertue manuscripts, a key to the 18th-century art world, was an unexpected bonus, the museum paying just £45 where Madden had been prepared to go to £150. Turner had bought them only 11 years previously from Thomas Thorpe, who had paid too much at the Strawberry Hill sale and allowed Turner to buy them for £100 – that is, £30 less than he had paid.[181] Madden's greatest headache was over the extra-illustrated Blomefield, which was to be offered almost at the end of the sale. Many people wanted to see it in the museum, but Madden's budget was not inexhaustible, and the need to conserve his energies meant that he had to place his bids carefully in the last two days of the auction. The price realised, £460, vindicated Madden's care and it came to the museum.[182] In all, the museum acquired about 18 per cent of the lots. Turner had already parted with most of his Books of Hours and other liturgical manuscripts at the auction in 1853, when they had been offered among a group of similar printed books. The better medieval manuscripts were kept back. The sale of 1859 provided the *Roman de la Rose* bought at Paris in 1814, which now went to Lilly for £17 10s., and appeared in a Quaritch catalogue in 1874. Sir Henry Spelman's 15th-century manuscript of Roger Bacon, catalogued as being of the 13th century, went to Chetham's Library in Manchester for 10 shillings.[183] The 15th-century missal, illustrated with 18 full-page miniatures and acquired by Turner from the library of William Barnes of Redland Hall in Surrey thirty-odd years earlier, went to Lilly for £23: Lilly gave it pride of place at the conclusion of his *Bibliotheca Elegantissima et Selecta* in 1860, pricing it at £52 10s. The Amiens *Horae* was bought by John Forster.[184] Turner's small collection of Persian manuscripts was shared between Thorpe and Quaritch.

As a book collector, Turner was both independent in his taste and yet deeply conservative. His career coincided with a generation imbued with bibliomania, which saw the Roxburghe sale of 1812 as the beginning of a new age of collecting and frequently of high prices. Peace with France not only made trade again possible. Thanks to the secularisation of monasteries, and the confiscation or dispersal of many foreign private libraries, there was also released into the British market an unprecedented wealth of foreign books ancient and modern, manuscript and printed. But Turner was no Phillipps, and no Heber. The 13 main sales, in London alone, of Richard Heber's books in 1834-7 proved too much for the market to absorb, and prices for some kinds of books slumped.[185] By the end of Turner's life, many of the books printed for the bibliophile market in the 18th and early 19th centuries were worth a fraction of their initial value. Time and again, autograph collectors found themselves bitterly disappointed when they tried to sell their collections. For the book trade, the 1830s and 1840s were at once times of plenty and times of very great difficulty. The dominant second-hand bookseller in London, Thomas Thorpe, was rescued with the help of a loan from Turner that had still not been repaid in 1848.[186] Samuel Sotheby (by this time, admittedly, retired from the family business) was bankrupt in 1836. Robert Harding Evans, who had conducted the Roxburghe auction in 1812, was bankrupt in 1846. Prices were depressed by mid-century. When in 1853 Turner parted with much of his library at auction, he was told that it sold well. Even so, he thought he had recouped only about a quarter of the books' cost.[187]

Turner's own published works had enjoyed mixed success. In 1838, the stock of J. & A. Arch, publishers of his *Fuci*, was auctioned by J.W. Southgate; and in 1841 hand-coloured copies of the work were still available, at a remainder price of 16 guineas rather than £36: the reduced price was said to be less than the cost of the colouring alone.[188] The residue of his privately published books and pamphlets, some in many copies, were sold in the auction of 1859, the family letting go of some copies bearing Turner's own notes as well as copies containing drawings by his daughters.[189]

His library was formed and dispersed within a generation. In some ways, thanks to the auctions in 1853 and 1859, it achieved an even wider influence after his death than it did during his lifetime, generous though he was in lending his books and in allowing people to consult them at Yarmouth. When, following the manuscripts sale of 1859, the London bookseller John Waller issued a catalogue containing much of Turner's autograph collection, and offered most of it not as groups but as single letters, he naturally lauded the collection which

> rivetted the attention and admiration of all true lovers of literature for many years. It was a sort of magnet, or Mecca, that drew crowds of loving literary pilgrims, from all parts of the world, to gaze and feast over its rich and attractive material. Its sale and dispersion, is regarded throughout Norfolk, but more especially at Yarmouth, as a national calamity.[190]

It was not much of an exaggeration. If, especially with his printed books, there was a lack of originality in the way that Turner emulated several of Dibdin's symptoms of bibliomania, in his taste for large paper copies, for illustrated copies, for unique copies and for copies printed on coloured paper or on vellum, he was nonetheless influential in his own right in other ways besides. In 1846 John Westwood, entomologist and author of the widely read *Palaeographia Sacra Pictoria* (1843-5), wrote to thank Turner for a complimentary letter and for two etchings. It was, explained Westwood, thanks to Turner's *Account of a Tour in Normandy* and to Dibdin's *Bibliographical Decameron* that he had taken up a career in what he called a branch of archaeology. 'I happened to meet with these works just after I left school, at a time when the mind receives its principal impulses in the way of science, and the great initial P, which figures in the title page of my Book was then ... copied from your Tour.' Though he had heard of the library at Holkham through the work of Gustav Waagen, it was thanks also to Turner that Westwood now learned of those at Blickling and Narford.[191]

Others who expressed their gratitude were less in the public eye. In 1842, G.J. Stevenson, recently arrived in Yarmouth as the manager of the printing office only a few yards from Turner's front door on Short Quay, finally summoned up courage to write. He had

> heard so often of the Bibliographic fame with which your name is always associated both in the book:world and in my own mind, I cannot longer forbear thus venturing to introduce myself to you – not as a veteran either in Bibliography, or in the more interesting field of Typography, – but as one possessed of the genuine *Bibliomania*, which I cannot satisfy from limited means, but should these means be extended — would only increase my desire.[192]

Not surprisingly, Dibdin was Stevenson's favourite author, while the historical link between the earliest printing and the 'present exquisite perfection' of what now came from the press only served to increase his enthusiasm. 'Book-madness is the height of my ambition,' he concluded. The by-ways of Dibdin's influence have yet to be properly explored. In 1876 the new firm of Chatto & Windus thought it worthwhile to publish a fresh edition of *Bibliomania* at a price of 17s. 6d., or £2 12s. 6d. on large paper, taking advantage of the fact that they had just acquired the stock, and blocks for printing, of Henry G. Bohn, publisher of the previous and more ambitious edition of 1842. The edition was a last link with the past, but the ideas that linked book collecting, printing and visual pleasure were firmly fixed in the minds of a much broader range of people, by no means all even reasonably well off. The so-called Roxburghe style of binding, quarter dark green roan, in which the 1876 edition of Dibdin's book was issued, was one that had passed from the hands of an élite book club and onto the shelves of the middle classes: dozens of ordinary trade books of an antiquarian turn were published in this style. By 1876, Turner had been dead almost twenty years. He had never been familiar with members of the Roxburghe Club apart from Dibdin himself. He had lived through a revolution not just in book-collecting taste, reflected partly in the fall in prices for some of the very kinds of books that he most valued. He had also lived to see a world in which bibliophily became an affordable pastime to innumerable members of the middle classes.[193]

David McKitterick

CHAPTER FIVE

The Banker

Introduction

Our information on Dawson Turner as a banker depends largely on the surviving records of the Yarmouth and Suffolk Bank. Our main records specifically relating to Yarmouth are the first customer ledger, the first private ledger, two partnership agreements, bills of exchange and banknotes, and a settlement book. There are very few glimpses of Dawson himself outside the figures in the ledgers.

Most of the information that has survived is from the records of Gurney and Company. This group, which included the Yarmouth and Suffolk Bank, was at the heart of a series of interlocking partnerships in East Anglia and became one of the founding banks in the formation of Barclay and Company in 1896.

The Parent Bank

John and Henry Gurney founded the Norwich Bank in 1775. The family fortune was based on the woollen and worsted trade.

By the 19th century, the Gurneys were one of the leading Quaker families in England. Their accumulated wealth, which stayed in the business, inspired confidence and increased the numbers of their customers.

The reason for forming interlocking partnerships rather than a head office with a network of branches, as we have today, lay in the laws governing banking. Limited companies could not be formed until 1826. Without the possibility of setting up a company with limited liability it was safer to set up interlocking partnerships. Each partner was liable for all the debts. One of the things potential customers had to think about was the reliability of the partners in the banks in their locality. Gurneys had an advantage in that they were Quakers, and it was known that Quakers would be 'disowned' if they became bankrupt. In addition, members of the Society of Friends had a reputation as reputable citizens whose word could be trusted. They also had extensive networks of fellow Quakers with whom they did business. This network was held together by marriage connections; for example Hudson Gurney, a partner in the Yarmouth Bank, was the son of Richard Gurney, the chief partner in the Norwich Bank, and of Agatha Barclay, daughter and heir of David Barclay, the prominent London merchant who entertained royalty at his Cheapside house in 1761.

The Yarmouth Bank was one of a group of banks known collectively as Gurney and Company. Following the establishment of Norwich Bank an associated bank was founded at Yarmouth in 1781 with its associated bank at Halesworth in 1782. Another venture was established at Lynn and its associated bank at Wisbech in 1782, followed a few years later at Fakenham in 1792. Gurneys also took over the Ipswich Bank (founded 1744) in 1878; and the Colchester Bank (founded 1774) in 1891.

The Group of Banks became so powerful that they were thus described in 1838:

> The money power of the Gurneys sprang out of transactions connected with manufactures. This family, seated at Norwich formerly, before spinning jennies were invented, carried on an extensive trade in buying the worsted, and we believe also the linen, yarns which were for ages made in the eastern counties of England, Norfolk, Suffolk, Essex, and Cambridgeshire, by the hand – it was the employment of the villages, cottages, as well as the towns of that district. These yarns were collected by the Gurneys, as well as by other local merchants, and sent by them for sale to Dublin and other parts of Ireland, where they were made into poplins, lastings, shalloons, and other stuff-fabrics, the manufacture of which was in the middle of the last century in great measure confined to that country. The power of machinery and the concentration of the means of ready sale and transport of goods, have in great measure annihilated this trade, and transferred it to Bradford, Leeds, Halifax and Manchester. The collecting of yarns from the numerous scattered manufacturers of the east of England, and holding them in stock to supply those who were employed in weaving them into their various textures in Ireland, was a very lucrative business, and we deliberately question whether the Gurneys did not at one time derive from it an annual income greater than is obtained by any Bank on the Island of Great Britain, including those of London, excepting not more than fifty or sixty out of the whole (about) thousand. In the course of dealing with the worsted-spinners for their yarns this family began to supply them with cash to pay the wages of labour and enable them to carry on their operations in business. Out of these circumstances arose the great Banking operations of this family, who in London and the country may now be described as exercising an influence and a power inferior to that of no banking establishment in Great Britain – that of the Bank of England alone excepted.

Description of the "Money Power of the Gurneys"
in *The Circular to Bankers*, October 1838

The Yarmouth Bank

Dawson Turner became a partner in the Yarmouth and Suffolk Bank in 1794 on the death of his father James Turner. The bank was founded in 1781 when James Turner went into partnership with Richard Gurney, Bartlett Gurney and Joseph Gurney. The relationship with the Gurney Bank goes back further than that. James Turner's account appears in the first ledger for the Norwich Bank in 1775-1776.[1]

The next ledger[2] continues the account with James Turner having a balance of £3,156 1s. 11d. in 1777 and £10,444 8s. 8d. in 1778.[3] James Dawson also had an account with the Norwich Bank. Dawson and company used Barclays as their London banker. Their company had a balance of £1,526 in 1774 and £3,317 in 1775. Clearly a relationship had been established between Dawson and Turner, the Gurneys and Barclays but no direct evidence survives to tell us why James Turner was asked to be the active partner in the first subsidiary bank the Gurneys opened in Yarmouth in 1781, other than his role as a prominent local merchant.

For the partnerships outside Norwich the Gurneys seemed to have looked for prominent local merchants. James Turner was an iron merchant in Yarmouth in partnership with his uncle, James Dawson. They imported iron from Sweden and sold it on to smaller tradesmen. To carry on the trade they needed access to funds. The normal method of finance in the 18th century was the use of bills of exchange. The

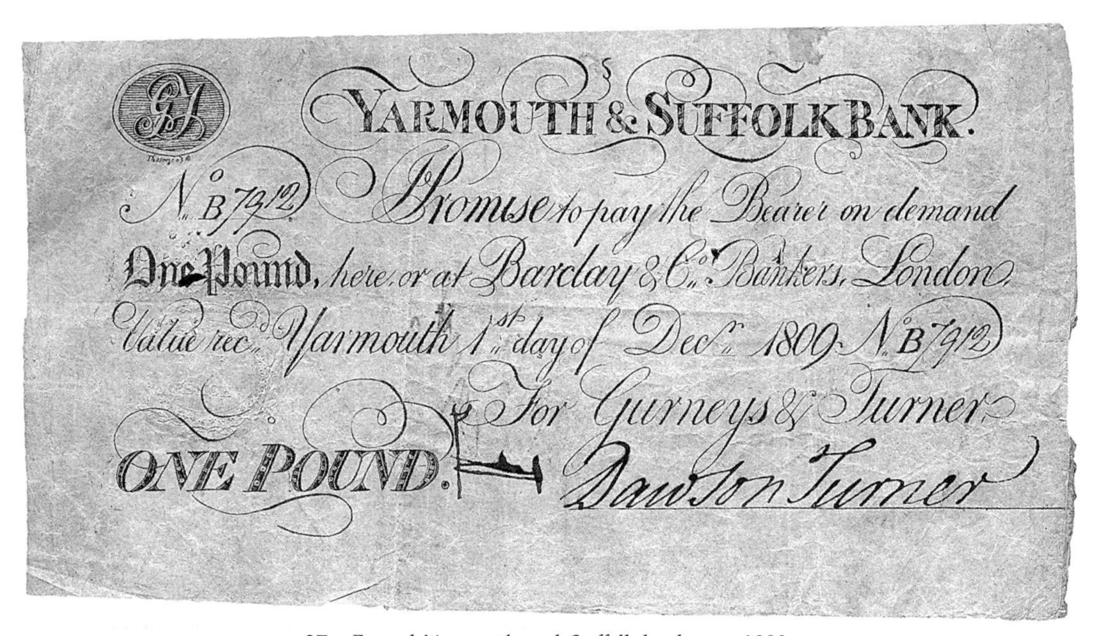

37 *Forged Yarmouth and Suffolk banknote, 1809.*

bill could simply be the equivalent of a banknote held by the owner or deposited in his London bank, or, more likely, it was discounted to provide the running capital for the business. London bankers discounted bills for a commission, so that the owner could use the money, and the bank would present the bill for payment when it became due. Bills were especially useful in foreign trade. Merchants like Dawson and Turner, who had a London account, frequently offered banking services to their own smaller clients who did not have such accounts. Dawson and Turner had carried out a successful business in Yarmouth from at least the 1760s. In addition to being an important local merchant, James Turner came from a family of good local standing. His father was a minister in Yarmouth for 40 years, and he himself was mayor in 1779. Although this was the type of person to whom the Gurneys turned to extend their banking partnerships, it is notable that the Turners were not Quakers or connected to the Gurneys by family ties, as so many other partners were.

Many country-banking partnerships grew out of the need of a merchant to set up an account for his business and found himself providing finance to his neighbours. The Gurneys themselves were wool merchants, as were the Birkbecks. Joseph and Jonathan Peckover of the Fakenham and Wisbech banks were merchants and shopkeepers; the Alexanders of the Ipswich Bank were shipowners engaged in the iron and corn trades.

The first ledger for the Yarmouth Bank dates from 22 December 1781, a date that agrees with the account of a letter from James Turner on 19 December 1781, 'I will give myself the pleasure of being at the bank on Friday morning at half past nine.'[4] The terms of the partnership were probably agreed then. The two opening accounts in the ledger are for Richard, Bartlett and Joseph Gurney, who put in £4,000 and James Turner who put in £1,800. In 1782 the balance of the Yarmouth Bank at their London bankers, Barclays, was £5,628. This same ledger covers the years 1781 to 1785. Accounts were held in the names of James Dawson, the Reverend Francis Turner, the Reverend Joseph Turner, and Thomas and William Palgrave. Other accounts included the charity school, the corporation, and the trustees of the Muster roll. No doubt many of the other names are significant in the history of Yarmouth.

While we do not have the original partnership agreement for the Yarmouth Bank we do have the one from 1785, as it was continued in 1793.[5] The partners agreed to continue the partnership for another seven years. The capital was to be £5,000, of which the Gurneys put up £3,750 and Turner £1,250. Profit and loss were to be distributed in proportion to the capital, so the Gurneys would have three quarters and Turner one quarter. The business was to be carried out in James Turner's house, with him as the active partner. The first place of business was in a house on the South Quay opposite the crane. Apparently this had been a public house called the *Three Cranes Tavern,* which James Turner closed down and turned into a bank house when he became a partner. In 1784 the bank moved to the present site of Barclays' Yarmouth branch. It too was the home of the Turner family. Dawson Turner occupied the upper part of the house as his residence. In the early 1850s the Bank House was rebuilt at a cost of £6,955 19s. 9d. and Stationers House for £1,135 5s. 9d. to designs by Anthony Salvin. By then the living-in partner must have been Brightwen, as the account included a beam ceiling for Mr Brightwen's bedroom.[6]

In an era when many banks over-stretched themselves the characteristic carefulness of Gurney business practice is shown in the seventh head of agreement. It said that an account was to be raised under the head of bad debts from 10 per cent of the profits each year. Careful attention was paid to what would now be called risk management in the eighth head of agreement, which said that a balance should be taken twice yearly and an annual settlement made.

While we do not have the agreement by which Dawson Turner took his father's place we do have one dated 1796.[7] This was between four Gurneys: Bartlett, Richard, Joseph and Hudson and Dawson Turner. The capital remained £5,000 with Richard, Bartlett and Joseph Gurney supplying £3,000, Hudson Gurney £1,000 and Dawson Turner £1,000. As before, profit and loss was to be in proportion to the capital put in. A new provision prohibited Dawson from entering into another banking partnership in Yarmouth on penalty of £10,000. Like his father, he was 'to be considered as the Partner, whose time and attention is to be given up to the Business, and upon whom the agency is principally to rest'. Provision was made for Dawson's death by saying that his share would revert to Richard, Bartlett and Joseph Gurney.[8] A memorandum by Dawson Turner in 1812 stated that his share of the bad debt fund would no longer revert to the Gurneys on his death, but would go to his family.

A tantalising glimpse of the Gurneys' attitude to Dawson's banking skills comes in a letter written from Yarmouth in 1815 about sorting out overdrawn accounts, saying, 'I must acknowledge that most of the persons on whom I call here had been previously applied to by D T – but he does not seem firm enough to follow up with sufficient spirit.'[9]

The Norwich Bank kept a set of settlement books for all their banks from 1826. The settlement book was the equivalent of the annual balance sheet. Because the country banks were privately owned the information was not made public. The table on p.116 shows the results for the Yarmouth Bank from 1826 until the death of Dawson Turner.

Yarmouth Bank Profits

Year	*Gurneys Bank*	*D Turner*	*J Brightwen*
1826	£5,500	£2,500	£2,000
1827	£4,950	£2,250	£1,800
1828	£4,400	£2,000	£1,600
1829	Not given	Not given	Not given*
1830	£3,850	£1,750	£1,400
1831	£4,400	£2,000	£1,600
1832	£4,400	£2,000	£1,600
1833	£3,850	£1,750	£1,400
1834	£4,400	£2,000	£1,600
1835	£4,950	£2,250	£1,800
1836	£5,500	£2,500	£2,000
1837	£5,500	£2,500	£2,000
1838	£4,400	£2,000	£1,600
1839	£5,500	£2,500	£2,000
1840	£5,500	£2,500	£2,000
1841	£5,500	£2,500	£2,000
1842	£4,950	£2,250	£1,800
1843	£2,420	£1,100	£880
1844	£2,860	£1,300	£1,040
1845	£3,960	£1,800	£1,440
1846	£5,500	£2,500	£2,000
1847	£6,600	£3,000	£2,400
1848	£4,400	£2,000	£1,600
1849	£3,190†	£1,450‡	£1,160§
1850	£2,970	£1,350	£1,080
1851	£3,300	£1,500	£1,200
1852	£2,750	£1,250	£1,000
1853	£3,300	£1,500	£1,200
1854	£4,950	£2,250	£1,800
1855	£5,500	£2,500	£2,000
1856	£6,325	£2,875	£2,300
1857	£6,325	£2,875	£2,300
1858	£4,400	£2,000¶	1,600

* Figure for division given as £7,000 but not what each partner received.
† 11/20.
‡ 1/4.
§ 1/5.
¶ To his executors.

Note the drop in the years 1843 to 1844, years in which many banks became bankrupt.

38 *Yarmouth Bank pre-1854.*

The figures for each bank show that Yarmouth was the most prosperous bank in the group, after Norwich. In 1826 Yarmouth had the highest balance sheet total at £13,939 followed by Halesworth with £9,476, Wisbech with £9,393, Fakenham with £5,698 and Lynn with £1,163. The position remained the same in 1858 with Yarmouth having a figure of £17,310 followed by Wisbech with £16,967, Halesworth with £14,139, Lynn with £14,061, Fakenham with £3,472 (£5,955 in May) and Aylsham with £1,742.

In 1816 John Brightwen was brought into the partnership. The Brightwens married into the Gurney and Turner families when John married Hannah, the granddaughter of Henry Gurney, and his son Thomas married another Hannah, the daughter of Dawson Turner. The memorandum of agreement[10] recorded that he would join the Yarmouth Bank under the name of Gurneys, Turner and Brightwen on 6 September 1816 and bring in capital of £1,000 on which he was to receive interest at five-ninths. For the first two years he was to receive £700 as his share of the profits, and after that one-fifth part of the Gurneys' shares of the profits, with a guarantee of a continuation of the £700 per annum if the profits did not reach that level. It was also agreed that he should become a partner in the Halesworth Bank under the firm of Gurneys, Turners and Brightwen. In that partnership he was to receive one-seventh of the Gurneys' profits, leaving it to them to increase that share at any future time. A letter from Samuel Gurney to Joseph Gurney illustrates the relationship between Brightwen and Dawson:

> I think John Brightwen will be of great use, he views these matters in a right point of view and as Dawson is pleased with him and consults him I think he will be found to effect more than if he was of a bolder nature and by that means raised a feeling of opposition in Dawson's mind.[11]

39 *Dawson Turner, lithograph by Hannah Sarah Turner after a drawing by J.P. Davis, 1816.*

The evidence of the surviving letters about the Yarmouth Bank and Yarmouth's own internal settlement book from 1853 suggests that Dawson remained the main partner, but left day-to-day administration to Brightwen. The partners who met to agree the settlement did not include Dawson Turner.

The Yarmouth partners had opened Halesworth Bank in 1782 and in 1809 James Turner, younger son of James Turner, became a partner. He remained there until his death in 1820. From the Halesworth Settlement Books it appears that Dawson Turner took over as the Turner partner in this bank. He appears in the list of partners' profits from 1841. The 1856 settlement saw him receive £1,100 profit while the share of Gurneys and Birkbeck was £6,200 and that of John Brightwen £1,100.

The Yarmouth Bank circulated notes in its own locality. Forgery was a risk and in 1802 the bank was warned about some poor forgeries (see fig.39, p.113). A letter in 1852[12] refers to 'an extensive forgery of our £1 notes' 40 years ago. One of these notes had turned up and it was decided 'it would be better quietly to pay it'. According to Bidwell, in 1810 the circulation was £46,000 in large notes and £2,000 in small notes; and in 1825 the circulation of £1 notes was £50,000 and high notes £35,000. By 1833 it had fallen to £24,000 and £1,500 respectively. The amount in circulation stayed fairly steady but the discrimination between large and small ceased in 1840 with a circulation figure of £21,500. By 1858 it had fallen slightly to £18,475. The circulation of notes at the sister bank at Halesworth, started in 1799, by 1833 was £36,800 and £12,000 in £1 notes. As at Yarmouth this fell to £18,525 in 1858.

The bank was very prosperous, as shown by the statistics for 1833 when the amount of deposits was £449,532, and advances £204,362. By 1858 this had risen to £548,134 (this figure included Beccles) and advances totalled £228,370. The number of Yarmouth accounts was 1,530 and of the Beccles branch four hundred and eighty.

The Halesworth Bank, which was under the management of the Yarmouth partners, was almost equally prosperous. In 1833 the deposits were £234,000 and advances £82,140. In the same year the deposits were £370,258 and advances £122,011. The Halesworth accounts were made up of 431 at Halesworth itself, 252 at Harleston, 170 at Eye, 260 at Bungay, 230 at Saxmundham and 290 at Framlingham.

We have an account book for Bungay branch[13] that suggests that it was opened in October 1783. It was an account between Messrs Gurneys and Turner and Matthew Abell. The front page described it as 'the Bungay branch of the Yarmouth and Suffolk Bank D Gambles's Banking Book as agent for Richard Gurney, Bartlett Gurney, Joseph Gurney and James Turner.'

The Yarmouth Bank opened a Lowestoft branch, probably in 1812. A little book[14] gives 'Characters of our Lowestoft Customers'. A flour and corn chandler was described as 'a steady and respectable man' in 1859 while another was described as having 'a quantity of Norway herrings on hand', thus allowing his note to be discounted for three months. Another asked for £50 'till he could sell his herrings'. The difficulty of raising money for shipping is pointed out and followed by a note 'this ship was lost, insured for £1,200'.

A branch was opened at Beccles under the partnership of Gurneys and Turner of the Yarmouth and Suffolk Bank, probably in 1823. A note on the expenses of the Yarmouth Agencies in 1843 has Beccles holding 500 accounts with credits of £138,000 and debits of £25,900. According to the note the Lowestoft accounts were mixed with the Yarmouth accounts, so separate figures could not be given.[15] The agencies under Halesworth were Bungay with 250 accounts, Harleston with 306, Framlingham with 237, Saxmundham with 240, and Eye with two hundred and two.

The settlement book for Yarmouth Bank recorded Dawson Turner's death on 21 June 1858. In July that year the total came to £17,310 16s. 4d., of which £1,462 was spent on salaries. In addition Palgrave received £350, Thomas Brightwen £700, clerks £100 and Dawson Turner's executors £2,000. The large sum of £3,491 2s. 9d. went to the bad debt fund. One of the reasons for the success of the Yarmouth Bank was the careful attitude of the partners to lending and provision for bad debts.

We have a statement for the bank in 1856, which states that the capital was £63,809 13s. 11d.: the fund for bad debts was £20,313 6s. 7d., of which £1,044 7s. 8d. had been written off. Deposits including Beccles amounted to £463,215, advances to £218,054, and notes in circulation £19,415. The number of accounts at Yarmouth was 1,475 and at Beccles four hundred and ninety-two. The bank's profit after paying the partners' share was £6,325.

The private ledger[16] records the final settlement of the executors of Dawson Turner's account with his bank. The executors were John Brightwen and William Worship. It records his last year's profit as it was shown in the settlement book as £2,000, along with £17,944 from the capital account, £3,696 from the bad debt fund with another one-eighth share of the fund of £2,174. The executors transferred £8,000 to Mary Anne Turner.

Background

In the early days of country banking there was no need to provide information for shareholders and regulators. Each partnership was regulated by private agreement and the success of the bank depended on the community trusting in the reputation of the partners. Many banks failed through making bad loans, so it was important to feel that your money was in the hands of men of financial standing and acumen. The circulation of banknotes in the community depended on local businessmen being happy to take notes in lieu of coin.

The Bank of England was founded in 1694. Before this some goldsmiths and scriveners in London had already extended their business into banking. Barclays PLC, the bank of which the Yarmouth and Suffolk Bank eventually became part, traces its history back to 1690 and a goldsmith's *shoppe* in Lombard Street. Country banks started to appear in the 18th century, as merchants set up London accounts and provided services to other smaller local tradesmen.

The failure statistics show banking to be a risky business. Between 1790 and 1826, 334 banks failed; and in 1825-6, 60 failed.[17] Reasons varied from economic crisis to over lending and issuing too many notes, leading to a run on the bank.

There was hardly any regulation until 1826 when joint stock companies were allowed for the first time outside London. For the original partnership banks reputation was vital. Members of the Society of Friends had an advantage because they were known for their probity and plain dealing. In addition it was known that a member who became bankrupt was 'disowned' and lost his standing in the society. Close family relationships were also important. The marriage bonds between the Barclay, Gurney, Bevan and Backhouse families in the early years of their banks were fostered by the Quaker rule that no-one could marry out. Consequently Quaker families had two incentives for intermarriage – to keep capital in the wider family and to remain members in good standing. Quakers flourished in business partly because the Test Acts prohibited them from many occupations until 1828.

Issuing banknotes was an important part of the business of a country bank. Many used pictures of local buildings or industries but by and large Gurney banknotes were not as flamboyant as some. The variety of notes caused some confusion and customers could have preference for

40 *Yarmouth and Suffolk banknote.*

one bank's notes over another. Some attempts were made to control the issue of notes by the various Acts. The sheer number of banks issuing their own notes only added to the problem. In 1808, the Government required any person issuing notes to take out a licence; 755 licences were issued in England and Wales. With so many different notes around, forgery must have seemed a relatively easy crime, but it carried a stiff penalty for those caught. Between 1797 and 1829, 618 people were sentenced to death for forgery. No fewer than 28,412 forged £1 notes were found in 1817 alone – presumably one of the reasons behind the Act of 1826. In 1832, the death penalty for forgery was replaced by transportation for life.

The Bank Charter Act of 1844 limited the right to issue notes to the Bank of England and those banks that had done so before 1844. However, with the exception of the Bank of England, the banks were only allowed to issue the average number of notes that they had issued in the 12 weeks before 27 April 1844. Once a bank stopped issuing notes, then the Bank of England was empowered to increase their note circulation by two-thirds of the amount withdrawn. Any banks formed after the Act were forbidden to issue notes.

However, it was easy for a bank to over-issue and for the notes to become worthless. To stop this practice, the Government passed an act in 1844 forbidding the establishment of new banks of issue.

Aftermath

The reputation of the Gurney Group suffered from the failure of Overend Gurney and Company in 1866. Overend and Gurney had been founded by Thomas Richardson as a bill-broking business in 1802. Members of the Gurney family became partners in the firm and lent it valuable support. The failure rocked the city and tarnished the reputation of the Gurney family. The Gurney banking partnerships had to be restructured to take out the members of the family involved in Overend Gurney and Company.

The Barclay, Gurney and Backhouse partners were interconnected through the Quaker tradition and intermarriage. The initial agreement to form a limited company was made between Gurney and Company, Barclay and Company and Jonathan Backhouse and Company on 30 March 1896. They agreed to invite other banks to join them and negotiations took place, which resulted in a number of other banks joining. Barclays and Company and Gurney and Company each put in £1 million in capital and reserve. Gurneys held £1,254,535 and Barclays £8,589,530 in deposits.

It is believed that the reason for the title of the new joint stock company formed in 1896 being Barclay and Company is the association of the name Gurney with Black Friday, as the collapse in 1866 was called.

After 1896 Yarmouth became a local head office in Barclay and Company. The partners became local directors. In 1936 the local head office was taken over by Norwich Local Head Office. Now the Yarmouth Branch of Barclays remains on the site of Bank House, marking the long and distinguished history of banking in the area and commemorating the part played by the Turner family.[18]

JESSIE CAMPBELL

CHAPTER SIX

A Tasteful Occupation?

The work of Maria, Elizabeth, Mary Anne, Harriet, Hannah Sarah and Ellen Turner

The Turner family was a largely female household, consisting of Dawson Turner, his wife Mary and eight children: Maria, Elizabeth, Mary Anne, Harriet, Hannah Sarah, Eleanor (known as Ellen), Gurney and Dawson William. Three other children had sadly not survived beyond infancy – two sons, both called Dawson, and another daughter, Katherine.[1] The achievements of the Turner women[2] have, however, been rarely written about. This chapter will look at their artistic output for, while not professional artists, all of them made significant contributions towards Dawson Turner's antiquarian projects as well as creating a large body of other prints, drawings and watercolours. From the daughters of an art patron and collector, one would expect some level of artistic activity among the Turners and certainly drawing was considered a necessary and fashionable accomplishment for young ladies of their social position. However, the sheer volume of work they produced is unusual and the ways in which much of it was encouraged and subsequently used are remarkable. In addition to a vast number of sketches of everyday life at Bank House, they produced several thousand drawings for their father for inclusion in his extra-illustrated edition of Francis Blomefield's *An Essay Towards a Topographical History of the County of Norfolk*, plus drawings and etchings for a variety of other projects. Many of their drawings were published, albeit privately and for a small audience, at a time when it was uncommon for women to have any sort of public artistic presence.

There is one main difficulty in discussing the Turners as artists in that much of their work is similar in appearance and is unsigned, making it difficult to attribute correctly. It is not ideal to discuss Maria, Elizabeth, Mary Anne, Harriet, Hannah Sarah and Ellen as one, but all of them appear to have had the same approach to drawing and the ways in which it was presented to a wider audience. Very little has previously been written about them as individuals – they are most often discussed in terms of being daughters, wives or mothers. Maria, for example, features in many

41 *Hannah Sarah Playing the Harp, September 1819. Attributed to Elizabeth Turner.*

articles written about her husband, Sir William Jackson Hooker, and Elizabeth similarly is mentioned in discussions about the Palgrave family, into which she married. This chapter is unconcerned with their marriages and children and will look entirely at them as women who are part of an exciting and significant development in female artistic endeavour during the early part of the 19th century.

The impression one might have of the type of family who would spend time creating thousands of images of antiquarian topics is perhaps a rather dull and dry one, and indeed the Turner family was noted for its industrious nature. The geologist Charles Lyell wrote home from Bank House that: 'What I see going on every hour in this family makes me ashamed of the most active day I ever spent … Mrs Turner has been etching with her daughters in the parlour every morning this week since half past six!'

Drawings of the family by Elizabeth, Maria and Hannah Sarah support this idea – in almost every sketch they are active: drawing, reading, playing the harp or piano, or teaching their younger brothers or nephews. Their heads are always bowed in concentration. The only respite seems to have been when they were ill and even then books and paper often lie strewn around the sick bed. The sheer amount of pictures they produced points towards a household in which there was very little time spent idle.

Frederick Madden, Keeper of Manuscripts at the British Museum, painted a quite dismal picture of the household when he visited in 1832:

> I feel myself quite lost. Everything is run in the house by clockwork. The young ladies, if I am a little late at breakfast, sit on thorns & the moment I have sipped the last cup of tea, all fly off as if I was a monster. It is the same

> thing in the evening. There is no amusement introduced. There is a harp and a piano, but no one touches either, & when I have succeeded in entering into a little conversation, the hour of ten arrives and away they go to bed! I call this misery. There is neither comfort not pleasure in such a system. I almost resent coming here.[3]

The Turners' own drawings and writings, as well as the recorded impressions of others who knew them, paint quite a different picture. Although the household was hard-working, it seems to have been far from dull and the Turner women were considered intelligent, witty and attractive, as well as diligent and proficient artists. Henry Crabbe Robinson considered Elizabeth to have 'more beauty, elegance, sense and taste united than I have seen for a long time' (22 May 1824), while Elizabeth's own sketch of her grandmother, dated 22 March 1821, shows a sharp eye for detail and rather a wicked sense of humour. All the Turners wrote to each other, almost incessantly it would appear, and their writings are full of engaging descriptions of places they have visited, people they have encountered and their impressions of them. Harriet's letters to Dawson Turner from Holland include a rather disgruntled description of: 'myriads of gnats, very large and very nimble, and quite on the alert; and they are everywhere: my gloves, one of which I pulled off to write, are full of them, and so is my bonnet.'[4] Sir Joseph Hooker, son of Maria and her husband William Jackson Hooker, recalled 'being carried there [Bank House] in my nurse's arms early in 1821 … I remember distinctly the railings before the Bank, its drawing room, and my aunts' seizing me from my nurse, dancing with me round the room and striking the harp to amuse me.'[5] These aunts would have been Elizabeth, Mary Anne, Harriet, Hannah Sarah and Ellen, who were all still living at Bank House. This conjures up the images of a happy and rather fun family, far removed from the silent, unfriendly experience recorded by Madden. In fact, Madden changed his mind about the family over the course of his visit, in particular about Hannah Sarah. His diary entries from Bank House chart a growing admiration for Hannah, in spite of her upbringing:

> Tuesday 17th The young ladies have become more sociable with me, & I begin to like them, particularly the second who is really a very nice creature – & excels in accomplishments that I should wish a wife to be … She is also what may be termed pretty, certainly very interesting, but her dress & style is not quite what I like. This, however, results from the manner in which she is brought up. A girl who gets up every morning in the dark, cannot be supposed to attend much to the nicety of her apparel, her hair or her person.

By the Friday of the same week, Madden was considering proposing, but decided to 'wait a twelve-month & see if I then retain the same interest for her'.

He did not propose though – his diaries also reveal his deep love for his dead wife and guilt at the thought of loving another, an issue that he appears to have been unable to resolve. Hannah went on to marry Thomas Brightwen, a banker from Great Yarmouth, in 1839.

Both Madden and Lyell's diaries describe the dedication with which the girls and their mother approached the business of drawing, as this entry by Madden makes explicit:

> Friday 13th Mr T has three unmarried daughters at home, all of whom are extremely clever and are brought up in a systematic plan adopted by Mr T for getting up at 7 or earlier, breakfasting at 8, drawing or studying all day, teaching at schools &c. dining at 5 and going to bed at 10. I confess, that the hours are very irksome to me, but I make a point of confirming to them.

This is the first clue that, within the household, drawing was not simply a leisure pursuit but may have had a more formal function and therefore places the Turners themselves in the position of being more than casual, talented amateurs.

By the early 19th century, drawing was just one of several 'accomplishments' young women of the upper and middle classes were encouraged to have, along with other activities such as needlework and playing an instrument such as the harp or piano. As a skill, drawing fulfilled a very specific social role, one which had very little to do with the type of publicly celebrated 'art' of the type exhibited at the Royal Academy and everything to do with socially acceptable notions of the feminine. A definite divide existed between art produced as 'high art' and recognised as artistic achievement, which was almost exclusively produced by men, and the type of art that women were encouraged to produce, which was seen very much as a leisure pursuit and not really containing true artistic merit. As a generalisation, male and female artistic endeavour can be seen as existing within two entirely separate spheres; the male within a public, commercial or professional and official context and the female very much within a private, unofficial, domestic arena. However, drawing fulfilled an important social function for women. Being able to draw implied an ability to observe, to interpret and to appreciate one's surroundings. It was suggestive of an artistic nature and the ability to appreciate works of art by others. This in turn indicated a certain type of upbringing, one that featured the money and leisure time to develop all of the above. Drawing, therefore, operated as a visible social indicator of wealth and suitable 'accomplishment' – important factors in the marriage market. It was not intended to be an expression of individual taste or interpretation and certainly not in any way an encouragement of true artistic ability or ambition; as Ann Bermingham has pointed out, 'the accomplished woman was understood to be artistic but not an artist.'[6]

Those women who were a little too skilled may even have been viewed with suspicion and certainly this was deemed to be an 'unfeminine' trait. In *Vanity Fair*, set about the same time that the Turners were drawing, Thackeray uses artistic ability to subtly suggest the characters of his two main protagonists. Amelia, who embodies the social ideal of the feminine, has been taught to draw at Miss Pinkerton's academy for young ladies but is sadly lacking in any ability – her attempts are described as 'feeble'.[7] By contrast Becky Sharp, who is socially transgressive in many ways, is rather gifted with the pencil, particularly at caricatures. The limitations social expectation may have placed on female artistic endeavour were not, however, mirrored by commercial developments. During the latter half of the 18th century, an entire industry aimed at the artistic female sprang up. Shops such as Ackerman's Repository lent out and sold prints of famous works of art for studying as well as books of motifs to copy into drawings. Manuals such as Brown's *New Treatise on Flower Painting, or Every Lady her Own Drawing Master* of 1799 and Ackerman's 1812 *New Drawing Book of Light and Shadow* were aimed specifically at the amateur female artist and drawing materials became more readily available. It was made more and more easy for women at a variety of social levels to make themselves 'accomplished'. Certainly, Dawson and Mary Turner encouraged and enabled their daughters to be typical in this way. Charming and lively sketches of the family, most often by Elizabeth and Maria, show them reading, playing musical instruments and drawing, always dressed in fashionable clothes, such as the drawing 'Hannah Sarah Playing the Harp, Sept 1819', by Elizabeth. There are several aspects of their lives that mark them out as different to this interpretation however, as hinted at by Madden's description of the 'systematic plan'. The way in which they were taught drawing and the ways in which their work was subsequently encouraged and used are significantly different to what one would expect.

The Turners had a very privileged art education, far beyond that which a drawing manual and shop-bought engravings could provide. Initially, John Crome was engaged as their drawing teacher and then from about 1811-12 was replaced by John Sell Cotman who came regularly to Bank House for the next 12 years. Both Crome and Cotman supplemented their income by teaching a variety of pupils and so their presence at Bank House is not surprising. It did mean, however, that the Turners had for drawing masters two of the leading local artists of the period. A fascinating insight to their education is provided by the list of 'Rules to be observed in Drawing' that Cotman prepared for them, which have as their introduction: 'Every good is to be expected from perseverance & attention. – from idleness, nothing.' An insight into how Cotman's tuition may have sometimes been received is also provided in rule two, which commands 'Implicit obedience to the remarks of those placed over you.' Perhaps Maria, Elizabeth and Mary Anne, his pupils when the rules were composed,[8] were not always as keen to learn as Cotman or their father might have wished! Cotman's rules also tell us that they were expected to approach drawing with serious dedication, suggesting that they were not being taught merely to become 'accomplished' but to enable them to create images with real skill and professionalism.

Cotman's rules encourage careful observation and a systematic approach for creating a final piece. He states as rule three: 'Examine well the subject before you, for it is only through a thorough knowledge of the subject you are about to copy, that accuracy, precision, ease and expedition can be acquired,' and goes on to set out a step-by-step process for then creating the picture, beginning with sketching in the entire subject, then adding in 'a clear, distinct and vigorous outline', moving on to completing the 'principal feature of your design' and leaving 'the subordinate parts, the sky, background & foreground to the last'. This approach can be seen clearly in the work of all the Turners, both for their father and in their own personal drawings, as well as in Cotman's own antiquarian work for Dawson Turner. It is an approach ideally suited to the factual recording of antiquities and buildings. Many of their drawings for the Blomefield project feature only a single object, such as a font, depicted in precise detail, with little or no background setting. Even in their sketches of each other, the main subject, a sister playing

42 *Lady Palgrave [Elizabeth] ill, by Maria Turner, 1834.*

the harp for example, will be drawn in isolation with no sense of the room around her. The watercolour by Maria of *Lady Palgrave* [Elizabeth] *Ill*, from 1834, illustrates the same method. The 'principle feature' here is Elizabeth, sitting up in bed (still looking rather industrious for an invalid) and has been completed in detail, in particular the table placed next to the bed. The rest of the room is much less precise, with pencil lines remaining to suggest the wood panelling. It merely exists to give a basic sense of context – we are not expected to pay it the same attention as the 'principle feature' and it has been treated accordingly.

In addition to their lessons from Cotman, the family was taught etching and lithography by William Camden Edwards and James de Carle Sowerby.[9] Even artists visiting Bank House appear to have been pressed into giving lessons. Elizabeth described one such occasion in a letter to Maria dated 5 October 1822:

> All this week we have been much & most delightfully employed in listening to & observing Mr Varley,[10] the water-colour artist, who has stayed with us while Papa was at Holkham. It is not enough to tell you that we have been delighted with this most singular man – Not only has he, with most unwearied diligence, sought to shew us every way of copying his drawings, he has also tried to make us compose, & explained to us all those principles of composition, which after many years of hard fagging, he has discovered himself.

The Turner family also had access to a range of art collections as Elizabeth's letter suggests in mentioning her father's visit to Holkham Hall. This was a major advantage at a time when there were practically no public art galleries, and most people had to rely on engravings to identify and study major paintings and sculptures. The primary source, of course, was Dawson Turner's own collection, hanging on the walls of Bank House and with which they would all have been familiar. Even in childhood sketches by Maria and Elizabeth, it is easy to identify individual paintings, such as the pencil sketch of the *West Side, Dining Room*, *c.*1811-14. Dawson Turner was also in contact with other local patrons and collectors, and this provided his family with the opportunity of viewing and studying other major works. A visit to Holkham Hall in 1817 is reflected in a series of etchings of the statues from the renowned sculpture gallery, published in the *Dawson Turner Family Etchings* of 1817, and again in these we see the attention to detail and focus on a primary subject taught by Cotman. Family journals and letters also relate trips abroad to view both private and public collections. In 1814 Dawson and Mary Turner, Elizabeth and Maria together with William Jackson Hooker and Charles Lyell, toured France and visited the Louvre several times: 'tho' we had three times run thro' it, we could not til today say that we had seen'.[11]

43 *West Side, Dining Room, by Elizabeth or Maria Turner,* c.*1811-14.*

Dawson Turner's later 'Rhenish Tour' of 1833, was undertaken in the company of his wife, Ellen, Elizabeth and her husband Sir Francis Palgrave. Dawson Turner kept journals of both these trips, which were later transcribed and written out 'in neat' by Hannah Sarah with the addition of watercolours and sketches made by various members of the parties. This type of upbringing enabled the Turners to look and think about art in a critical way, and instilled in them a love of art that lasted for the rest of their lives. Harriet's letters from Holland of 1834 include descriptions and opinions about a wide range of sculptures, buildings and paintings. Of the painting *Five Large Heads* by Karel du Jardin in the Amsterdam Museum, Harriet wrote:

> ... and if the five heads had been cut out of card-paper, and pasted on the canvas, they would have looked as like life, and have formed as good a picture. As it was, they proved how completely different portrait-painters and artists are, and how possible it is to be the one, and yet not the other, according to Mr Cotman's old opinion.

Harriet is clearly confident in her own ability to appraise paintings and hold informed opinions about them. Her considerable knowledge of major works of art, which we can assume was common to all the family, also comes through in these letters:

> We were waked about three this morning by a furious splashing, occasioned by two men who were washing wool in the canal. They stood under a little shed, built by the water-side, having piled their wool, which they carried in large and very pretty baskets, just like those in Rubens' [*sic*] *Gathering of the Manna* ...

Harriet's art education informs how she views the world, likening a commonplace event to a very specific detail from a major painting, with which she was evidently very familiar. Her letters also indicate the function she considered drawing to have: 'This little sketch, vile as it is, will give you a better conception of my idea of the mouth of the Maas, than any description I could write.'

She sees drawing as a reliable indicator of fact, an objective rather than subjective approach. All the Turners include sketches as part of their correspondence to each other, and it is rare to find a letter that does not contain at least one drawing. Throughout their lives, all of them used drawing as a means to what they saw to be objective communication. This is, of course, entirely in keeping with the way in which Harriet and her sisters were taught to draw by Cotman and the context in which many of their drawings were produced.

This context, for much of their lives at Bank House, was of course the production of drawings for Dawson Turner's edition of Blomefield's *Norfolk*. Published between 1805 and 1810, *An Essay Towards a Topographical History of the County of Norfolk* was a massive 11-volume account of Norfolk's past, detailing every town and village in the county. Dawson Turner conceived the notion of adding illustrations to his copy to produce a fuller record of Norfolk's material history. This project began in *c.*1814 and lasted for at least thirty years – the last dated drawing in the Turner Blomefield is 1848. Other Grangerised, or extra-illustrated, versions of Blomefield exist. The so-called 'Norfolk Collection' was created by James Bulwer (1794 -1879), a Norfolk clergyman, during the mid-19th century. Bulwer employed 23 artists, including John Sell Cotman, Miles Edmund Cotman and Frederick Sandys, to produce watercolours of Norfolk churches and their interiors, local monuments and archaeological artefacts that would illustrate his copy of Blomefield alongside his own watercolours.[12] A later version known as the Todd Collection (now in Norwich Castle Museum & Art Gallery), uses prints as illustrations. Todd collected a vast array of illustrations, which range from original etchings by John Sell Cotman and John Crome to mass-produced prints cut out from local newspapers. The Todd Collection was clearly a very different project from Bulwer's rather more professional approach and both of them differ greatly from Dawson Turner's own project, of which they must both have been aware. The thousands of images that illustrate the Dawson Turner Blomefield (now in the British Library), were almost all created by his daughters. Part of their drawing lessons involved the Turners copying from Cotman's own drawings and most of these ended up in the Blomefield. In fact, Dawson Turner as Cotman's patron had encouraged the artist to sketch details from every church in Norfolk and it is these sketches that the Turners were copying. The copies are very accurate, as is evident if a Cotman original and a Turner version are compared. Why Dawson Turner decided not to purchase the Cotman sketches and instead have his daughters create images for the Blomefield is, however, unclear. There could have been financial motivation – rather than paying Cotman for the finished group of sketches, simply have his family create the same images for free, but, this seems underhand and unlikely. There may have been the intention of creating an endeavour to pass his daughters' time suitably, but as various accounts indicate, they were also busy with other pastimes and occupations as well as drawing and etching for other projects. Certainly, it is clear that Dawson Turner considered his daughters quite capable of producing images for such a large antiquarian project and so having them create only copies seems rather odd. One theory is that, in order to make original sketches, they would have had to travel across Norfolk to sketch in other towns and in the countryside, and this was perhaps considered unsuitable for young women. However, Cotman took the girls and their mother on regular sketching expeditions,[13] and the sketches featured in Dawson Turner's various foreign journals are all original rather than copies and so must have been sketched 'on the spot'. Dawson Turner even seems to have commended this approach, as his entry for 1 August 1833 in the Rhenish Tour Journal records:

> (Bruges) Our fellow travellers, the Miss Rickmans, though they had never been on the Continent before gave us an admirable specimen of that determined industry & energy & good sense for which they are remarkable, by continuing seated in the midst of the street, & making sketches of the most interesting objects in the town, notwithstanding the crowd by which they were constantly surrounded & occasionally teazed.

The reason for making copies rather than original illustrations remains somewhat of a mystery but nevertheless the Turner Blomefield remains a remarkable achievement, both as a record of Norfolk's past as seen through the eyes of early 19th-century antiquarians and as a record of the artistic endeavours of the Turners themselves. A note written in pencil by Dawson Turner in the *Index of Illustrations arranged by Parish* (1859),[14] states: 'In this printed Index about 5400 illustrations. Since added (Feb 1846) about 1800.' This brings the total number of illustrations up to an astounding 7,200. Sadly, most of them are not signed or even initialled, apart from some very early images by Elizabeth, Maria and Mrs Turner but, while all the family contributed, it is likely that a greater number were carried out by Mrs Turner and by Mary Anne, who was unmarried and remained at home with her father until his remarriage. Some later additions are clearly by other artists and have been added in the absence of the Turners to carry out the work.

The Turners were also busy creating images for a variety of other projects. Books of *Dawson Turner Family Etchings* were published for 1812-14, 1817, 1818, 1819, 1820, 1821 and 1824. These featured portraits of the family and what the family called 'celebrities', local antiquities, buildings and copies of famous paintings all etched by the Turners and their friends. In total the books contain 667 different images. Typically

44 *Mrs Turner, by Elizabeth Turner, 22 March 1821.*

45 *Ellen ill with cat, by Elizabeth Turner, December 1828.*

these images were the work of two people, drawn by one and etched by the other. This could be a variety of combinations; of two sisters, such as *Melrose Abbey* published in the 1817 book, which was 'etched by ET [Elizabeth], drawn by Mrs WJ Hooker [Maria], 1815', or with their husband or friend. Others were based on drawings by more famous artists – the 1817 volume includes *Miss O'Neil* 'drawn by Fuseli and etched by Mrs Turner'. More complex involvement occurs with some of the architectural images, where a member of the family has copied a drawing by, for example, Cotman, and another has etched it, so that three people have contributed towards the final image. The family published various other books, each time only in small numbers and for private circulation. In 1826, 20 copies of *Eighty Copies of Architectural Antiquities in Norfolk. By Miss Ellen Turner from the Originals by JS Cotman* were printed. Hannah Sarah's *Sixty Portraits from Drawings on Stone after Unedited Originals* appeared in 1840. Several of the Turners continued similar projects as adults – Mary Anne wrote and illustrated a *History of Caistor Castle* and in 1849 *Drawings by Mrs Gunn* [Harriet] *of Mural Paintings in Crostwick Church* was published, both funded by Dawson Turner. Journals of foreign tours were also produced, such as *Lady Palgrave's Italian Journey* of 1837 and 1839. The Turners seem to have inherited many of their father's interests, from travel and art to antiquarianism, particularly in relation to their home county. Most of the publications and projects reflect these private interests and activities and tell us what sort of lifestyle they had – Mary Anne, for example, who remained at home in Yarmouth, developed more of an interest in local history while Elizabeth was able to travel to the Continent. Most of the books discussed above were published on a small scale and distributed to members of the family and friends, and it is probably fair to say that they appealed only to this type of audience. Mary Anne's *History of Caistor Castle* stands apart and indeed did have a wider circulation and there is also the 1840 *Outlines in Lithography*, which is different from the majority of the family publications. *Outlines in Lithography* is a record of Dawson Turner's art collection, in which each painting is illustrated by Hannah Sarah or Mary Anne, and described in detail by Dawson and Mrs Turner. Illustrations of private art collections were quite common and Dawson Turner therefore was not unusual in having this book published. Once again though there is the fact that, rather than have a professional artist copy the paintings, he had his daughters execute the work and it is interesting to wonder why this was. Just as with the Blomefield project (on which we can assume Mary Anne and Hannah Sarah were also working at the time), the questions arise as to whether this was a cost-saving exercise, a devised project to occupy the time, or a combination of both. Again, the fact that Dawson Turner saw his daughters as proficient enough artists to carry out this project is also clear, although, as with the Blomefield illustrations, they were essentially copying the work of others.

In fact, the Turners' work divides itself into two categories – those illustrations produced for their father's various projects and for the family publications, almost all of which are copies; and the sketches

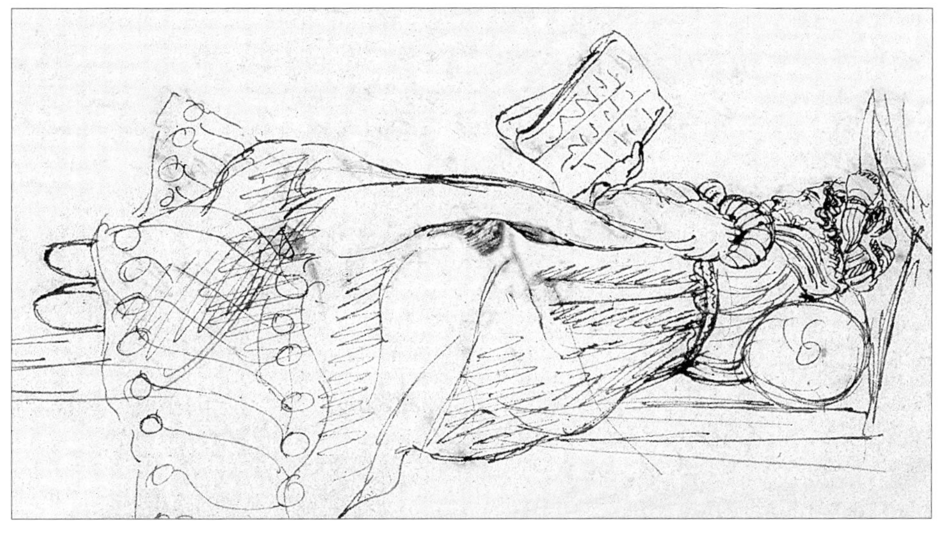

46 *Mrs Turner reading, by Elizabeth Turner, 1820.*

and watercolours they did for their own amusement and interest. Within the family there existed a definite notion of images intended for 'public' consumption and a life beyond that of the artist. A scrap book entitled 'Sketches, for the greater number not made to be preserved, Of and by different individuals of the Family of Dawson Turner Esq., 1813-1824' makes this divide clear. These show the family at home, reading, playing musical instruments, drawing, teaching and playing with the younger children. They also provide a fascinating record of not only the family, but of fashions and lifestyle in early 19th-century Norfolk. The sketches depict in detail the rooms and furniture at Bank House and reveal an interest in fashion, although the clothes are perhaps slightly behind the very latest styles, as one would expect from a country family. One sketch of Mrs Turner reading, dated 1820, shows her wearing a Turkish-style turban headdress of the type that would have been very fashionable a few years earlier but, in London, was now being supplanted by a more French-influenced mode of dressing. These casual sketches were made by the Turners for their own enjoyment in the hours they had free from working on their father's projects and are very different in feel from the sometimes rather turgid illustrations produced for the Blomefield and books such as *Outlines in Lithography*. This divide is interesting, in that the illustrations commissioned by Dawson Turner and produced for a specific purpose and for wider dissemination are all copies and therefore an indication of artistic proficiency only, while other sketches made casually and not intended for 'preservation' were produced independently of Dawson Turner's direction and are more of an artistic expression of someone viewing and interpreting her surroundings. This very much ties in with the idea discussed above that women were expected to be artistic but not artists and suggests that the Turners were perhaps seen by their father in this way. What they themselves thought is not really clear – no references to any of the major projects they were engaged in have so far been unearthed, but Elizabeth's letter concerning John Varley's visit to Bank House gives some indication of how she saw herself in relation in this regard:

> Alas! All his endeavours are in vain! We can copy & that is all. And Mr Varley's kind efforts & example have only showd to prove to us the strong line of demarcation which separates the artist from the draftsman, the one who, with a principle of beauty firmly impressed in his mind, goes out & arranges the materials nature affords according to his pre-conceived idea, & the other who draws for ever, it may be beautiful scraps, without ever making a picture, or raising any feeling in the spectator. We alas! have merely the dead letter, the law without the spirit, the body without the soul! But it is not Mr Varley's fault if we are not all now Michel Angelos.

47 *Stringing Currants. Attributed to Hannah Sarah Turner, 10 July 1830.*

This description shows us how Elizabeth saw a clear divide between two modes of artistic endeavour, the notion of being an 'artist' as opposed to being merely 'artistic'. Within her letter and, more importantly, in relation to wider society, this division also extends to being between the 'professional' and the 'amateur' and therefore between men and women. This was, of course, a mainstream idea of the day and one of which Elizabeth must surely have been aware. In addition is the fact that here she is comparing herself, a 21-year-old female amateur, with an acclaimed 58-year-old professional male artist and is likely to have compared herself unfavourably. Certainly her remarks can be read in the same, rather self-effacing vein as Harriet's description of her quite skilful sketch of the mouth of the Maas as 'vile'.

The way the Turners' work can be interpreted is therefore problematic. One cannot escape the fact that, although clearly seen by Dawson Turner as artistically proficient, they were employed essentially as copyists for his various projects, and that their original work was, by and large, considered by him to be of lesser importance. The lack of clarity around why they were only permitted to make copies adds to this. Certainly, some visitors to Bank House viewed their artistic output as little more than a hobby. Henry Crabbe Robinson wrote in 1826 that: 'The moment breakfast was over, Mr Turner went to the bank, Mrs Turner to her writing desk and every one of the young ladies to drawing or some other tasteful occupation.'

Their drawing is clearly seen by Crabbe Robinson as only a fashionable and suitable 'accomplishment'. This seems a somewhat patronising view, when one remembers that at this time Mary Anne, Harriet, Hannah Sarah and Ellen[15] would have been getting up at 7am or earlier to work on the thousands of Blomefield illustrations. Luckily, their contribution did not go unappreciated by their father, who wrote in the preface to the completed grangerised edition:

> To speak of them, and of the active zeal & steady perseverance with which they and their mother have joined in my pursuits and forwarded my views, can be in no wise, I am aware, be needed. In the words of Sir Christopher Wren's well known epitaph 'Si monumentum queris, circumspice'. A single glance at the Index of whatever page it may be opened will attest the fact. The acknowledgement, however, which may not be required as necessary, may be allotted to the feelings of an affectionate and grateful parent, the pride of whose heart it has always been, that if he has had the good fortune to produce what may be of service and give pleasure to others, he has mainly owed his success to those connected with him by the nearest and dearest ties.

Others too saw their work as something to be applauded; the 1859 sale catalogue entry for the Dawson Turner Family Etchings books describes:

> 5 Volumes of Etchings executed in the House of Dawson Turner Esq. An Unique Series, with Impressions of the Plates in every stage of the Progress. Of the Variety of these Prints it is needless to speak, as a series this Collection is probably unexampled as a monument of Artistic Skill in one Family.

The entry for the Blomefield goes further, describing the Turners' work as exhibiting:

> all the practised skill of the artist in handling, and being executed alike ... and prompted by a high degree of knowledge and taste in the executants, accuracy and minuteness of detail are nowhere sacrificed to mere picturesque effect. While the drawings are, on the one hand, elegant pictorial representations, they are no less the delineations which will satisfy the most exact and literal archaeologist.

There are, however, a few examples of their original work being published – Mary Anne's *History of Caistor Castle* and Harriet's illustrations of the Crostwick Murals. The Dawson Turner family etchings, although not entirely original, also represent a body of work produced for no real purpose in the manner of the Blomefield illustrations. These examples, together with the sale catalogue entries, indicate that perhaps their work was considered to have some sort of artistic merit after all.

There is one important example that has not been mentioned yet, and that indicates that at least one of the Turners was considered artist enough to produce work for a large-scale publication, and that is the possible illustrations Maria executed for inclusion in her husband, W.J. Hooker's botanical publications. The early sketchbook belonging to Maria and Elizabeth and dated 1811-14 includes two exquisite watercolours of a Yew and of *Rubus Caesius the Dewberry*. The Dawson Turner Family Etching book for 1817 also contains three pages of plants etched by W.J. Hooker and drawn by Maria. At this time, Hooker was planning the illustrations for his *Muscologia Britannica* and had written to a colleague that he and Maria had:

> tried to etch a few mosses ourselves & I believe we can very well draw & complete one species a day ... And if these are good enough for publication as I verily believe some of them are I should save a considerable expense (9 November 1815).[16]

W.H.C. Edwards completed the final engravings for the book but some of the original drawings were possibly by Maria who was skilled enough at botanical illustration to have done them. If she had, this puts her work into a far more public arena than we have seen before and suggests that she was considered talented enough to produce work for a major publication, with a significant readership.

It becomes clear that, whilst the Turners might initially appear to be rooted in a feminine, domestic tradition of art production, they were in fact moving towards a very different mode of artistic endeavour. They cannot be claimed as revolutionaries, but are certainly different from most of their contemporaries. At the very least, we must appreciate the quite incredible dedication they put into the drawings and etchings for the various projects they embarked upon throughout their lives. The vast body of work they produced can perhaps be seen as a monument to unacknowledged female artistic endeavour – their own and that of many other women of whom little is known or written about. To have created such a vast body of work alone moves them out of the sphere of mere amateurs. Much of their work was published, albeit for small audiences, and this indicates that both they and their peers considered the work to be good enough to have a public presence and some sort of artistic value. It is important to remember that the Turners themselves did not see themselves as 'Michel Angelos' and certainly much of their work was copied. However, they also produced a significant body of original work in their lively, detailed sketches of Bank House and of themselves. Drawings of this nature seem to have had a clear function for them as means of recording and interpreting their surroundings and they must therefore have ascribed some sort of value to their ability. The whole family seems to have been almost obsessed with recording their daily experiences for posterity – endless diaries, journals and letters describe their lives in minute detail, so much so that one wonders how they ever had the time to do anything but write. Some were selected by the family as being of particular interest or importance and were either published, as were Harriet's letters from Holland, or written out 'in neat' to make it easier for future readers. Of course, within the letters and diaries are numerous sketches and watercolours and they must have been aware that future generations would see these images as well as read their writings, and therefore produced them with at least some sort of public presence in mind. The Turners can then be seen as a group of women who were moving beyond the accepted uses and roles of drawing. Their 'tasteful occupation' was subtly pushed to its limits.

JANE KNOWLES

CHAPTER SEVEN

Mary Turner – Wife of Dawson

Men who achieve much are often supported by a woman of equal resolve and, frequently, equal talent, even if this goes unrecognised. This would appear to be very much the case with Dawson Turner. He married a woman who had striking talents of her own but also helped and supported him in his many areas of interest and, with her tender motherly influence, also encouraged their talented children to contribute much to his work. Mary Palgrave married Dawson in 1796 and was with him for over fifty years until her death.

Hers was the legacy of a fascinating family, members of which leave reverberations with us today. Without her influence upon her children and grandchildren, some of the plants we now have in our gardens would possibly not be there, and Kew Gardens would not be the renowned place it is today without the efforts of her son-in-law Sir William Hooker. Another of her sons-in-law, Francis, contributed significantly to the development of the Public Records Office, and his son in turn became Francis Palgrave of 'Golden Treasury' fame. Another of her grandchildren was Clerk to the House of Commons. Another was well known in economic circles, acquiring part ownership of *The Economist*. Her grandson William Gifford Palgrave ('Giffy') became known as 'Palgrave of Arabia', travelling to exotic places and becoming a Jesuit missionary and diplomat. Her children and grandchildren travelled far and wide; Joseph Hooker on perilous plant collection and her 'scruffy little' Gurney as a missionary and surgeon to the Bishop of Calcutta. Her daughters, who inherited her artistic talents as well as her beauty, were devoted wives and mothers.

We know little of Mary's life before she married, only that she was the daughter of a well-respected corn merchant, William Palgrave, and spent a happy childhood at Coltishall Hall in Norfolk. Born in 1774, one of 11 children, her home was a large pleasant house looking over gently sloping meadows to the Yare, where the river was a hub of trade, alive with commercial shipping, feeding the port of Great Yarmouth where Dawson had his bank. It was probably through his banking connections with William that Dawson was introduced to Mary. On her marriage, she moved to Bank House at the better end of the Quay at Great Yarmouth, overlooking the tall ships crowded into the estuary. The building still stands today and is a branch of Barclays. Although later made welcome at many of the large Norfolk mansions, she did not aspire to a grand house herself, but spent her entire married life living 'over the shop'.

Home at Bank House

Children were born almost annually in what was a bustling, vibrant household. Behind the tall elegant building was a garden full of curiosities and the graves of much-loved dogs. There were no ha-has or grand vistas here, just a small grassy patch where children loved to play on a swing hanging from a whalebone jaw. Bank House was scattered with fascinating objects, packed with books and hung with remarkable paintings and specimens of seaweed, Dawson's earliest botanical interest.

However, there was not much time for play in the Turner household, for the father was a demanding parent, resolved that his children should utilise their talents to the full. Rising as soon as light would permit, they were expected to devote themselves to their drawing and other studies. Art played a major part in Mary's life and that of her family and there was scarcely a moment when they were not occupied with lessons and artistic activities. 'This house is the most agreeable I ever visited. No visit would be unpleasantly long here,' wrote Henry Crabbe Robinson the barrister, in his diary of 26 October 1826.[1] 'The moment breakfast was over,' he reported, 'Mr Turner went to the bank, Mrs Turner to her writing desk, and everyone of the young ladies to drawing or some other tasteful occupation.'

Charles Lyell the geologist, who visited the Bank House aged 20, wrote to his father:

> What I see going on every hour in this family makes me ashamed of the most active day I ever spent ... Mrs Turner has been etching with her daughters in the parlour every morning this week at half past six! Harriet (who was then 11) has as much talent as all the others united, & her knowledge of Latin is astonishing. She has a more perfect conception of Virgil than I had at 14, and earns a shilling at least 3 times a week by doing her Latin composition without a fault, and does all with energy and good will.[2]

There were other visitors, like Sir Frederic Madden the antiquary and paleographer, who found the life rather irksome. 'The young ladies,' he wrote, 'if I am a little late at breakfast sit on thorns and the moment I have sipped the last cup of tea all fly off as if I were a monster.'[3]

48 *Portrait of Mary Turner, by Cotman. (Reproduced by kind permission of the Victoria and Albert Museum.*

Life could never have been easy for Mary, her husband being a demanding taskmaster. He kept his family, and many visitors to the house, metaphorically pinned to their drawing boards, like his botanical specimens on their setting boards, producing illustrations for his lavish volumes.

The master of Bank House had the knack of getting people to acquiesce with his requirements. He kept his future son-in-law, William Hooker, working for him for years until his ambitions to travel the world were whittled away and he admitted defeat. Instead, he stayed and married the eldest daughter, Maria.

Yet both parents were much loved by the children. They were devoted to their mother and numerous letters to their father also bear evidence of the love as well as duty they felt to him. In the preface to a book of letters written by his daughter Harriet, Dawson Turner wrote that he had been 'Blest by the Almighty with a numerous family'.[4]

This is epitomised by an exquisite portrait by Thomas Phillips RA of Mary, together with Dawson and two of her beautiful daughters, when she was in an advanced stage of pregnancy, showing her exuding beauty and tranquillity.

The Artist

In spite of much self-doubt as to her abilities, Mrs Turner was an artist of some talent and her work can still be seen in the National Portrait Gallery. Together with some of her daughters, she took drawing and painting lessons from John Crome, John Sell Cotman and the accomplished portraitist Thomas Phillips. Dawson was patron to both Crome and Cotman. Today 25 of her etchings reside in the National Portrait Gallery, along with two lithographs of Mary herself by Richard James Lane (after Elizabeth Eastlake, née Rigby). When Manuel Canova made his celebrated trip to London, Phillips painted him, and she in turn produced a lithograph of him.

The practice of etching had begun to spread in the 17th century and was very popular in Mary's time as a means of lending flexibility, sensitivity and delicacy to the work. She produced a book of 100 etchings, most of them of well-known figures of the time, such as Charles Burney, the popular and charming brother of Fanny, Dominic Serres and John Hall. These were based upon other artists' work, as was the practice of the day and included delightful portraits of Thomas Phillips' wife and daughters, lifelong friends of the Turner family.

She also made etchings of William John Burchell, explorer and naturalist, 'after Cotman'. Copying was the favoured method of tuition with many artists. Cotman carried with him hundreds of specimens for his student families to work from.

Throughout her marriage, despite many trials and tribulations, she attempted to make good use of her artistic talents, not least to please her husband: 'I go on regularly and slowly with my old St Anthony but he is a tedious fellow with his dignities and formalities.'[5] Even throughout a long illness, she persevered with her work, helped in particular by the engraver W.H.C. Edwards.

Forty-nine copies of the book of a hundred etchings were privately printed. Referring to an etching of W.H.C. Edwards, a note states: 'This plate although begun by Mrs Turner, was finished by Mr Edwards himself … to whose teaching she is principally indebted for whatever success may have attended her in this department of art.'

It was not in Mary's nature to trumpet her own achievements and, like many women of the time, she was overshadowed by her husband's activities and demands. While attempting to run her busy household on oiled wheels, she attended to his whims and wishes while he indulged his intellectual pursuits when not working at the bank.

Dawson Turner, banker and polymath, passionately followed these activities: botany, book collecting, antiquities and autographs, manuscripts, illustrated missals and the acquisition of glorious paintings. He possessed an institution-sized library to which many people came. He was obsessed with collecting, illustrating and recording. Mrs Turner used her considerable talents helping him in this work. Throughout their long marriage her dedication contributed significantly to his output. Together with William Hooker, she dedicated many hours helping to catalogue and illustrate his work on *Fuci*.[6] The illustrations are striking examples of the water-colourist's depictions of flora.

Accompanied by her daughters, she would go trotting in a pony cart around the Norfolk lanes, endlessly pausing to make drawings of churches and writing up lengthy and detailed descriptions. At every possible opportunity, the women of the family were out ranging the county, making topographical sketches for the extra-illustrated copy of Blomefield's *History of Norfolk*. By the time the Turner ladies had completed this work, it comprised, with indices, 56 bound volumes, 11 boxes of deeds and a case of seals. It was ultimately purchased by the British Museum for £460.

In the library at Bank House, the family would have observed books of prints in large number, which prepared them for what they would see on their future travels. Thus the influence of great masters such as Titian, Bellini, Rubens and Cuyp would have made a considerable impression upon them. Already they would be familiar with the collections of the Louvre, galleries at Florence and Naples, the Doge's Palace and the Sistine Chapel as well as many notable cathedrals. In 1814, Dawson bought the magnificent altarpiece *The Madonna and Child Enthroned with Saint Peter and Saint Paul* by Giovanni Bellini (Birmingham Museum & Art Gallery). He acquired a choice collection of paintings by the Norwich school and pictures from Dutch, Flemish and Italian schools. In 1840 he published his collection of paintings in *Outlines in Lithography*.[7]

Mary and her daughters enriched their father's library with sketches, engravings and autograph letters, much of it their own work. The girls transcribed and translated, emblazoned coats of arms, mounted prints and drawings, catalogued and indexed. Life revolved round the library where some project was always going on. All this while the masts of tall ships could be seen just outside the long windows of the drawing room.

In the summer of 1814, Dawson, Mary, Maria, Hooker and Elizabeth, together with Charles Lyell the geologist, left London on Whit Monday, 20 May, bound for a Paris *en fête*, celebrating what was thought to be the end of the war that had torn Europe apart. Eleven years after English travellers had last been allowed to set foot on French soil, they were to leave a prosperous England and see a very different France. Even before they left Dover, the party were sketching furiously so as not to miss the sights. Dawson made side notes in his diary: 'See sketch by Maria,' and 'See sketch by Hooker.' They remained in Paris for a month. He recorded in his diary with some satisfaction that they had 'seen it all'. Back home at Bank House, Mrs Turner's dedication to her art still continued in spite of the many distractions and responsibilities: '19th April 1825 I have been so variously engaged today with perpetual calls for directions to whitewashers, whitesmith masons & [etc.] that I have not done Dr Johnson's head.'[8]

The proliferation of artistic talent in the Turner family was continued down through the generations. Their plant-gathering grandson, Joseph Hooker, was presented to Queen Victoria and Prince Albert on 4 October 1843, the occasion being a visit to see the expansion of the gardens at Kew. The Queen and the Prince both spoke to him and the latter 'begged to see more of his drawings either at Buckingham Palace or at Windsor'.[9]

Travels

It was a time of science, letters and art. After the Napoleonic Wars, travels abroad were once again becoming fashionable for people to enhance their children's education. During such travels the artistic talents of the Turner family were used to record and capture the scenes they discovered. These still exist in their fascinating journals.

Dawson was frequently away from home. He spent much time in London. A member of several distinguished clubs and societies, he enjoyed social gatherings. As a member of the Royal Society, together with his friend Thomas Phillips, he would be acquainted with a circle of people of diverse talents, including Humphrey Davy, Lyell, Byron and Babbage.[10] He also loved to travel abroad, enjoying the cultural sights, collecting works of art and visiting influential people. In his frequent absences he could be secure in the knowledge that his wife would manage everything, including attending to the entertainment of various people whose influence he wished to acquire. He left minutely detailed instructions as to the running of the household and the welfare and education of the numerous children, which she endeavoured to follow to the letter. In 1825 he set off on his 'grand tour', along with Phillips, to explore Italy. Mary wished him well, but her tone was wistful: 'Harpley Sat. June 11th.1825 to Yarmouth: It would be a nice trip to go to Italy, & especially with a man like Phillips.' She hopes that he will take Mary (her daughter Mary Anne) and Harriet for 'it is not in her assuredly the love of rambling, or of variety, but as laudable a curiosity as cd. be found in the best educated of the other sex'. She assures him her own state of health should not prevent them from going.[11] During his absences, she held the family together with the aid of various relations and servants, a perpetual headache for her, for good ones were always hard to procure. She kept the children at their studies and their art and attempted to control the family dogs who also missed their master when he went on his long journeys: 'Don begged for admittance this morng. at my door before I was up and gained it too – I spread for him his Master's dressing gown, havg. tried with his nose, he very complacently took possession of it.'[12]

Mary also felt his absence keenly and wrote him numerous letters, frequently expressing her wifely devotion. He had firmly informed her as to exactly when and where letters should be sent. She tried to be a faithful correspondent, becoming desperately worried and apologetic if she failed: 'I send this letter dear Dawson sooner than you and I had agreed upon.'[13] Family letters, having done the rounds, came home to roost according to his strict instructions and were lovingly and meticulously bound by his wife and daughters. As her husband was away for months at a stretch, she had to endure difficult and lonely times. However, strength often triumphed over timidity and she had her own ideas on what should be done: 'I have assumed the authority of both parents and we get on very well.'[14] Sometimes, naturally enough, Mrs Turner would allow her irritation at her husband's prolonged absences to creep in:

> On Sunday or Monday at farthest I look for yr. return.[15] With regard to the 13th. depend upon it Mr Sparrow does not want you as much as we; and if he did, he has not an equal claim to yr. attention.[16]

And to Fladong's Hotel London, forwarded to Rouen from Great Yarmouth, 'I hope in yr next [letter] to hear the time *absolutely* fixed for yr return.'[17]

At other times she was keenly aware that her letters might have been more of a hindrance than a help: 'I fear my long letters may be more trouble than profit to read pressed as you are.'[18]

> You will come home (I hope) on the Sunday – you can't squeeze out another day? However that's out of the question – I fear you will be worried out of health as well as enjoyment.[19]
>
> I have had so little to tell you of, nothing likely to interest you ... that I doubt you are disappointed in every one you receive.[20]

News of his homecoming was always well received:

> My dear Dawson. I frequently thought of you rolling homewards, as you proceeded on your course, through the night – I am greatly comforted at the thought of your return to the dear children especially the bearer of good news as you were happy enough to be – I know too I had your thoughts on this return of the 16th, & I thank you for the kind wishes you have sent towards me-we all reckon much on tomorrow's post to bring us news of your safe arrival, – Accept my thanks dear Dawson for the satisfaction which the seeing you has given me & us, & believe me to be Yr affectionate wife MT.[21]

But she was not always left behind. In the early days especially, when not borne down by ill health, pregnancy or other family duties, she travelled with her husband at home and abroad. It was an age of uncomfortable travel when you rejoiced to get an inside seat in a carriage and hoped not to have to share it with too many others. Accompanying Dawson on a trip to Wales in 1802, she scaled mountains in her flowing skirts and wrote in her journal: 'After the fatigue of the preceding day we lay in bed till late about 11.'[22] Her charms could not, however, always keep him in bed. He wrote in his diary, 'Before breakfast, I returned to my examination of Mr Davies' herbarium.' For Dawson the botanist, pleasure had to be combined with business and he took with him letters of introduction, enabling visits to various distinguished persons and fine botanical gardens.

Although her opportunities were far less than her husband's, on occasions Mary travelled abroad with the children, leaving him to conduct his affairs at home. These excursions, designed to widen their education, were no holidays. There was continual pressure to produce prolific and detailed records of all they had seen. They sat inside and outside churches, sketching architectural details: Norman doorways, Gothic windows, fonts, screens and pillars, people and street life. The beams on the ancient buildings look so real one feels the need to touch them, as with William Hooker's wonderful illustrations of seaweeds. The whole party painted, sketched, catalogued and bound their work. On returning home their recollections were copied out immaculately and embellished with sketches, news cuttings and delightful watercolour paintings. We can observe these in fascinating journals, which still exist. The travels without her husband gave rise to opportunities for letters home that give us an insight into her journeys abroad. There are descriptions of the people and places from a keenly observant eye that still seem fresh today. From her *Journal of a Tour in France 1814*:[23] 'they [the French] drink *vin de pays* mixed & water. The number of miserable dirty people, particularly women, now about the streets is inconceivable. Most of them have large loose cloaks of materials of all kinds and colours & full of a thousand holes. The old women are … ugly ragged & filthy.'

A trip to France in 1818 is fairly typical of the family's foreign travels and provides insight into the daily rigours of such expeditions. Mary Turner, now aged 44, and the elder girls accompanied by Mr Hooker (now married to Maria) set forth for France. It was a particularly hot summer and drought, which was encountered in both England and France, added to the normal tribulations of such journeys:

Fécamp, 9 June 1818 to her father at Coltishall:[24]

> My dear Father, … safe arrival at Dieppe after a fine passage of 12 hours. I say fair in the sailor's use of the term. Small vessel. London so excessively hot we were unwilling to wait another day.

They had not waited for inside places so suffered a lively journey ('I was never so situated in my life before.'). And later on in France: 'the horses go at their utmost speed … not very tranquillizing to look upon'.

From Yvetot (10 June 1818) to Dawson at Yarmouth when they had climbed, among other exploits, the eminence upon which the castle was situated:

> I thought Eliz wd. have fainted; & had not Mr Hooker got a bottle of wine from the village to refresh the party, we shd. have been quite unfit to hold a pencil.[25] As it was we made but a poor business of one of the grandest objects I ever saw.

On 11 June after the receipt of a letter from Dawson: 'The enervating heat of the weather, the fear that one at least of the objects of this journey will be frustrated, indeed has been so at Fécamp, the extreme difficulty of speaking French, altogether makes me so uneasy, that I can hardly see any comfort before me.'

Mary clearly wished for Dawson's company. 'I begged you in my first letter & in every letter to join us as soon as possible – things wd. not fail to go on better.'[26]

15, 17-18 June 1818, Mary to DT & Maria Hooker on a letter from Hannah Sarah Brightwen:[27] 'You can't imagine how much we wish for and want you especially now that the prospect of Mr Hooker's leaving us is so near.'

However, the presence of *any* men folk in the party was clearly welcome. Elizabeth begs her father to bring with him 'some gentleman or other because there is great need with so large a party of females.

Should you beat up a volunteer you will take especial care that it be a proper one.'

Mary's letters also expressed difficulties in coming to terms with the French people, 'Private lodgings are difficult to obtain so it is likely they will stay on in the same hotel' However, 'tis a house of great resort for the English but we have seen very odd opinions of our countrymen & not very gentlemanly French. M & Md Trimolet are tolerable well mannered, rather cool and indifferent as it appears.'

A letter from Rouen (20 June 1818) to Miss Palgrave, her sister Jane at Coltishall, shows this sojourn to be fairly typical of all they endured in the cause of education and art.[28]

> The curiosity of the people is a great hindrance to our comfortable progress – do what we can there is something about our appearance that bespeaks us foreigners, tho' we gradually conform to the costume of the people here – indeed drawing in public is of itself sufficient to proclaim us animals of a strange class & very disagreeable it is; not thro' their impertinence or insolence but from mere curiosity – one person observes another lookg. earnestly & thinks of course it must be at something very interesting.
>
> The other morning we had no fewer than 38 grown people upon our backs and shoulders without reckoning children. – those who can draw best and quickest, such as Mr H. & Eliz, mind it least; but to me who am embarrassed with my own peculiar difficulties, tis an absolute hindrance.

The weather continued to be oppressive: the sun 'glaring' onto her daughter Mary's drawing paper made her faint so she took to her bed soon after her return.

On one occasion she leaves the children with Mr Hooker and comes back to the hotel, which she much prefers to do: 'for you know there is no drawing by means of the Camera Lucida with a bonnet on'.[29]

But, probably to live up to her husband's expectations, they carried on regardless, going to see a certain church 'should it be in your list of desiderata.' They climb Mont St Catherine and have a lovely view of the town, 'the dirt of the streets being no longer visible'.

They travelled to Havre de Grace: 'a very fine country. For 'twas Dawson's wish that we shd. make this detour in order to see it.'[30]

All the while Mary was very aware of the need to supervise the children and concerned at her own shortcomings as indicated by her writing: ''Tis no endeavour I wd. spare to gratify you in such matters & set a good example to the children,'[31] and 'I find myself, my dear Dawson so at a loss in drawing except for the most simple subjects that I am quite unhappy.'[32]

She also recorded: 'there are certainly dear Dawson so many desirable objects to see & copy in this neighbourhood, that being on all hands so kindly urged by friends here, to which, as it seems, you add your approbation, I am inclined to think I shall prolong my stay – yet I am likewise much drawn homeward – this is a habit of mind I cannot get over'.[33]

The extra burdens of boarding the girls in a convent school are also evident: 'There is very little care taken of keeping the children clean or their clothes tidy.' She has the same problem: 'It is the greatest trouble possible to get linen out of the washerwoman's hands – she has had ours now a fortnight.' Additionally, 'they have ruined their silk frocks with ink as well as dirt' so will dear Dawson 'attempt to get new gingham ones made and bring them with him.[34]

Struggling to feel independent, when she travelled without her husband she stayed in less than salubrious conditions to save money, leaving vivid accounts of her thoughts on the matter: 'People who are rash enough, however, to leave their secure and commodious home ought not to be alarmed at little difficulties, or shocked at trifles; I am an old traveller besides.'[35]

Yet she gained in strength as she went, penning lively and very detailed commentaries. Disappointed at not being able to find lodgings 'in a respectable family of a reputable class – such never admit strangers at Rouen', she had instead to dine at the hotel (Hotel de Normandie) but 'shall decline dining at the Table d' Hote – to our ideas it does not look quite well for three ladies to intermix among strangers ... This is a hindrance to our mixing in French society as we had hoped to do in a respectable private house, & frustrated one main object of coming hither.'[36]

She had little time for the English 'who are flocking to the continent to get rid of their money and their ennui ... chattering away carelessly in their bad French'. Her impressions of French urban life were equally disparaging: 'The town of Rouen besides is very ugly, dirty and stinking ... There is not a single thing in Rouen made by human hands that is not disgraceful and disgusting ... 'tis altogether discreditable to a polished people who ought to possess good taste and delicacy enough to alter these things.'[37]At such times she welcomed the arrival of her friends, Thomas Phillips and Cotman. She would find support from other members of the family when Dawson was too preoccupied with his own affairs to join her. 'We are now about to part with Mr Hooker who has been a most kind brother and son,' she wrote to her sister Jane from Rouen on 20 June 1818, 'but the near prospect of Mr Hooker's leaving us, I believe, in some degree, affected my mind. I do not in general trouble myself much about what can't be helped, & I shall get on pretty well I don't doubt; but let them who stay at home congratulate themselves on a freedom from care, anxiety and extreme fatigue to which those who leave a quiet home are subject.'[38]

Throughout this expedition there remained the heat. She writes, 'The French have not known such heat for twenty years.'[39]

The whole *hot* trip seems to be torture, attempting to please her husband, coping with accommodation arrangements and desperately uncomfortable modes of travel, trying to be talented at drawing, grappling with the camera lucida, supervising the children, including the torment of placing them in a convent, coping with the French, the fleas, the food and above all the money. The impression seems to be one more of endurance than of pleasure.

* * *

Between trips abroad, London still played a significant part in Turner family life.

Dawson Turner consorted with some of the leading artists of the day, visiting exhibitions and collecting a vast number of catalogues. As the children grew, they became more involved with their father's engagements in the city. Trips to enrich their art education were considered essential and occasionally their mother accompanied them: London, June 1819.'I left Eliz with Mrs Phillips & accompanied the Lyells to Lord Grosvenor's, & saw the pictures … I remained an hour and 10 minutes with the watch in my hand.'[40]

As their daughters married and spread their wings, their resettling in London and Edinburgh gave both parents the opportunity to see more of lively and fashionable society. Staying at the Hookers' smart house near the Thames made a change for Dawson from one of his various clubs or *Fladong's Hotel*, a watering hole better known for its being frequented by sailors than wives of the genteel. Mary has left us lively accounts of visits to music halls and shopping arcades in the vibrant city of the time.

* * *

In 1833 foreign travels were resumed with a Talbot steam packet to Ostend, the party consisting of Sir Francis Palgrave, Elizabeth, Mary and the two Misses Rickman.[41]

There were looking glasses outside the windows so that people could see without putting their heads out. This Rhenish tour, with Mary now aged 59, seemed somewhat reminiscent of her earlier ventures in that there was much art and history to observe, but also the heat of August at Ghent to be endured. Her views on 'modern art' are aired. At Antwerp, she finds a picture by the alcoholic artist Frank Floris, *Fall of the Rebel Angels*, kept behind a curtain 'lest it should frighten the children'. She comments that this, like most other pictures of the time, is 'debased by absurdity bordering on the burlesque'.[42]

As she grew older, in poorer health, the difficulties of foreign travel seemed too much to cope with, and her husband would travel more and more without her. As mentioned some years before, she felt her inadequacies keenly: 'I should join with those who congratulate you on yr. successful accomplishment of many things, rather than echo your lamentation at having done so little. At least my powers are never commensurate with your endeavours & inclinations & I suppose you do more by yrself than with me to drag forward.'[43]

But the wandering husband on his travels did not forget his wife and family. Throughout their lives, whenever he was away, correspondence winged its way back to England with some frequency, containing many references to his concern for their health and well-being and his missing them all. His letters, while conveying his excitement at the sights, also revealed his affection for and appreciation of his wife. On 8 September 1825, at the foot of the Jura, he wrote of 'the grandeur of the mountains' and the 'dazzling silvery whiteness of Mont Blanc',

> The wonders which I have seen or am likely to see have not at all diminished my wish to be at home again ... Oh if I wished for you then, I have done so till now ... Could you but come to me without that detestable passage through France how glad I should be. Could I but be again at home how much more glad.[44]

In London without her, he still found time in his crowded life to write to his wife at least once a day. Letters were sandwiched between trips to galleries with friends, complicated and arduous travel arrangements and sociable meals with colleagues and acquaintances. And Mary would respond in kind:

> Harpley May 28 1823
>
> My dear Dawson, We were made very happy yesterday by the receipt of yr. letter & by hearing of your safe arrival – I hope that the hurry & worry then experienced have left no unpleasant effects upon you, & that you are sufficiently recovered to enter with enjoyment upon the various exciting objects of a London campaign.[45]

Tragedy and difficulties

Amid the travels and the artistic life at Bank House, times could be hard for the Turners. Tragedy struck on more than one occasion. It was a time of long nightgowns and open fires. Many children died as a result and the Turner family did not escape. Mary desperately mourned the loss of her little son in 1806, aged only four, as did the devoted father. 'My poor dear Dawson' (his namesake) he wrote in his diary, above four anguished lines.

His wife also wrote: 'Oh dear Dawson that our late great misfortune may bring us nearer to God! We shall not fail in our duty or affection to each other nor in which I most fear my failure, regard & kindness to Harriet Mitchell – your love & solicitude have been very apparent in this late trying affliction.'[46]

Harriet Mitchell was a family servant of long-standing and looking after the child at the time of the accident.

> Mary had gone to her parents' house at Coltishall and corresponded with her husband, who was at home with the remaining children: I long to be back again with you tho' that house I fear will never be so wholly comfortable as I could wish home to be. It seems to me as if I could never love it again. However your society will do much I know, for there is no one else that I have such a confidence in & such a respect for, nor anyone that can enter into my feelings as you, an unhappy sharer of them can.

Such anguished messages are a reminder of how close the couple could be.

Another baby, Dawson, was born and died in 1809. She wrote to her husband on his loss:

> Dear Dawson, John will have informed you before you read this of the heavy affliction that has befallen us – you will feel enough for yr. own share as a parent to the dr. innocent, but do not let yr. grief be augmented by any thought of me – I trust it is a wholesome affliction to us & if it can awaken in us a livelier sense of the duty we owe each other & the dear children that are left to us he will have been taken from us in mercy – as merciful & wise & good I assuredly esteem it.
>
> Be assured I am with sympathy, esteem & love
> yr. affectionate wife MT.[47]

Next a daughter Katherine lived less than a year. In all they had had 11 children of whom eight survived.[48]

Worries about money

Times were often hard in other ways, too. Money was always an issue for the family. Throughout their marriage Dawson had lavished large sums on his collections. His dealings with the bank had sometimes been problematical. He admitted that he had overstretched himself. He wrote to a friend in 1831: 'Not only have I with my books invaded every closet in every room but, in this library ... all the chairs but three are covered with books: the same is the case with the sofa, the same with the four tables and window seats and then on the floor, I have sixty volumes which have been there for months and for which I have no place whatever.'[49] In 1849 he wrote, 'I had very unwisely expended more than £20,000,'[50] on the library.

He did at times keep a close eye on family finances. A detailed economic account of travels can be seen in his Welsh journal.[51] Each section of the journey was minutely accounted, including such items as 'postillion', 'letters' and 'blotting paper'.

For Mary, the cost of things on a daily basis was a perpetual headache.On 27 May 1809 she wrote from Yarmouth to Bedford Coffee House, London:

'If you buy anything for me, for I fear you will … I do not wish, indeed I shd. be sorry you shd. throw away yr. money for superfluities.'[52]

When travelling without him, she lived in fear and dread of overspending. She felt she could only justify the expense if she was achieving 'good' art but she had little faith in her own ability. Even before they have embarked for France in 1818 her doubts are very close to the surface. From the *Spread Eagle* at Midhurst on 4 June she wrote to her husband at Yarmouth,

> This opportunity which you have thrown in our way. You will not I trust think that I make idle or false causes for business left undone thro' indolence or negligence – I can truly say that I have attempted more than I have been equal to … You are about to incur a very heavy expense & I feel confident that you will be disappointed in yr. expectation of advantage from it.[53]

And on the other side of the Channel she wrote: 'Rouen June 11th: This is a very elegant Hotel …but we do not occupy the better parts because of the expense.'

She had been recommended apartments for the party at a boarding school. 'You must not think that we are over fastidious … but it won't do at all,' was her comment on their accommodation being approached along dirty, stinking passages, and added, 'Everything is uncomfortable and unpromising looking.' To get to their tiny rooms they would have traversed rooms packed with children (and fleas). She concluded, 'So I am afraid we shall have to continue here & there is no particular objection except as to the expense.'[54]

On 1 July she wrote: 'Yesterday the dear children left us and I asked Mr Hooker to ask for the bill since we gave up one chamber.' She lists the prices in great detail and has 'kept the girls on two meals a day telling them no one eats more in France'.[55]

She protests that she would love to do more 'for we are here at great expense and I feel that the whole responsibility lies on me for Mr H. is very indulgent as you know'.

Mary's letters to Dawson Turner continued at Rouen, on Saturday 4 July 1818: 'I hope you [Dawson] will have had patience with me – I may say it now when no longer sensible to the same disappointment, that the mortification of finding little done, & health & money wasted made me very wretched indeed.'[56] She once again labours the point that she has these concerns. In a long and almost despairing passage she reiterates her concern over his wasting money on her. She has to compromise her usual standards in order to save funds, expressing her horror at dirty strawberries and the French lack of manners. She writes to her sister Jane:

> Rouen, July 24th 1818, the fleas here as with you for they abound in France. J.M. Hooker says more still in Italy. Tis for that reason I suppose that the

> chamber floors are laid with pavements of hexagonal form for the … sake I suppose they are layered over with a composition resembling the … floors of the library at Holkham. This makes the chambers cool; and you could imagine it were agreeable to march about … on going to bed; but no the floors are too dirty to admit of this, unless you give your feet a second washing immediately before stepping into bed.[57]

She tells Dawson on his way to join them, to 'stay at Delarius' house where the charges are very reasonable' and 'nothing additional for Fanny who lives in the kitchen'.[58]

A postscript to one of her letters to him reads: 'I took £50 on the 1st July. This is the third £50 we have had since our arrival in Rouen. I pay our Hotel bill weekly – the journey to St. Georges etc. was not dear; for the carriage 50fr. & our other expenses 35fr.4 which was not much for 4 people – I do not include the postillion, whose expenses and horses were all included in 24fr. per day.'[59]

There are many references to the cost of things in Mary's letters. Money clearly was an object for the Turner family.

> London July 17th 1823 Sent to North Yarmouth
>
> My dear Dawson, this letter will reach you on your birthday & I beg you will receive my sincere wishes for your health & prosperity during many succeeding years – I say prosperity 'tho the events of the last 5 & the present gloomy prospect may well render the fulfillment of that wish doubtful yet there are other modes of prosperity than by getting money, & these I heartily wish you.'[60]

Old Age

In old age, Mary found life exceedingly difficult. Persistent illness, money worries and family concerns had taken their toll. She became less able to accompany Dawson on his travels. Although not robust himself, he persisted in his desire for adventure. As he made plans to travel with some of the children but clearly not her, she assured him that her own state of health should not prevent their going. He travelled more and more frequently without her, sending her sketchy and self-obsessed letters, swiftly scrawled and barely legible. Although there were times when he keenly expressed his absence, these tender sentiments were soon superseded by absorption in the sights he had seen.

Mary remained at Bank House, seeing less and less of her family. Only one daughter, Mary Anne, remained unmarried and took over the running of the household as her mother grew older and in poorer health. After a lifetime's devotion to her large family she felt redundant and inadequate.

Towards the end of her life, Dawson's funds had been endlessly drained. His involvement with a brewery and the purchase of expensive collections had left the family in a state of penury. He had been forbidden involvement in any dealings with the bank. Mary had to make do and mend, writing letters on scraps from those of other people, scrimping, darning and repairing clothes. A year before she died she wrote to her daughter Hannah, 'I have not, not even a penny, *"dans mon poche"*.'[61]

In spite of her own difficulties, she still showed practical care and compassion for the poor, and was supportive of her husband to the end. Deeply religious, she had taken to heart all sentiments contained in the word 'obey.' From her constant bible reading she had absorbed the injunction: 'To be discreet, chaste, keepers at home, good, obedient to their own husbands that the word of God be not blasphemed.'

A letter from Elizabeth to Tom Brightwen, her brother-in-law, after her mother's death, mentions her 'deep humility ... her constant preference for the lowest place' and 'her habitual self-denial. ... Through many years of failing health, to the very close of life, she would only have the plainest fare, nor did she taste of more than one dish even when sinking in strength.'[62]

There remains a poignant account of how, on her death-bed, she attempted to return to her husband their wedding ring. Her daughter Mary Anne relates that she had 'reached out with the most decided action to my father ... she had drawn off her wedding ring in the night in order to return it to my father upon their wedding day, the completion of 54 years of married life.'[63] But the ring had slipped from her hand into the bed. Despite extensive and frantic searches of the bedding, the 'little thin circlet' was never found.

Despite the hardship she had endured, at her death, Bank House was still home to a large collection of valuable works of art. On 22 March 1850, Dawson wrote from Yarmouth to Charles Konig at the British Museum:

> Exceedingly kind do I feel it in you to have so promptly sent me yr. affectionate condolences in my present bereavement and very heartily do I thank you for it. In cases like this every fibre of the heart is necessarily open; and the assurance of the sympathy of a friend is a precious balm.
>
> With me the desolation cannot be but great: she whom I have lost has been the partner of my life for 54 years and had most cheerfully entered into all my pleasures and pains & pursuits, so that, turn where I will, I find a vacuum & a void never to be filled; for it is idle for a man of 74 to think of forming new connexions or acquaintances or friendships, or of engaging in new studies, or of diverting his mind by new subjects ... It is quite true as you justly observe, that I ought to have been prepared for my poor wife's death; but I really never could anticipate the disruption of an union which has existed so long; and even now I can scarcely believe her really dead; seeing her, as I do, altogether unchanged after six days, and still with the same tranquil countenance & the same lovely expression which you and I knew 40 years ago.

> But my grief is quite selfish: I am happy in the assurance that she is safe in the bosom of her Maker, after a life spent in the uniform practice of every virtue.[64]

After her death Dawson's extensive collections were dispersed in two Sotheby's sales lasting 21 days.

Mary Turner, self-effacing and dedicated to her husband and family, is perhaps less recognised than she deserves to be. A year after her death he remarried. The scandal divided the family, and eventually he and Mary were buried far apart. Dawson lies beneath a 'pyramid' in Brompton Cemetery. Of her burial place in Yarmouth, there remains no trace. Thus parted after death, Dawson, in spite of his drive and determination, without her sacrifices and dedication, would not in life have been able to achieve so much.

WENDY KETT

Travels and Tours from which material has been gathered:

1802 Tour of Wales MT & DT
1814 Paris, France MT & DT
1818 Normandy MT and elder children later joined by DT
1819 Normandy DT and elder children later joined by MT
1825 Italy DT partly with Phillips
1833 Ostend DT, Elizabeth & Francis Palgrave
1833 Rhenish Tour DT & MT and family members
1836 Rhenish Tour DT & MT and two daughters
1848 Antwerp DT

Acknowledgements

The author wishes to thank the following for the provision of original manuscripts and help in researching this work: C.P. Barker, C.N. Goodman, Mr & Mrs G. Barker, D. McKitterick, J. Smith, Wren Library, Trinity College, Cambridge; Dr A Moore, Miss. N. Watt, Castle Museum, Norwich; the staff at Norfolk Record Office, Norwich.

Notes

Chapter 1: Introduction

1 Sadler, Dr T. *Diary*, vol. 2 (1869), pp.365-9.
2 Inglis Palgrave, R.H., in *Annals of an East Anglian Bank*, Bidwell W.H. (1900), p.294.
3 Kitson, Sydney D., *Life and Letters of John Sell Cotman* (1937), p.162.
4 Lyell, Sir Charles, *Life and Journals* (1881), p.42.
5 Haydon, Benjamin Robert, *Diary*, ed Pope.
6 Norwich Public Library Ms 5287 (7).
7 I am indebted to John Heath for this example of Dawson Turner's friendship.
8 Munby, A.N.L., *The Cult of the Autograph Letter* (1962).
9 Goulburn, E.M., *John William Burgon* (1892), p.68.

Chapter 2: Dawson Turner: Art Patron, Connoisseur and Collector

1 MS letter, WG to DT, 4 May 1821, Trinity College Library.
2 MS letter, Norfolk Record Office.
3 *Outlines in Lithography* (1840), p.14.
4 Mary Anne and Harriet Turner, after John Sell Cotman, *Drawings of Architecture and Scenery in Normandy, 1822, fifty one drawings in a volume*, Sotheby's 11 July 1985.
5 Quoted in Rajnai, M. (ed), *John Sell Cotman 1782-1842*, Arts Council (1982), p.21 ('Cotman and his patrons' by M. Pidgeley, no reference given).
6 Kitson, S.D., *The Life of John Sell Cotman*, London (1937), p.176.
7 J.S. Cotman to D.T., 3 September 1841, quoted in Hemingway, A., *Cotman's 'Architectural Antiquities of Normandy': some amendments to Kitson's Account, Walpole Society*, XCVI (1978), p.179.
8 J.S. Cotman to DT, 3 September 1841, Norfolk Record Office.
9 Exhibited Royal Academy 1815 (16).
10 Quoted in Miller, C., *Thomas Phillips RA FRS FSA, Portrait Painter*, MA Report, Courtauld Institute, May 1977, p.44.
11 *Outlines in Lithography* (1840), p.55.
12 Ibid.
13 Exhibited Royal Academy, London 1825 (292).
14 See below.
15 Druery, J.H., *Historical and Topographical Notices of Great Yarmouth*, London (1826).
16 MS letter, Phillips to DT, 25 June 1815, Trinity College Library.
17 MS letter, Delahante to DT, 4 August 1814, Trinity College Library.
18 MS letter, Phillips to DT, 10 July 1815, Trinity College Library.
19 MS letter, Phillips to DT, 28 January 1826, Trinity College Library.
20 Pope, W.B., *The Diary of Benjamin Robert Haydon*, 5 vols, entry for August 1817.
21 *Outlines* (1840), p.28.
22 Norwich Castle Museum & Art Gallery, Art Department, has Dawson Turner's MS Journal of his 1814 trip to Normandy in the company of his wife Mary and two daughters, Charles Lyell and William Hooker. They set off from London to Canterbury on 30 May 1814, returning to Yarmouth on the evening of Wednesday 6 July, in time to see the Yarmouth illuminations celebrating peace.

23 Turner, Dawson, *Journal of a three week tour, with Thos. Phillips Esq. R.A. from London, through Rouen, Vernon, & Montes to Paris, in the Autumn of 1815*, introduction. MS. Christopher Barker Collection.
24 *Ibid.*, p.11. It was at Dieppe that Turner received his passport, erroneously filled out for Monsieur Danton Turner. There he is described as aged 39, 1.72 metres tall, with brown hair, a high forehead, brown eyebrows and chestnut brown eyes, a turned up nose, a large mouth, a brown beard and a square chin, set within an oval, florid (*coloré*) face. MS. Christopher Barker Collection, inserted in 1815 Journal.
25 *Ibid.*, pp.32-3.
26 *Ibid.* p.34.
27 *Ibid.*, p.38.
28 *Ibid.*, pp.41-2.
29 *Ibid.* p.50.
30 *Ibid.*, p.53; The Holkham painting is now in New York, Metropolitan Museum, no.36.29.
31 *Ibid.*, p.64.
32 See *Outlines* (1840), pp.234 for his assessment of local collections.
33 Christopher Barker Collection; lodged with Trinity College Library. This was inserted in a copy of the sale catalogue for Turner's Library. Thanks go to David McKitterick.
34 *Catalogue of the valuable collection of Pictures by Italian, Flemish, French, Dutch, and English masters; The property of the well-known Collector, Dawson Turner, Esq., F.R.S. and removed from Great Yarmouth: which will be sold by auction, by Messrs. Christie & Manson, at their Great Room, 8, King Street, St. James's Square, on Friday, May 14, 1852, lots 1-79.*
35 An MS note records of the valuation of £5 for the *Titian & Mistress* attributed to Padovanino: 'so says Murch 1819'.
36 See below ref. acquisition of Homfray's paintings.
37 Goodman, Alexandra, *Dawson Turner: Patron and Collector. A study of his debt to Thomas Phillips*, Dissertation, Trinity College, Cambridge, April 1990, p.55.
38 Kitson, S.D., *The Life of John Sell Cotman*, London (1937), p.204.
39 MS letter, JH to DT, 31 August 1811, Trinity College Library.
40 MS letter, JH to DT 29 September 1811, Trinity College Library.
41 *Outlines* (1840), pp.5-6.
42 *Ibid.*, pp.13-26.
43 *Ibid.*, pp.55-8.
44 Turner, Dawson, MS, *Journal of a Tour in France, 1815-16*, Woodward family and Arley Gift, Norwich Castle Museum (1970); a second account is in the Christopher Barker Collection, see note 2 above.
45 *Outlines* (1840), pp.87-90.
46 *Ibid.*, pp.83-4.
47 *Ibid.*, pp.53-4, now private collection.
48 *Ibid.*, pp.63-4.
49 *Ibid.*, pp.75-6.
50 *Ibid.*, pp.39-40, now Foundation E.G. Bührle Collection, Zurich.
51 *Ibid.*, pp.85-6.
52 *Ibid.*, pp.69-70, now Wallace Collection, London.
53 *Ibid.*, pp.3-4.
54 *Ibid.*, pp.29-30.
55 *Ibid.*, pp.27-8.
56 *Ibid.*, pp.65-6; now Yale Centre for British Art, Paul Mellon Collection.
57 *Ibid.*, pp.11-2.
58 *Ibid.*, p.71.
59 Now Isabella Stewart Gardner Museum, Boston.
60 *Outlines* (1840), pp.1-2; now Birmingham Museums & Art Gallery (1977), P.227.
61 *Remarks upon the Pictures in this Volume, by Artists, Connoisseurs, & Picture Dealers, in their own words*, MS 28 pp. (inserted in a bound volume of the *Outlines*), Family Collection. The other visitors recorded, some of whom are local to Norfolk, are Henry Barlow; Mr Brown; Mr R. Buttery of Manchester; J. Douce; W.G. Edwards; Rev G. Elwin; the Rev J. Forster; Mr Farrer; Mrs Holmes; Mr Isaacs; Mr Mawson; Anthony Merry (1755-1835), former ambassador to Sweden and America; Rev N. Nicholls; Viscountess Weymouth; Mr Wiggers; William Woodburn; Mr Yates.
62 Beechey's opinions were recorded on 5 July and 15 September 1824, 8 and 28 June 1837.
63 Poussin's brother Claude Lorraine Richard Wilson Nursey (1820-73) became Headmaster of the Norwich School of Practical Art, 1854-9.

64 13 November 1837.
65 It is not clear in the MS that this opinion was actually given at Bank House.
66 5 April 1841; also 9 April 1841, when he commented of Turner's *Christ Among the Doctors*: 'Certainly Ferrarese.'
67 7 July 1842.
68 Waagen, G., *Treasures of Art in Great Britain, Being an Account of the Chief Collections of Paintings, Drawings, Sculptures, illuminated MSS, &c., &c.* London, John Murray (1854) (supplement 1857).
69 *Ibid.* (1854), letter xxxii, pp.437-8.
70 Exhibited Royal Academy 1825; Christopher Barker Collection.
71 Waagen saw also the hand of Ludovico Caracci in this work.
72 *Norwich Mercury*, 31 October 1829.
73 A coloured drawing of the drawing room at Bank House was enclosed with Harriet Brightwen's letter to Dawson Turner of 7 March 1835, Trinity College Library. Another letter, from John Burgon, included a drawing of the interior of the library at Bank House, JB to DT 19 April 1838, letter now missing.
74 Christopher Barker Collection.
75 *Outlines* (1840), p.96.

Chapter 3: Nature's Treasures: Dawson Turner's Botanical Collections

1 Turner left London on 30 May 1814 (Turner, D., *Journal of a Tour to France*, MS, 2 vols (1814), acc. no. NWHCM: 1970.483.11, Norwich Castle Museum & Art Gallery). In the event, the peace was interrupted when Napoleon escaped from Elba and returned to France in March 1815 until his defeat at Waterloo in June of that year.
2 Turner to Ellen Hutchins, 24 July 1814, Archives of the Royal Botanic Gardens, Kew (hereafter RBGK). For the gathering of natural history collections in Paris by the Jacobins during the Revolution, and the moral and social improvement that was believed to result from displaying them to the public, see Spary, E., *Utopia's Garden: French Natural History from Old Regime to Revolution* (2000), pp.227-35.
3 Journal (*op. cit.*, n.1), vol. 2 (1814) p.190.
4 Pearce, S.M., *On Collecting: An Investigation into Collecting in the European Tradition* (1995), p.256.
5 Turner to Hutchins, 19 April 1808, RBGK.
6 Turner, D. and Dillwyn, L.W., *Botanist's Guide*, 2 vols, vol. 1 (1805) p.i.
7 Walford, T., *The Scientific Tourist through England, Wales, & Scotland*, 2 vols, vol. 1 (1818) pp.i, vi.
8 Turner showed his appreciation of Wigg by naming a rare marine plant *Fucus Wiggii* in 'Description of Four New Species of Lichens', *Transactions of the Linnean Society of London*, vol. 6 (1802), pp.125-36, and also by appointing him a clerk in the bank of Gurney and Turner in 1802. Although the position was subordinate and poorly paid, it did, however, secure Wigg's future and he remained in the job until his death in 1828 at the age of seventy-nine. See Glasspoole, H.G., 'A Memoir of Mr Lilly Wigg', *Transactions of the Norfolk and Norwich Naturalists' Society*, vol. 2 (1874-9), pp.269-74.
9 Turner, D., *Synopsis of the British Fuci* (1802), p.ix.
10 Goodenough to William Withering, 1 May 1796, Royal Society of Medicine, MSS 534, fols. 171-2.
11 Turner, D., 'Remarks upon some parts of the Hedwigian system of mosses, with a monograph of the genus Bartramia,' *Annals of Botany* vol. 1 (1805), p.517. Turner's claim that his opinions were based on personal experience was also borne out by the fact that he had travelled to Ireland to collect materials for his *Muscologiae Hibernicae Spicilegium* (1804).
12 Hooker to Turner, 24 April 1808, WJH/2/1, Letters from Sir William Hooker, 28 December 1805-11 December 1832 fols. 35-36, RBGK. Hooker drew 234 of the 258 figures in Turner's work. Turner himself produced only one.
13 Turner to Hutchins, 12 Nov 1809, RBGK.* Hutchins' drawings were used for six of the plates in Turner's work.
14 For the way in which these correspondence networks functioned in order to make such participation possible, see Secord, A., 'Corresponding interests: artisans and gentlemen in nineteenth-century natural history,' *British Journal for the History of Science*, vol. 27 (1994), pp.383-408.
15 Sowerby, J. and Smith, J.E., *English Botany; or, Coloured Figures of British Plants, with their*

Essential Characters, Synonyms, and Places of Growth (1790-1814), vol. 36, p.v.

16 Price, J.H., 'Bibliographic notes on works concerning the Algae V. A note on aspects of the *Fuci* ... (Dawson Turner, 1807-1819),' *Archives of Natural History*, vol. 11 (1984), pp.440-2. Turner's monograph, *Fuci, sive Plantarum Fucorum Generi a Botanicis adscriptarum Icones, Descriptiones et Historia* or *Fuci, or Coloured Figures and descriptions of the Plants referred by Botanists to the Genus Fucus* (hereafter *Fuci*) included descriptions in both Latin and English.

17 L.W. Dillwyn to Turner, 1 February 1814, Trinity College, Cambridge (hereafter TCC).

18 Journal (*op. cit.*, n. 1), vol.2 (1814), p.264.

19 Dillwyn to Turner, 13 August 1814, TCC.

20 Lyell to Turner, 10 January 1814, TCC. The Bourbons briefly regained the French throne with the restoration of Louis XVIII a few months later.

21 Hooker to Turner, 14 October 1815, WJH/2/1, Letters from Sir William Hooker, 28 December 1805-11 December 1832, fols. 200-201, RBGK. Hooker and Maria Turner were married on 12 June 1815.

22 *Journal of a Tour to France in 1815*, pp.78-80 (privately owned). With respect to the shells, Turner added that the French, keen 'to preserve every thing that is unique' had 'just completed a negotiation to this effect, giving in exchange their own duplicates'.

23 *Ibid.*, p.79. The Prussian occupation is discussed in Mansel, P., *Paris between Empires 1814-1852* (2001), pp.84-93.

24 *Journal* 1815 (*op. cit.*, n.22), p.85. One volume of Humboldt and Aimé Bonpland's *Voyage aux Régions Equinoxiales du Nouveau Continent* had been published in 1814; the second eventually appeared in 1819 from a different publisher, and yet another publisher produced the third and final volume in 1825.

25 Turner to Hutchins, 25 March 1811, RBGK.*

26 Samuel Goodenough to J.E. Smith, 7 February 1814, quoted in Price, J.H., 'Publication in parts: a background to the concept, efficacy and taxonomic complexity,' *Archives of Natural History* vol. 10 (1982), p.449. Goodenough makes reference to specimens provided by Joseph Banks, Amelia Griffiths, Elizabeth Hill, and Ellen Hutchins.

27 Draft letter from James Sowerby to Hugh Davies, *c.*September 1814, and Davies to Sowerby, 8 October 1814, quoted in Price (*op. cit.*, n. 26), pp.449-50.

28 J.E. Smith to Samuel Goodenough, 1 December 1812, quoted in Price (*op. cit.*, n. 26), p.449.

29 The quotations derive from the history of Borrer and Turner's collaboration as charted in extracts from their correspondence in Hawksworth, D.L. and Seaward M.R.D., 'New Introduction' (1978) to *Specimen of a Lichenographia Britannica* by Turner, D., and Borrer, W., a reprint of the page proofs produced between 1809 and 1814 that were published by Turner in 1839, to Borrer's horror.

30 Lyell to Turner, 31 July 1815, TCC.

31 For Roscoe's difficulties, see his letter to Turner, 16 March 1816, TCC. See Edmondson, J., *A Growing Concern: William Roscoe and Liverpool's First Botanical Garden* (2005), p.10, for the fate of some of the botanical works from Roscoe's library. For the financial and social standing of bankers, and for the vicissitudes in banking in the early 19th century, see Hilton, B., *A Mad, Bad, & Dangerous People? England 1783-1846* (2006), pp.129, 152-6.

32 *Fuci* vol.1 (1808), p.14.

33 Turner, D., *Synopsis of the British Fuci* (1802), p.xvi.

34 *Ibid.*, p.xv.

35 *Ibid.*, p.xxix (quoting from Goodenough, S. and Woodward, T.J., 'Observations on the British Fuci, with Particular Descriptions of each Species,' *Transactions of the Linnean Society*, vol.3 (1797), pp.84-235), and p.xxii. For the extreme variability of seaweeds, see *Fuci*, vol.3 (1811), p46, p122.

36 *Fuci*, vol.1 (1808), p.102.

37 Turner to Hutchins, 28 April 1808, RBGK.*

38 *Fuci*, vol.3 (1811), p.4.

39 Turner to Hutchins, 17 October 1810, RBGK.

40 Hutchins to Turner, 9 November 1810, TCC.

41 Hutchins to Turner, 7 December [1812], TCC.

42 Brown to Turner, 24 November 1815, TCC.

43 *Fuci*, vol.4 (1819), p.4.

44 *Journal* (1815) (*op. cit.*, n. 22), p.79. Lamouroux's *Essai sur les Genres de la Famille des Thalassiophytes Inarticulés* of 1813 proposed some of the groups still recognised in modern classifications. Lamouroux was the first to claim that these algae possessed two types of reproductive organs, whereas Turner believed that the two types corresponded to different stages of the

same organ. For the history of ideas concerning reproduction in the cryptogams, and the later 19th-century elucidation of their complex life cycles in terms of the alternation of generations, see Farley, J., *Gametes & Spores: Ideas about Sexual Reproduction 1750-1914* (1982).

45 *Fuci*, vol.4 (1819), Advertisment.

46 *Ibid.*, p.120.

47 *Ibid.*, Advertisment.

48 Murray, G., *An Introduction to the Study of Seaweeds*, p.2 (1895); Berkeley, M.J., *Introduction to Cryptogamic Botany* (1857), p.177.

49 Brewster D. (ed.), *The Edinburgh Encyclopaedia*, 18 vols (1830), vol.10, pp.2-3. Although the volume bears a publication date of 1830, the article by Patrick Neill was written in 1815.

50 Lyell writing to Turner, 13 Dec 1815, TCC, asked 'Who ever examines a Moss that wd. not prefer a Latin description? Neatness, perspicuity & brevity give it the advantage over English.' For the pleasure generated by the plates in works like Turner's *Fuci*, and the high cost of both producing and purchasing such books, see Secord, A., 'Botany on a Plate: Pleasure and the Power of Pictures in Promoting Early Nineteenth-Century Scientific Knowledge,' *Isis* vol. 93 (2002), pp.28-57, especially n. 15. When completed, *Fuci* cost £21, or £36 for the large paper edition.

51 Turner to James de Carle Sowerby, 30 January 1816, quoted in Price (*op. cit.* n. 26), p.446.

52 Dawson, W.R., 'Sir Joseph Hooker and Dawson Turner,' *Journal of the Society for the Bibliography of Natural History*, vol. 2 (1950), p.219 n. Many of these portraits were made by Turner's wife Mary, as the eminent French botanist Augustin-Pyramus de Candolle recorded (Hooker, J.D., *A Sketch of the Life and Labours of Sir William Jackson Hooker* (1903), p.xxiv).

53 Dawson, W.R., 'Dawson Turner, F.R.S. (1775-1858),' *Journal for the Society for the Bibliography of Natural History*, vol.3 (1958), p.306; Mabberley, D.J., *Jupiter Botanicus: Robert Brown of the British Museum* (1985), p.274. Turner revealed his opinion of Banks's character when describing Alexander von Humboldt in his *Journal* (1815) (*op. cit.*, n. 22), p.84. Turner's transcriptions of Banks's correspondence are now in the Natural History Museum, London. In 1835 Turner did publish *Extracts from the Literary and Scientific Correspondence of Richard Richardson*, showing, as David McKitterick argues in this volume, the emphasis he placed on correspondence for historical understanding.

54 Gascoigne, J., *Joseph Banks and the English Enlightenment: Useful Knowledge and Polite Culture* (1994), pp.10-19; Carter, H.B., *Sir Joseph Banks 1743-1820* (1988), pp.536-46.

55 *Fuci*, vol.1 (1808), p.2.

56 *Fuci*, vol.2 (1809), p.2.

57 Borrer to Turner, 21 July 1808, WJH/2/1, Letters from Sir William Hooker, 28 December 1805-11 December 1832, fols. 43-44, RBGK.

58 Samuel Goodenough to J.E. Smith, 19 January 1807, quoted in Price (*op. cit.* n. 26), p.448.

59 Pope, W.B. (ed.), *The Diary of Benjamin Haydon*, 5 vols (1960-2), vol. 2, p.127.

60 *Fuci*, vol.2 (1809), p.88. Daniel Matthias Heinrich Mohr (1780-1808), professor at Keil, with Friedrich Weber, had proposed a subdivision of the genus *Fucus* in their *Beiträge zur Naturkunde*, published in parts between 1805 and 1810.

61 Turner to Brown, 24 November 1808, British Library Add MSS 32439, fols. 272-3; Turner to Hutchins, 13 November 1808, RBGK.

62 Dalton to Turner, 6 December 1808, TCC.

63 Smith, P. (ed.), *Memoir and Correspondence of the late Sir James Edward Smith*, 2 vols (1832), vol. 2, pp.115-6. Turner's struggle to regard his son's death 'in the true light which I believe that duty to my Maker requires' was eased by the fact that his wife and other children were saved from the fire through the 'mercy of Divine Providence'. According to Hilton (*op. cit.*, n. 31), p.177, the interpretation of tragic bereavements of this sort as examples of the way in which 'God smiteth those he loveth', and thus as tests of faith, was characteristic of the evangelical renewal of the late 18th century.

64 Smith (*op.cit.*, n. 63), pp.279-80.

65 James Hurdis's poem, first published in 1794, was also included in *Poems by the Rev James Hurdis*, 3 vols (1808). Turner described the poem as 'exquisite' in his *Journal* 1815 (*op. cit.*, n. 22), p.8.

66 For notions of the family in this period see Jordanova, L., 'Naturalizing the family,' in Jordanova, L. (ed.), *Languages of Nature: Critical Essays on Science and Literature* (1986), pp.86-116.

67 Turner to Hutchins, 11 July 1811, RBGK.* Eleanor Jane Turner (called Ellen) was born on 10 July 1811.

68 Hutchins to Turner, 19 July 1811, TCC.

69 Turner to Hutchins, 17 October 1813, RBGK.*

70 *The Art of Employing Time to the Greatest Advantage, The True Source of Happiness* (1822), which went through two editions in the first year of publication.
71 Butler, M., 'History, Politics, and Religion,' in Grey, J.D., *The Jane Austen Handbook* (1986), p.204. Butler argues that this form of evangelicalism was characteristic of the gentry and professional classes, and should not be confused with the lower-class evangelicalism of the Victorian period.
72 Haydon (*op. cit.*, n. 72), p.128.
73 Spary, E., 'Codes of Passion: Natural History Specimens as a Polite Language in Late 18th-Century France,' in Bödeker, H.E., Reill, P.H., and Schlumbohm, J. (eds), *Wissenschaft als kulturelle Praxis, 1750-1900* (1999), pp.105-35. See also Outram, D., 'Life-paths: Autobiography, Science and the French Revolution,' in Shortland, M. and Yeo, R. (eds), *Telling Lives in Science* (1996), pp.85-102.
74 Turner to Hutchins, 2 September 1808, RBGK.
75 Turner to Hutchins, 4 July 1811, RBGK.
76 Turner to Hutchins, 12 July 1810, RBGK.*
77 Turner to Hutchins, 22 December 1809, RBGK.
78 Turner to Hutchins, 2 March and 19 April 1808, RBGK.
79 Hooker, W.J., *British Jungermanniae* (1812-16); *Musci Exotici,* 2 vols. (1818-20); and, in collaboration with Taylor, T., *Muscologia Britannica* (1818).
80 In a letter to Robert Brown, 2 November 1813, British Library Add MSS 32440, fols.15-16, Hooker stated that now he was 'doomed to stay at home quietly', Turner had offered him his collections of mosses to undertake a 'general Muscologia'.
81 Haydon (*op. cit.*, n. 59), p.128.
82 Lyell to Turner, 24 April 1816, TCC.
83 Lyell K., (ed.), *Life Letters and Journals of Sir Charles Lyell,* 2 vols (1881), vol. 1, p.42.
84 Allan, M., *The Hookers of Kew 1785-1911* (1967), pp.75-6, 105. See also Drayton, R., *Nature's Government: Science, Imperial Britain, and the 'Improvement' of the World* (2000).
85 Turner to Hutchins, 4 July 1811, RBGK.
86 The precarious state of Joseph Hooker's scientific career at this point is clear from Burkhardt, F., Smith, S., *et al.* (eds), *The Correspondence of Charles Darwin,* vol. 5 (1989), p.57; vol. 13 (2002), p.375, and Huxley, L., *Life and Letters of Sir Joseph Dalton Hooker,* 2 vols (1918), vol.1, p.351.
87 Harvey to Jane Loring Gray (wife of Harvard botanist Asa Gray), 15 January 1852, in Ducker, S.C. (ed.), *The Contented Botanist* (1988), p.19.
88 See Endersby, J., *Imperial Nature: Joseph Hooker and the Practices of Victorian Science* (2007). William Hooker was also a paid botanist, but he had obtained his positions through an older network of patronage; a system despised by his son Joseph.

Chapter 4: Dawson Turner and Book Collecting

1 Now British Library MSS Add.19398-402. Turner had published privately a description of them in 1843 as *Descriptive Index of Five Manuscript Volumes, Illustrative of the History of Great Britain.*
2 Bidwell, W.H., *Annals of an East Anglian Bank* (1900); Matthews, P.W., *History of Barclays Bank Limited,* ed. Tuke, A.W. (1926), pp.140-2.
3 Munby, A.N.L., *The Cult of the Autograph Letter* (1962), pp.57-8. Munby did not make use of the five albums of invoices and letters from booksellers, auctioneers, printsellers, bookbinders and printers, dating between the 1790s and the 1840s and now in the Victorian Studies Centre, Saffron Walden Public Library.
4 Munby, *Cult of the Autograph Letter,* p.59.
5 Dawson William Turner (b.1815) was Turner's youngest child. His slightly older brother Gurney died at Calcutta in 1848.
6 Druery, J.H., *Historical and Topographical Notices of Great Yarmouth* (1826), pp.74-6, provides the most detailed account in print of the hanging of the pictures, but see also Palgrave, G.F., *Francis Turner Palgrave; His Journals and Memories of his Life* (1899), pp.10-14. For Turner's family and his descendants, see Palmer, C.J. and Tucker, S.I., *Palgrave Family Memorials* (1878).
7 Haydon, B.R., *Diary,* ed. William Bissell Pope, 5 vols, vol. 2 (1960-3), p.128.
8 Elizabeth Palgrave to Turner, 1 August 1834: Trinity College, Cambridge, additional Turner papers. See also Palgrave, *Francis Turner Palgrave,* pp.14-16.
9 Janet Ing Freeman, *The Postmaster of Ipswich; William Stevenson Fitch, Antiquary and Thief* (1997). The extent and variety of Fitch's activities had not previously been documented. For his theft of the Lauderdale papers from Ham House, see Adams, S., 'The Lauderdale papers, 1561-1570:

the Maitland of Lethington state papers and the Leicester correspondence', *Scottish Historical Review* vol. 67 (1988), pp.28-55, and Freeman ch.2.

10 Fitch died in 1859, 13 months after Turner. Unfortunately, the correspondence of the two men in their last years does not seem to have survived. The obvious question remains of whom else, and to what extent, Fitch was associated with, or was able to dupe. A number of other papers from Helmingham and Ham turned up in the auction of the library of Fitch's friend, and fellow collector, William Powell Hunt (d.1873), formerly steward of the Helmingham estates: see Freeman, *Postmaster of Ipswich*, pp.83, 165.

11 Freeman, *Postmaster of Ipswich*, p.97; *Municipal Corporations (England and Wales); Appendix to the First Report of the Commission* part iv (1835), paras 2,302, 2,339.

12 Freeman p.102. See also Arthur Freeman and Janet Ing Freeman, *John Payne Collier; Scholarship and Forgery in the Nineteenth Century*, 2 vols (2004), pp.220-4. The manuscript is now Huntington Library MS HM 3: see Dutschke, C.W., and others, *Guide to Medieval and Renaissance Manuscripts in the Huntington Library*, 2 vols, vol. 1 (1989), p.81.

13 Freeman, *Postmaster of Ipswich*, p.42.

14 Sir Frederic Madden, Diary, 18 February 1847; quoted in Freeman, *Postmaster of Ipswich*, p.106.

15 de Ricci, S., *English Collectors of Books & Manuscripts (1530-1930) and their Marks of Ownership* (1930), p.102.

16 The main parts of Upcott's library and autograph collections were eventually sold at auction in three sales in 1846. Long before, in 1831, he had hoped to sell his autographs to the Duke of Sussex or perhaps the British Museum. By the mid-1830s he had hopes of the Guildhall Library in the City of London and then, in what must have been some desperation since he faced a notoriously dilatory payer, with Sir Thomas Phillipps. See Munby, *Cult of the Autograph Letter*, pp.25-7, based largely on Upcott's letters to Turner now in Trinity College.

17 *Catalogue of the Manuscript Library of the Late Dawson Turner, Esq., M.A., F.R.S., F.S.A., F.L.S., etc., Formerly of Yarmouth … which will be Sold by Auction by Messrs. Puttick and Simpson … June 6, 1859, and Four Following Days* (1859).

18 Cf. Cristiano, F., *L'Antiquariato Librario in Italia; Vicende, Protagonisti, Cataloghi* (1986), p.41.

19 Druery, *Historical and Topographical Notices of Great Yarmouth*. Cory's books were auctioned at Yarmouth on 19 October 1840 (copy of sale catalogue in the British Library).

20 When in 1840 Thorpe sent to Turner a complete set of the *Gentleman's Magazine*, he consigned it by the *Romona*. But because of a muddle in London it went to the wrong wharf and was put on another, later, ship, the *Ailsa-Craig* (or, as it was called by some, the *Elsiecraig*). The effort required in London to discover the missing consignment, and the delay in Turner's receiving it when Thorpe was particularly keen on prompt payment in order to meet another bill, added to Thorpe's anger. Thorpe's letters on the subject are in Saffron Walden.

21 White, W., *History, Gazetteer, and Directory of Norfolk*, 2nd ed. (1845), p.292.

22 Elizabeth Palgrave to Turner, 1 August 1834: Trinity College, additional Turner papers.

23 George Burrell to Turner, 28 December 1817: Trinity College MS O.13.14 (157).

24 See for example Buchanan to Turner, 9 August 1851, Trinity College MS O.14.50 (93). For Buchanan's bankruptcy, see the attached newspaper cutting of 10 July 1852. For his earlier career, see Brigstocke, H., *William Buchanan and the 19th Century Art Trade: 100 Letters to his Agents in London and Italy* (1982).

25 Hering to Turner, 2 August 1830: Saffron Walden.

26 Lilly to Turner, 3 December 1838: Saffron Walden. For the publisher G.B. Whittaker and his use of this method to promote Cuvier's *Animal Kingdom*, see *First Report from the Select Committee on Postage* (Parliamentary Papers 1837-8 XX.1), evidence para.3,718.

27 John Rylands University Library of Manchester MS Eng. Mis.71, fo.51, quoted in Lister, A., 'George John, 2nd Earl Spencer and his "librarian", Thomas Frognall Dibdin', in Myers, R. and Harris, M. (eds), *Bibliophily* (1986), pp.90-120, at p.97.

28 Turner to Dibdin, 25 June 1815: Houghton Library MS Eng 1177*, f.87.

29 Turner's copy of J. Dawson's *Stranger's Guide to Holkham* (1817), annotated by Turner and Benjamin Robert Haydon, and recording observations on the paintings by Haydon, Thomas Phillips and R.R. Reinagle in 1814-17, is in Trinity College, Cambridge. For the library, see Mortlock, D.P., *Holkham Library; A History and Description* (2006).

30 The 1859 auction of his printed books included about half the edition. Lot 799 was a copy with the plates on India paper and with extra illustrations including drawings in gold and colour besides various notes by Turner's accomplice in the scheme, Archdeacon George Glover. In 1860, Joseph Lilly (*Bibliotheca Historica et Topographica Anglicana*) offered 'Mr Dawson Turner's reserved copy' for £6 16s. 6d. The project remained unpublished; but see *A Handlist of Manu-*

scripts in the Library of the Earl of Leicester at Holkham Hall, Abstracted from the Catalogues of William Roscoe and Frederic Madden and Annotated by Seymour de Ricci (1932). For correspondence on the project, see the letters from Coke, Roscoe, Madden and others in Trinity College, and Bodleian Library MS Eng.Misc.d.99. See also Graham, J.E., 'The cataloguing of the Holkham manuscripts', *Trans Cambridge Bibliographical Soc.*vol. 4 (1965), pp.128-54.

31 Haydon, *Diary*, vol. 2, p.127.

32 *Catalogue of the Principal Part of the Library of Dawson Turner, Esq. ... which will be Sold by Auction by Messrs. S.Leigh Sotheby & John Wilkinson .. March 7th, 1853 & Five Following Days, and March 17th, and Six Following Days* (1853); *Catalogue of the Remaining Portion of the Library ... which will be Sold by Auction by Messrs. Puttick & Simpson ... May 16th, 1859, and Seven Following Days ...* (1859).

33 Munby, *Cult of the Autograph Letter*, pp.59-60, offers the most convenient summary of most of the various series. Almost all of the close family letters, and those from John Sell Cotman, were removed from the albums now at Trinity prior to their presentation to the college in 1890. Since then, the college has acquired some of the excised family letters. The Norfolk Record Office has recently acquired several letters from Cotman formerly in the series now at Trinity College; eight others, 1825-41, were to have been auctioned by Bonhams on 8 November 2005 (lot 559), but were withdrawn before the sale. Further of Cotman's letters to Turner are in the British Museum (Dept of Prints and Drawings) and the National Library of Scotland.

34 James Poole to Turner, 29 August 1814, with a list of pictures and Turner's notes of provenance: Trinity College MS O.13.11 (50). Poole died on 15 September 1814.

35 Druery, *Historical and Topographical Notices of Great Yarmouth*, pp.365-82.

36 Turner's letters to Mertens are now in the Hunt Botanical Library at Pittsburgh (Archives 54). The manuscript of Mertens's *Algae Aquaticae*, including drawings, was sold in the Turner sale of May 1859, lot 1,665: the auction catalogue prints Turner's opinion of Mertens, copied from a note in the book.

37 Turner's own dedication copy of Hooker's *British Jungermanniae* (1812-16) was offered by Antiquariat Botanicum (Lynden, WA) in 2005.

38 Kaempfer, E., *Icones Selectae Plantarum quas in Japonia Collegit et Delineavit E.Kaempfer* (1791).

39 von Humboldt, A., *Plantes Equinoxiales, Recueillies en Méxique* etc. (Paris, 1808-9); idem, *Monographie des Melastomacées et Autres Genres du Même Ordre* (Paris, 1816-23).

40 Schaaf, L., 'The first photographically printed and illustrated book', *Papers of the Bibliographical Society of America* vol. 73 (1979), pp.209-24; Larry Schaaf, 'Anna Atkins' cyanotypes; an experiment in photographic publishing', *History of Photography*, vol. 6 (1982), pp.151-72. Turner seems to have possessed six parts only.

41 Reeve to Turner, 19 December 1846: Saffron Walden.

42 Letters from Escher, 1798 etc.: Saffron Walden.

43 These figures are taken from the account, 30 September 1809, from John and Arthur Arch for nos 13-24: Trinity College MS O.13.7 (95). This gives the number of large-paper coloured copies as 11, where other sources give 12: it is possible one copy was included free of charge. Presumably other copies were coloured subsequently, as plain copies are now rare. I am grateful to John Collins for this observation. For a full list of Turner's publications, see Dawson, W.R., 'A bibliography of the printed works of Dawson Turner', *Trans Cambridge Bibliographical Soc.* vol. 3 (1961), pp.232-56. Most of the Dawson Turner collection belonging to the late A.N.L. Munby is now in Trinity College, Cambridge.

44 de Ricci, *English Collectors of Books & Manuscripts*, p.72.

45 Norwich Castle Museum 11.583.970: Tour to France, 1814. 2 vols. Vol. 2, ff.212-13. Turner's dismay at the lack of catalogues from de Bure was perhaps provoked by knowledge of the catalogue of the de la Vallière library (1783-8) and those of the de Brutelle library (1802 and 1805). J.G. Treuttel and J.G. Würtz, both born at Strasbourg, eventually had branches at Paris, Strasbourg and London (opened in 1817): see Edmond Werdet, *De la Librairie Française* (1860), pp.286-8.

46 Presumably lot 1,878 in the 1853 sale, when on the basis of an inscription it was described as having belonged to Jean Claude de Preaulx. Turner's manuscript and printed Books of Hours and other liturgical manuscripts were grouped together in this sale, lots 1,866-83. After 1814-15 he bought such books only rarely: in 1825, Arch supplied a small quarto missal for five guineas, and a printed *Horae* (1532) for three guineas (Saffron Walden).

47 Nepoeu invoice, 14 November 1814 (Saffron Walden); 1859 manuscripts sale, lot 402.

48 Nepoeu invoice, 14 November 1814 (Saffron Walden); 1859 manuscripts sale, lot 221, now British Library MS Add.22937.

49 Turner, Memoir of Phillips, quoted by Peach, A., art. 'Thomas Phillips, 1760-1851', *Oxford*

Dictionary of National Biography. See also Kitson, S.D., *The Life of John Sell Cotman* (1937), pp.190-1.

50 For summaries of the contradictions and hopes surrounding the post-war restitutions, see for example Pommier, E., 'Réflexions sur le problème des restitutions d'oeuvres d'art en 1814-1815', in *Dominique-Vivant Denon, l'Oeil de Napoléon* (1999), pp.253-7, and Bénédicte Savoy, '"Le nauffrage de toute une époque"; regards allemands sur les restitutions de 1814-1815', *ibid*, pp.258-67.

51 Rajnai, M. and Allthorpe-Guyton, M., *John Sell Cotman; Drawings of Normandy in Norwich Castle Museum* (1975); Kitson, *Life of John Sell Cotman*, pp.201-17.

52 Dawson Turner, *Account of a Tour in Normandy* 2 vols, vol. 1 (1820), pp.210-17 (Rouen), vol. 2, pp.210-11 (Caen).

53 David McKitterick, *Cambridge University Library; A History. The Eighteenth and Nineteenth centuries* (1986), pp.404-6.

54 Note in his copy of Pseudo-Cyril Thessalonicensis, *Speculum Sapientiae* [Vienne, c.1481], Trinity College, Cambridge VI.13.145.

55 Pointon, M.R., 'The Italian tour of William Hilton, R.A. in 1825', *Journal of the Warburg and Courtauld Institutes* vol. 35 (1972), pp.339-58, and Turner, J.M.W., *Correspondence*, p.97. Dawson Turner's appetite for looking at paintings required a leavening with other activities.

56 Brussels, Bibliothèque Royale, MS 9008; the Bibliothèque Royale in Brussels was created in 1837: see *Bibliothèque Royale; Mémorial, 1559-1969* (1969).

57 Brussels, Bibliothèque Royale, MSS 9242-9244 and 9511, 9026.

58 Norwich Castle Museum 13.483.970. Journal of a Rhenish tour, 1833. This is quite separate from the tour made by his daughter Harriett Gunn in 1834, recorded in her letters to Turner and published privately by him in 1834 as *Letters Written During a Four-Days' Tour in Holland in the Summer of 1834*. Turner's own copy of this, illustrated by his daughter, is in Norwich Castle Museum, 24.483.970.

59 Huntington Library MS HM 1144: see Dutschke, *Guide to Medieval and Renaissance Manuscripts in the Huntington Library* vol. 2, pp.465-8.

60 Manuscripts sale, 1859, lots 373, 376, in a section of eight lots of Persian manuscripts. For Turner's notes on the Chinese drawings, see British Library MS Add. 50487, f.7r. In July 1823 John Shalders in Yarmouth was paid to bind these two Persian manuscripts; in January 1827 his work included the binding of an unspecified Chinese manuscript and a group of Chinese drawings (Saffron Walden).

61 A transcript of this letter is in Trinity College MS O.13.11 (23); the original was presumably that inserted in the copy of *Bibliotheca Spenceriana* sold in 1853 (lot 990).

62 Dibdin to Turner, 29 October 1817: Trinity College MS O.13.14 (100). Despite his reputation in influential bibliophile circles, not everyone judged Lewis's binding to be of the best. On seeing the *Bibliographical Decameron*, George Burrell wrote to Turner: 'I think it might have been more generalized, as your Library will afford specimens of "bibliopegistic" excellence, not surpassed by any London binder, and Jones our bookbinder, who has been and is engaged in binding many of Mr Coke's valuable manuscripts, beats Lewis hollow. I have seen a copy of the Decameron bound by Lewis, which so far from being superior to, is absolutely worse than many common specimens of country binding.' (Burrell to Turner, 28 December 1817: Trinity College MS O.13.14 (157).) Thanks to the connections of William Roscoe, John Jones, binder for the Liverpool Athenaeum, was currently engaged in a large programme to rebind the manuscripts at Holkham, belonging to Thomas Coke. For Charles Lewis, see for example Nixon, H.M., *Five Centuries of English Bookbinding* (1978), pp.192-3; for Jones, see Ramsden, C., *Bookbinders in the United Kingdom (outside London), 1780-1840* (1954), p.99, and Mortlock, *Holkham Library*, p.102.

63 For an assessment of Cotman's relations with Turner in this enterprise, see Andrew Hemingway, 'Cotman's "Architectural antiquities of Normandy": some amendments to Kitson's account', *Walpole Soc.* vol. 46 (1976-8), pp.164-85; idem, '"The English Piranesi": Cotman's architectural prints', *Walpole Soc.* vol. 48 (1980-2), pp.210-44. Turner's copy containing all the states of the plates is in the British Museum, Dept of Prints and Drawings 166.d.24-27.

64 Turner's interleaved and annotated copy of this book, part of Great Yarmouth parish church library, is now on deposit in Norwich Cathedral Library.

65 British Library MS Add.50487, ff.66r, 67r.

66 Invoice from Samuel Sotheby, 24 May 1809: Saffron Walden.

67 Invoice from J. and A. Arch, April-May 1810: Saffron Walden.

68 The Grafton sale, beginning 6 June 1815, was anonymous; the Devonshire sale, beginning 29 May 1815, and which contained many 15th-century books, was announced as consisting

of duplicates.

69 Cotman's earliest surviving letter to Turner was written from Castle Acre, Norfolk, 9 August 1804, when he was on a sketching tour. He moved to Great Yarmouth in 1812. See Rajnai, M. and Allthorpe-Guyton, M., *John Sell Cotman, 1782-1842; Early Drawings (1798-1812) in Norwich Castle Museum* (1979).

70 1853 sale, lot 3,197; see also Turner, J.M.W., *Collected Correspondence*, ed. John Gage (1980), p.291.

71 Stothard, Mrs C., *Memoirs ... of the Late Charles Alfred Stothard* (1823), pp.36-7 etc. The portrait included in this volume of de Coster, who became celebrated as Napoleon's guide at the battle of Waterloo, was etched by Mrs Dawson Turner after Stothard's drawing.

72 'Nothing came amiss to Mr Edwards' graver; but the greatest number of his plates are portraits; in these Mr Edwards has the greatest pleasure, and on them he grounds his hopes for fame ... In all his works there is a knowledge of the subject which places him deservedly in the rank of eminent engravers.' (Puttick & Simpson sale 1859, lot 813, note attributed to Turner.) Others have been less enthusiastic about his reworking of John Crome's etched plates: see for example Moore, A., *The Norwich School of Artists* (1985), p.28.

73 British Library MS Add. 50486, f.11r.

74 Lot 109 in the 1853 sale, including a letter from Bewick (now untraced).

75 This copy was sold in the 1853 sale, lot 449. See also Bentley jr, G.E., *Blake Records Supplement* (1988), who adds that 'Turner is not known to have bought any work by Blake' (p.72).

76 Blake to Turner, 9 June 1818: William Blake, *Letters*, ed. Geoffrey Keynes, 3rd ed. (1980), pp.142-3 (original in the Rosenbach collection, Philadelphia); see also Bentley, jr, G.E., *Blake Bibliography* (1977), p.281, and, for a further letter, *Blake Bibliography Supplement* (1995), pp.95-100. Lilly invoiced Turner for 30s. for *Job* on 3 December 1838: Saffron Walden.

77 British Library MS Add.50487, f.15r.

78 British Library MS Add. 50487, f.47r.

79 *The Douce Legacy; An Exhibition to Commemorate the 150th Anniversary of the Bequest of Francis Douce (1757-1834)* (1984). Mary Turner's etching after a medallion portrait of Douce was not universally considered a success. In 1834 Turner was among the recipients of a mourning ring under the terms of Douce's will: his letters to Douce are in the Bodleian Library.

80 Mauquoy-Hendrickx, M., *Les Estampes des Wierix*, 3 vols in 4 (1978-82), nos 1989-2141.

81 For the 18th-century background, see for example Pointon, M., *Hanging the Head; Portraiture and Social Formation in Eighteenth-Century England* (1993), pp.53-78; Peltz, L., 'Engraved portrait heads and the rise of extra-illustration: the Eton correspondence of the Revd James Granger and Richard Bull, 1769-1774', *Walpole Soc.* vol. 66 (2004), pp.1-161; Peltz. L., 'Facing the text: the amateur and commercial histories of extra-illustration, c.1770-1840', in Myers, R., Harris, M. and Mandelbrote, G. (ed.), *Owners, Annotators and the Signs of Reading* (2005), pp.91-135.

82 David Langton (Clothworkers Hall) to Turner, 25 October 1842: Trinity College MS O.14.33 (105).

83 Charlotte Sutherland to Turner, 23 April 1834: Trinity College MS O.14.12 (86). For the Sutherland books in the Bodleian Library, see Macray, W.D., *Annals of the Bodleian Library, Oxford* 2nd ed. (1890), pp.331-5. The Clarendon and Burnet are now in the Ashmolean Museum: see 'The transfer of the Sutherland collection of prints and drawings', *Bodleian Library Record* vol. 3 (1951), pp.115-16.

84 Thomas Strong (117 Long Acre) to Turner, 23 December 1848: Trinity College MS O.14,45 (177).

85 Blackie & Sons to Turner, 10 June 1837: Trinity College MS O.14.18 (159).

86 It was bought by Turner in Upcott's auction, 15 June 1846, lot 69, price £4 15s.

87 Upcott to Turner, 13 September 1837: Trinity College MS O.14.19 (54).

88 Summarised in Puttick and Simpson MSS sale 1859, lot 68: the description occupies pp.288-94. Now British Library MSS Add.23013-23066, 29738, Add. Charters 14509-15012. The project seems to have begun to take on its final form by about 1846-7: on 20 September 1847 Charles Sloman, printer in Great Yarmouth, supplied 40 title pages to illustrate the work. The invoices from J.W. Diboll for about this period include several charges for binding volumes of Blomefield. (Saffron Walden.)

89 Turner's volume of 'Dibdiniana', including Dibdin's own collection of reviews of this book, is now in the Houghton Library: see (Jackson, W.A.) *An Annotated List of the Publications of the Reverend Thomas Frognall Dibdin* (1965), p.21.

90 Now in the Brotherton Library, University of Leeds. See Windle, J. and Pippin, K., *Thomas Frognall Dibdin, 1776-1847; A bibliography* (1999), p.56.

91 Dibdin, T.F., *Reminiscences of a Literary Life*, 2 vols, vol. 2 (1836), p.977.

92 Sold in 1859, lot 500, to Lincoln, for 2s.
93 Sold in 1859, lot 499, to Booth, for 2s. 6d.
94 Sold in 1859, lot 498, to Booth, for £2 18s.
95 For a summary of some of these catalogues, see also Dawson, 'Bibliography of the printed works of Dawson Turner', pp.243-4.
96 Phillipps MSS 14812, 14813 (now in the Grolier Club, New York), 14822, 14825, 14826, sold in the Phillipps sales at Sotheby's, 1893-6.
97 Sold in 1859, lots 496, 497, to Turner, and thus retained by the family. Lot 497 in the manuscripts sale, Turner's draft in six (not five) volumes, is now British Library MSS Add.50484-9.
98 This summary is based on that given in the sale catalogue of his manuscripts, Puttick & Simpson, 6 June 1859 etc., lot 496.
99 John Martin, *Bibliographical Catalogue of Works Privately Printed* (1834).
100 No longer in the correspondence files at Trinity College. For Cole's involvement in postal reform, see Bonython, E. and Burton, A., *The Great Exhibitor; The Life and Work of Henry Cole* (2003), pp.54-65. Turner followed its progress closely.
101 Turner to Dibdin, 25 June 1815: Houghton Library MS Eng 1177*, f.87.
102 For a gilt binding by Shalders on the *Catalogue of the Books Belonging to the Public Library ... of Norwich* (1825), see Maggs catalogue 1,014, *Provincial Bookbinding in Great Britain* (1981), no.59, with illustration.
103 Reeve Brothers to Turner, 7 December 1846: Saffron Walden. For caoutchouc bindings, where single leaves were bonded together on the spine with rubber, see Middleton, B.C., *A History of English Craft Bookbinding Technique* (1978), pp.30-2. As innumerable wrecked volumes of plates now testify, it was almost universally unsatisfactory as a long-term binding.
104 Note in sale catalogue of printed books, 1859, lot 1,606. For another example of Downes's inventiveness, see Nixon, H.M., *Broxbourne Library; Styles and Designs of Bookbindings from the Twelfth to the Twentieth Century* (1956), p.208.
105 Dawson, 'A bibliography of the printed works of Dawson Turner.'
106 The Pinkerton papers offered in the 1859 catalogue of Turner's manuscripts (lot 385) formed a substantially larger collection than what was published in 1830.
107 Freeman, *Postmaster of Ipswich*, pp.70-1. For this English translation (now in the Courtauld Institute of Art), and a French translation, see Muller, J.M., *Rubens: The Artist as Collector* (1989), pp.91-146.
108 British Library MSS Add. 19398-19402.
109 Bohn to Turner, 18 September 1847: Saffron Walden.
110 When in 1849 Samuel Leigh Sotheby was arranging the sale of Upcott's autograph collection, he discovered over a hundred letters from Turner. Rather than risk spoiling a friendly and useful relationship, he sought Turner's view of the subject. Sotheby to Turner, 31 December 1849: Trinity College MS O.14.47 (231). Many of Turner's letters to Upcott were included in the sale of Turner's own manuscripts, 1859, lot 509.
111 See Sadleir, M., *Archdeacon Francis Wrangham, 1769-1842* (1937).
112 Munby, A.N.L., *The Catalogues of Manuscripts & Printed Books of Sir Thomas Phillipps; Their Composition and Distribution* (*Phillipps studies* 1) (1951); Holzenberg, E., *The Middle Hill Press; A Checklist of the Horblit Collection* (1997). When in 1830 Phillipps sent Turner some sheets for the first time, he explained that he had had only 12 copies of the first sheet printed: Phillipps to Turner, 26 March 1830, Trinity College MS O.14.5 (61). This cannot have been the copy of the later edition (1837 etc.) sold in the Turner sale at Puttick & Simpson, May 1859, lot 2,143.
113 Phillipps to Turner, 27 June 1833: Trinity College MS O.14.10 (114).
114 Phillipps to Turner, 10 October 1844: Trinity College MS O.14.37 (119).
115 Agnes Strickland, to Turner, 11 February 1841: Trinity College MS O.14.27 (38), transcript. The original of this letter was sold by John Waller, *Catalogue of 5,000 Choice Autograph Letters, &c., Collected with Great Care, and Illustrated with Portraits, Private Plates, &c., by the Late Dawson Turner ... also Interesting and Important Manuscript Collections* (1859), no. 1,859. The first volume of Strickland's *Lives of the Queens of England* had appeared in 1840.
116 John Mitford, 'Advertisement' to Thomas Gray, *Poetical Works*, p.xiii.
117 In his letter to Turner, 20 August 1842, Mitford stated that the 'important volume ... which contained a few notes & a Poem', on which Pickering bid up to 20 guineas at the sale, was bought by Mr Soper of Guildford for £21: 'he has since destroyd the poems.' (Mitford to Turner, 20 August 1842: Trinity College MS O.14.33 (46)). The much more important sale of Gray's papers, from the family, took place later, on 27 November 1845.
118 Mitford to Turner, 20 August 1842: Trinity College MS O.14.33 (46). Gray's letters to Nicholls formed Lot 219 in the 1859 sale of manuscripts, and are now in Eton College Library: Gray,

T., *Correspondence* ed. Toynbee, P. and Whibley, L., with corrections and additions by Starr, H.W., 3 vols (1971). An apparently further letter from Nicholls was inserted in a copy of Mitford's edition of the *Correspondence of Thomas Gray and the Rev Norton Nicholls* (1843) offered in Pickering & Chatto catalogue 708 (1993), item 149, with no details of the date. The 1859 catalogue of printed books, lot 761, offered a copy of T.J. Mathias's edition of Gray (1814) with various insertions including letters from Norton Nicholls. For letters to Mitford respecting his editorial work, see Houghton Library MS Eng.116.4.

119 1859 catalogue of printed books, lot 413.

120 For 19th-century interests in newspaper collecting, both by libraries and by individuals, see for example Harris, M., 'Collecting newspapers; developments at the British Museum in the nineteenth century', in Myers, R. and Harris, M. (ed.), *Bibliophily* (1986), pp.44-62.

121 Now British Library 8225.bb.78.

122 Now British Library N. Tab. 2012/6 (formerly 1889.d.14). Part of the collection, which extends beyond Turner's death to 1861, was assembled by Joseph Diboll, one of Turner's bookbinders in Great Yarmouth.

123 A memorial to Hume (d.1855) is in Winterton church.

124 Upcott to Turner, 2 January 1838: Trinity College MS O.14.20 (1).

125 Four of these volumes, numbered in manuscript 1, 3, 4, 8, are now in the British Library, 1879. b.1.

126 See also Munby, A.N.L., 'Dibdin's reference library: the sale of 26-28 June 1817', in *Studies in the Book Trade in Honour of Graham Pollard* (1975), pp.279-314, including a facsimile of the Dibdin sale catalogue, and list of prices and buyers. A further copy of the Dibdin catalogue, not noted by Munby and with various manuscript amendments, is in Cambridge University Library, SSS.56.20.

127 Some copies of the sale catalogue of Richard Mead's library in 1754 were printed on large paper.

128 Gregory died in 1847, having worked for Turner for over twenty years: his invoices are in Saffron Walden.

129 Dibdin to Turner, 14 November 1817: Trinity College MS O.13.14 (112).

130 These were described in some detail in the manuscripts sale in 1859. Of the lots sold then, lot 134 (assorted papers relating to Dibdin's life) is now Houghton Library MS Eng.1177.2*; lot 136 (papers relating to *Bibliomania*) is British Library MS Egerton 2974; lot 137 (papers relating to the *Bibliographical Decameron*) is Houghton Library MS Eng.1177*; lot 138 (papers relating to the *Bibliographical Tour in France and Germany*) is in the collection of Robert S. Pirie, New York; lot 141 (MS *Horae Bibliographicae Cantabrigiensis*) has been published in facsimile, ed. Rabaiotti, R. and McKitterick, D. (1989); lot 143 (papers relating to the *Reminiscences*) is Bodleian Library MS Eng. Misc. d.85-6.

131 1853/2796 noted that at the sales of these libraries the copies fetched £30 9s. and £46 4s. respectively. See also Schoenbaum, S., *Shakespeare's Lives* (1970), pp.193-233, and *idem*, *William Shakespeare; Records and Images* (1981), pp.117-36.

132 *Oxford Dictionary of National Biography*, s.v. 'Ryland, William Wynne', by Clayton, T.

133 Harris, E.M., 'Experimental graphic processes in England, 1800-1850', *Journal of the Printing Historical Soc.*, vol. 4 (1968), 33-86, at pp.66-74: this includes references to contemporary literature concerned with security printing of banknotes.

134 In 1818 Moyes printed Hooker's uncompleted *Pomona Londinensis.*

135 Saffron Walden: volume for '1847-1848'.

136 Joseph Lilly, invoice 6 July 1847, price eight guineas: Saffron Walden. The same invoice includes two manuscripts, described as a quarto *Missale Romanum* and an octavo *Horae.* Lot 2,985 in the 1853 sale described a *Speculum Vitae Humanae* said to have been printed at Verona in 1472, 'letteris gothicis'.

137 J.D. Downes invoice, 23 May 1803: Saffron Walden.

138 Payne & Foss invoice, 4 June 1813, price £3 13s. 6d. (Saffron Walden); Walsh, J.E., *A Catalogue of the Fifteenth-Century Printed Books in the Harvard University Library* 5 vols (Binghamton, 1996), no.3837. The Payne & Foss invoice described it as 1495. In the 1859 sale (lot 235) it was misdescribed as of 1485 and as the first edition,

139 Invoice in Saffron Walden.

140 Lilly to Turner, 2, 19 August 1844: Saffron Walden. de Ricci, S., *A Census of Caxtons* (1909), no.12, records five known copies. The other two known to Lilly were presumably those in Cambridge University Library and in the Spencer collection; the one on offer must have been that formerly belonging to Francis Wrangham (his sale, 1826; de Ricci 12.8).

141 STC 15842.

142 Lot 533 in the sale of 1859 (unsold in 1853). Now in the Folger Shakespeare Library, Washington: see Kuhta, R.J., 'Thys Boke Is Myne: further reflections on the subject of provenance', *Gazette of the Grolier Club* vol. 54 (2003), pp.5-58, at pp.23, 46.
143 Letters from Wilkin in Saffron Walden. The books sold ranged from the 16th to the 19th centuries.
144 John Arch to Turner, 6 July 1839: Trinity College MS O.14.23 (2).
145 Sotheby to Turner, 11 July 1837: Trinity College MS O.14.19 (11). *The Typography of the Fifteenth Century* was published in 1845, and *Principia Typographia* in 3 vols in 1858. Sotheby had also been declared insolvent in 1825.
146 Trinity College MS O.14.27 (94).
147 Britton, J., *Autobiography*, 2 vols vol. 2 (1849-50), Dedication to Turner.
148 Mayer to Turner, 15 July 1850: Trinity College MS O.14.49 (14).
149 Molini to Turner, 20 August 1850: Trinity College MS O.14.49 (35).
150 Invoice from Diboll, 4 November 1851: Trinity College MS O.14.50 (134).
151 William Worship to Turner, 28 October 1851: Trinity College MS O.14.50 (131).
152 Trinity College MS O.14.50 (143a).
153 For Gurney, see the article by Peter Osborne in the *Oxford Dictionary of National Biography.* Many more of Gurney's letters to Turner, and his correspondence with Sir Francis Palgrave, have since been acquired by Trinity College.
154 Hudson Gurney to Turner, 29 September 1851: Trinity College, Turner papers.
155 Sir John Boileau, of Ketteringham and Thursford, is a central figure in Chadwick, O., *Victorian Miniature* (1960).
156 Sir Francis Palgrave to Hudson Gurney, 13 April 1852: Trinity College, additional Turner papers.
157 Palgrave to Gurney, 26 March 1852: Trinity College, additional Turner papers.
158 He remained a partner until his death: Bidwell, *Annals of an East Anglian Bank.*
159 Palgrave to Gurney, 3, 4,11 March 1852: Trinity College, additional Turner papers.
160 Palgrave to Gurney, 3 March 1852: Trinity College, additional Turner papers.
161 Palgrave to Gurney, 25 May 1852: Trinity College, additional Turner papers. The sale of his pictures was at Christies on 14 May.
162 Palgrave to Gurney, 11 June 1852: Trinity College, additional Turner papers.
163 One of these was offered in 1859, lot 1,971.
164 Palgrave to Gurney, 1 March 1853: Trinity College, additional Turner papers.
165 Palgrave to Gurney, 1 March 1853: Trinity College, additional Turner papers.
166 It was bought in under the name 'Pasmore'. See de Ricci, S., *A Census of Caxtons* (1909), no.40.5. The book is now in the Pierpont Morgan Library, PML 699: see also *Catalogue of Manuscripts and Early Printed Books from the Libraries of William Morris, Richard Bennett* [etc.] *now Forming Portion of the Library of J.Pierpont Morgan*, 3 vols (1907), no.699.
167 Joseph Lilly offered it in 1860 for £84, noting that the work had cost over £300 to assemble and have bound: Lilly, J., *Bibliotheca Historica et Topographica Anglicana* (1860), p.60.
168 Lilly subsequently offered the vellum copy for £31 10s.: *Bibliotheca Historica et Topographica Anglicana* (1860).
169 Goodall's books were auctioned at Eton by Sotheby on 8 June that year.
170 Quaritch catalogues 61 (no.15, *Horae*), 62 (nos 45-64, Normandy books) (1853).
171 The further Puttick & Simpson auction, on 3 April 1869, was of the residue of the 3rd, 4th and 5th series of Turner's collection of autographs. These had been bought by Holloway, the bookseller, in 1859 (lots 677-9) for £741, and apart from the papers he either kept for himself or sold to his British customers, he sent the German letters to Leipzig and the French ones to Paris before consigning the residue to Puttick for re-sale. The remains of the albums were sold as individual lots. (Puttick to Mary Turner, 19 April 1869, in the collection of Christopher Barker.)
172 Madden's account is in his diary, Bodleian Library MS Eng. Hist. c.172, pp.166-76. The late A.N.L. Munby's interleaved and annotated copy of the catalogue is in Cambridge University Library, Munby c.92.
173 Munby, A.N.L., *The Formation of the Phillipps Library from 1841 to 1872* (*Phillipps studies* 4) (1956), pp.83-4. For the sale of some of Libri's manuscripts in March 1859, and the sumptuous catalogue prepared for the occasion, see also Ruju, P.A.M. and Mostert, M., *The Life and Times of Guglielmo Libri (1802-1869), Scientist, Patriot, Scholar, Journalist and Thief; A Nineteenth-Century Story* (1995), pp.293-4.
174 A summary of the Lauderdale and other Tollemache papers stolen by Fitch, and offered in the Turner manuscripts sale, is provided in Freeman, *Postmaster of Ipswich*, pp.160-4, together

with such modern locations as could be discovered in 1997.

175 Cf. Houghton Library MS Eng 1177-1177.2.

176 Now Chantilly MS 1378: see *Chantilly; Le Cabinet des Livres: Manuscrits* 2 vols (1900), no.28. The Duc d'Aumale was buying regularly at London sales during this period.

177 British Library MS Add.22937.

178 British Library MS. Add.22934.

179 British Library MS Add.32555.

180 This is now in Christ's College, Cambridge: see Beal, P., *Index of English Literary Manuscripts*, vol. 2: 1625-1700, part 2 (1993), p.76.

181 Thorpe to Turner, 28 March 1848: Saffron Walden.

182 British Library MS Add.23013 etc.

183 Ker, N.R., *Medieval Manuscripts in British Libraries. vol. 3. Lampeter — Oxford* (1983), pp.366-7.

184 Now Victoria & Albert Museum Forster collection 271: see Ker, N.R., *Medieval Manuscripts in British Libraries. vol. 1. London* (1969), p.378.

185 For the sales, see Hunt, A., 'The sale of Richard Heber's library', in Myers, R., Harris, M. and Mandelbrote, G. (ed.), *Under the Hammer: Book Auctions Since the Seventeenth Century* (2001), pp.143-71.

186 Thomas Thorpe (the elder) to Turner, March/April 1848: Saffron Walden.

187 Letter to Charles Roach Smith, 26 March 1853, quoted in Munby, *Cult of the Autograph Letter*, p.50.

188 Bohn, H.G., *Catalogue of Books* (1841) remainder section.

189 Lot 1,202 (sold for £35) was the family copy, containing the original drawings, of the record of the family trip to Normandy in 1820; lot 1,244 was Turner's interleaved and annotated copy of his *Sepulchral Reminiscences of a Market Town* (1848); lot 1,608, the interleaved and annotated copy of his first book, *A Synopsis of British Fuci* (1802), is now in the Natural History Museum.

190 John Waller, *Catalogue of 5,000 Choice Autograph Letters, &c., Collected with Great Care, and Illustrated with Portraits, Private Plates, &c., by the Late Dawson Turner ... also Interesting and Important Manuscript Collections* (1859), preface.

191 Westwood to Turner, 10 November 1846: Trinity College MS O.14.41 (130). The initial to which Westwood referred was reproduced from the manuscript of William of Jumièges at Rouen: *Tour in Normandy*, vol. 2, plate opposite p.211.

192 Stevenson to Turner, 1 June 1842: Trinity College MS O.14.32 (79)

193 This summary is part of a larger study of Turner and his books that I have in preparation. On this occasion I am especially grateful to Christopher Barker, John Collins, Martyn Everett, Janet Freeman, Adam Green, Eric Holzenberg, the staff of the Houghton Library, Andrew Moore and the staff of Norwich Castle Museum, Fernando Pena, the staff of Saffron Walden Public Library, Anne Secord, Katherine Spears and Gudrun Warren for their active interest and help.

Chapter 5: The Banker

1 BGA 3/383.

2 BGA 201/1.

3 BGA 201/1.

4 Bidwell, W.H., *Annals of an East Anglian Bank* (1900).

5 BGA 3/3147.

6 BGA 3/2364.

7 BGA 1248/156.

8 BGA 1248/156.

9 BGA 3/1864.

10 BGA 1248/156.

11 BGA 3/2364.

12 BGA 3/2364.

13 BGA 3/2591.

14 BGA 3/1866.

15 BGA 3/2364.

16 BGA 3/943.

17 Pressnell, L.S., *Country Banking in the Industrial Revolution* (1956).

18 Goodman, Rupert, 'The Role of County Banking in the Industrial Revolution with specific reference to the Turner Gurney Bank of Great Yarmouth', dissertation, Trinity College Cambridge, 1984.

Chapter 6: A Tasteful Occupation?

1 Maria, 1797-1872; Elizabeth, 1799-1852; Dawson, 1801-6; Mary Anne, 1803-74; Harriet, 1806-60; Hannah Sarah 1808-82; Dawson, May 1809-June 1809; Katherine, May 1820-February 1822; Eleanor (Ellen), 1811-95; Gurney, 1813-48; Dawson William, 1815-85.
2 Hereafter, for the purposes of this essay, called the Turners, unless specifically referred by name.
3 *Journal of Sir F. Madden*, Bodleian Library, MS ENG HIST c.148.
4 *A Four Days Tour in Holland, in the Summer of 1834*, letters from Harriet Gunn (née Turner) to Dawson Turner. Dawson Turner had the letters printed so they could be read by the rest of the family – a plan unknown to Harriet until they appeared in print. The date given on the published version is 1863; however, Dawson Turner had died five years before and Harriet three years before. In the introduction, Dawson Turner says that he is 'all but a sexagenarian', meaning that the correct date of publication must have been 1834 or 1835. My thanks to Nigel Goodman for pointing this out.
5 Sir J.D. Hooker, speech given at the anniversary dinner of the Royal Society, 30 November 1887.
6 Bermingham, A., *Learning to Draw: Studies in the Cultural History of a Polite and Useful Art* (2000).
7 Thackeray, W.M., *Vanity Fair: A Novel without a Hero* (1877).
8 At the time the rules were written in about 1812, Harriet would have been about six, Hannah Sarah four and Ellen only one, and therefore not old enough to be having lessons.
9 W.C. Edwards (1777-1855) worked mainly as a portrait engraver; Sowerby (1787-1871) was a renowned natural history illustrator and part of the Sowerby family of natural historians, who were major figures in British natural history writing, publishing and illustrating throughout the 19th century.
10 Elizabeth is referring to John Varley (1778–1842).
11 *Dawson Turner's Tour to France* (1814).
12 For a fuller discussion of Bulwer's Norfolk Collection, see Elzea, B., *Frederick Sandys: A Catalogue Raisonne* (2001).
13 Thanks to Nigel Goodman for this information.
14 British Library ADD MS 23068
15 Maria and Elizabeth were married by this date and not therefore living at Bank House.
16 British Library Add MSS 324400, fols. 95-96. I am grateful to Dr Anne Secord for bringing this reference to my attention.

Chapter 7: Mary Turner – Wife to Dawson

1 Henry Crabbe Robinson diary of 26 October 1826, Dr Williams' Library, 14 Gordon Square, London.
2 Charles Lyell correspondence, Edinburgh University Library.
3 Allen, M., *The Hookers of Kew (1785-1911)* (1967).
4 Private Collection: DT preface to unpublished letters 'A four-days tour in Holland, summer 1834', Harriet Gunn née Turner.
5 Dawson Turner Correspondence, Wren Library, Trinity College, Cambridge: letter from MT 9 February 1819
6 Turner, D., *Natural History of Fuci* (1808-19).
7 Dawson Turner, *Outlines of Lithography, Illustrated Catalogue of Pictures Acquired in the Previous Decades*, 1840.
8 Dawson Turner Correspondence, Wren Library, Trinity College, Cambridge: letter from MT 19 April 1825.
9 Allen, M., *The Hookers of Kew (1785-1911)* (1967).
10 Hamilton, J. (ed), *Fields of Influence: Conjunctions of Artists and Scientists 1815–1860* (2001).
11 Dawson Turner Correspondence, Wren Library, Trinity College, Cambridge: letter from MT June 11 1825 to DT.
12 *Ibid.*, 2 August 1841.
13 *Ibid.*, 24 May 1823.
14 *Ibid.*, 12 September 1825.
15 *Ibid.*, 5 June 1806.
16 *Ibid.*, 21 June 1818.
17 *Ibid.*, 9 February 1819.
18 *Ibid.*, 24 June 1819.

19 *Ibid.*, 31 May 1806.
20 *Ibid.*
21 *Ibid.*, 16 January 1825.
22 *Journal of a Tour Made by Dawson Turner Esq. in Company with Mrs Turner* (1802), Castle Museum, Norwich.
23 Turner, M., *Journal of a Tour in France 1814*, Castle Museum, Norwich.
24 Dawson Turner Correspondence, Wren Library, Trinity College, Cambridge: letter from MT 9 June 1818 to her father at Coltishall.
25 Dawson Turner Correspondence, Wren Library, Trinity College, Cambridge: letter from MT 10 June 1818 to DT.
26 *Ibid.*, 11 June 1818.
27 *Ibid.*, 17 June 1818.
28 *Ibid.*, 20 June 1818 to her father at Coltishall.
29 *Ibid.*, 10 June 1818 to DT.
30 *Ibid.*, 9 June 1818 to her father at Coltishall.
31 *Ibid.*, 4 July 1818 to DT.
32 *Ibid.*, 20 June 1818 to her sister at Coltishall.
33 *Ibid.*, 11 June 1825 to DT.
34 *Ibid.*, 4 July 1818.
35 *Ibid.*, 19 June 1818 to her sister at Coltishall.
36 *Ibid.*
37 *Ibid.*, 17 June 1818 to DT.
38 *Ibid.*, 19 June 1818 to her sister at Coltishall.
39 *Ibid.*
40 *Ibid.*, 16 June 1819 to DT.
41 Turner, M., *Journal of a Visit to Ostend 1833*, Castle Museum, Norwich.
42 Turner, M., *Journal of a Rhenish Tour 1833*, Castle Museum, Norwich.
43 Dawson Turner Correspondence, Wren Library, Trinity College, Cambridge: letter from MT, 1 June 1812.
44 *Ibid.*, letter from DT, 11 Sept 1825 to MT.
45 *Ibid.*, letter from MT, 28 May1823 to DT.
46 *Ibid.*, 31 January 1806.
47 *Ibid.*, 2 June 1809.
48 Palgrave, D.A., *The History and Lineage of the Palgraves* (1978).
49 Munby, A.N.L., *Dawson Turner*, lecture notes 22 November 1960.
50 Bean, M., 'Dawson Turner FRS', *Journal of Yarmouth Archeology*, 1995.
51 *Journal of a Tour made by Dawson Turner Esq. in Company with Mrs Turner* (1802), Castle Museum, Norwich.
52 Dawson Turner Correspondence, Wren Library, Trinity College, Cambridge: letter from MT 27 May 1809 to DT.
53 *Ibid.*, 4 June.
54 *Ibid.*, 18 June 1818.
55 *Ibid.*, 1 July 1818.
56 *Ibid.*, 4 July 1818.
57 *Ibid.*, 24 July 1818 to her father.
58 *Ibid.*, 10 June 1818 to DT.
59 *Ibid.*, 4 July.
60 *Ibid.*, 17 July 1823.
61 Private Collection Letter from M.T. to Hannah Brightwen, 2 August 1849.
62 Private Collection Letter from Elizabeth Palgrave to Tom Brightwen, 1850.
63 Private Collection Letter from Mary Anne Turner to Dawson Turner, 1850.
64 Private Collection Letter DT to Charles Konig, 22 March 1850.

Index

Page numbers in **bold** refer to illustrations.